Democratic Governance and Social Inequality

A project of the
Latin American Program
of the Woodrow Wilson International
Center for Scholars

Democratic Governance and Social Inequality

edited by

Joseph S. Tulchin
with Amelia Brown

LYNNE
RIENNER
PUBLISHERS

BOULDER
LONDON

Published in the United States of America in 2002 by
Lynne Rienner Publishers, Inc.
1800 30th Street, Boulder, Colorado 80301
www.rienner.com

and in the United Kingdom by
Lynne Rienner Publishers, Inc.
3 Henrietta Street, Covent Garden, London WC2E 8LU

Library of Congress Cataloging-in-Publication Data
Democratic governance and social inequality / edited by Joseph S. Tulchin,
    with Amelia Brown.
    Includes bibliographical references and index.
    ISBN 1-58826-003-8 (alk. paper)
    ISBN 1-58826-028-3 (pbk. : alk. paper)
    1. Democracy—Economic aspects. 2. Economic development—Political
aspects. 3. Democracy—Case studies. 4. Economic development—Case studies.
5. Equality. 6. Social justice. I. Tulchin, Joseph S., 1939–   II. Brown, Amelia.
JC423 .D466 2002
321.8—dc21   2001048643

British Cataloguing in Publication Data
A Cataloguing in Publication record for this book
is available from the British Library.

Printed and bound in the United States of America

     The paper used in this publication meets the requirements
 ∞   of the American National Standard for Permanence of
     Paper for Printed Library Materials Z39.48-1984.

 5 4 3 2 1

Contents

Acknowledgments

The editors would like to thank former Wilson Center public policy scholars Bolivar Lamounier, Chung-in Moon, and Steven Friedman for their intellectual leadership in developing this project. Former Latin American Program Associate Ralph Espach was also instrumental in shaping this volume. Finally, thanks are due to the following Latin American Program interns for their meticulous work in preparing the manuscript for publication: Craig Fagan, Micah Bump, Audrey Yao, Nikki Clemente, and Julie Ensiki.

1

Introduction:
Globalization, Social Inequality,
and Democracy

Bolívar Lamounier

As we begin a new millennium, we confront challenges that in some ways are much less severe than those of the twentieth century and in other ways are new and more daunting. The likelihood of state-to-state conflict, such as occurred with the two world wars of the previous century, has diminished dramatically. On the other hand, the potential reach of terrorist attacks, by hijacked airplane, nuclear weapon, or biological agent, creates a widespread sense of malaise. In the past forty years, we have seen a notable expansion of electoral-based democracies—what some scholars label a "universalization" of this form of government—a trend in stark contrast with the once-plausible prediction that totalitarianism would become the dominant political system in the world. The difficult choices that face societies today are no longer about war versus peace or dictatorship versus democracy. In an era of relative peace and the expansion of democracy, national concerns focus instead on how to improve governance and quality of life, and how to preserve national cohesion against centripetal forces that threaten to tear apart the social fabric.

It is in this context that this volume examines the challenges that social inequalities present to democratic governance around the world. The authors in this work view the issues of poverty and social inequality, and the difficulties in dealing with them, not as lingering leftovers of the nineteenth century, but rather as issues that are becoming even more important in the twenty-first century. Among the themes that this volume seeks to address are the following: (1) the effects of globalization on the distribution of income and wealth within national frontiers; (2) the impact of inequality on the stability and/or the quality of democratic governance; and (3) the future of democracies as redressers of social wrongs, especially in light of the apparent decline in the capacity of the public sector to take effective action to reduce inequality.

A central, if not primary, focus of the debate surrounding the issue of inequalities in income and wealth distribution is the relationship between the recent geographic expansion of democracy and the economic phenomenon of globalization. Democratization and globalization are not only simultaneous processes, but also, many would argue, mutually reinforcing processes. The more optimistic scholars see globalization as a solution to inequalities, not a problem—or, at least, believe that the problems that eventually arise or are aggravated by globalization can be resolved by more globalization. The pessimists contend that globalization will only serve to amplify inequalities and that this widening of income gaps will create ever-growing tensions that will challenge democratic governance by reducing or nullifying the capacity of national governments to act as redressers of social wrongs.

Although reality may not be as bleak as the pessimists portray, latent economic and political instabilities in the current international system should be taken seriously. On the one hand, as Steven Friedman points out in his contribution to this volume, there exists much greater accord among countries today on the requirements for economic growth, as the centrally planned economies of Eastern Europe have collapsed and the import-substitution policies of Latin America have been abandoned. However, the new surge of prosperity resulting from the shift toward more liberal economic policies has not been experienced uniformly among the countries that have adopted the new system. And it is questionable whether this prosperity will lead to the reduction of poverty and the reduction of existing inequalities in income and wealth.

On the political side, electoral democracy has never been as widespread. In the case of Latin America alone, almost all of the populace today lives under constitutionally established governments, and there has been a general reduction in factional antagonisms over the course of the past two decades. Countries with a rather spotty tradition of true democratic pluralism, such as Mexico or Paraguay, have been taking giant steps in this direction. Throughout the region, legislators, political parties, and judicial institutions are supervising and tracking performance and working together in a significant way with businesses and private organizations of many kinds to attempt to create governments that are more accountable for their actions. However, the notable geographic expansion of electoral democracy during these last three decades should not blind us to the fragility of this system in many parts of the world. In Latin America, grave problems persist in Colombia, Venezuela, and Peru. In Africa, among the countries that were seen as the most promising for the advancement of democracy, some, such as the Congo (Kinshasa) and Sierra Leone, are showing signs of backsliding. In all of the countries with a majority or strong Islamic presence, Western-style democracy, where it existed at all, is beginning to recede, as indicated by recent events in Indonesia, Pakistan, or the Philippines. By the same token, in countries that were once part of the USSR the process of building a democratic system is getting bogged down and halted entirely, as evidenced by recent history in Ukraine, Belarus, or any of the Central Asian republics. The fragility of democracy in many countries can lead to tensions that are only heightened by strong social inequalities.

Social Inequality as a Threat to Democracy

Contemporary political science is rather inattentive to the subject of social inequality.[1] This inattentiveness seems to be part and parcel of excessive confidence in the triumph of democracy as a political and social system around the world. The persistence of posttransitional democracies in Latin America and many other parts of the world, rather than the reversal that many feared, and their robustness in the face of tensions that before would have undermined them, has given scholarship on democracy a celebratory tone. In line with this thinking is the belief that social inequalities no longer pose the threat they once did to democracy.

This exuberance may, however, be premature. Steven Friedman observes in Chapter 2 that many new, and even some old and well-established democracies, are having difficulty carrying out fundamental tasks such as ensuring public safety. As these cases illustrate, there is a significant difference between providing opportunities to participate in the political system and having the capacity to satisfy expectations of social well-being and to reduce social inequalities.[2] "Illiberal" democracies, as Larry Diamond has argued in his work, are all too common today. Competition, true competition, is not a term that can be applied to their electoral processes. These states do not fully qualify as democracies, especially when the elected authorities are not really accountable and laws are not equitably enforced and are often at sharp variance with social behavior. In the case of Latin America, illiberalism is most frequently attributed to the historical legacy of colonialism and Iberian culture. In this framework, social inequalities arise from the rigid social stratification that developed as an integral part of colonialism. The image of society viewed through this historical lens is one of a social system based upon repression as well as deeply rooted behavior patterns of deference and obedience—a troubled and anachronistic system destined to fall to pieces in the face of capitalist urban modernity. The problem with this view is that modernity alone cannot reduce the inequalities present in *objective* conditions, such as education, skill development, income, and wealth. Modernity does, however, transform day-to day social interactions and increase close or informal social contacts between classes. The result can be increased social conflict, as the social rules that once helped to prevent conflict start to fall away and as the focus on the objective inequalities that still remain becomes more intense. Given these new and complex realities, democratic leaders cannot quickly or easily eliminate the inequalities that Diamond refers to, even with the many human and material resources at their disposal. And because illiberalism is not only a product of remote historical factors but also of contemporary realities that reproduce themselves continually, some even gaining in intensity, it is not likely to disappear anytime soon.

But, is social inequality detrimental to democracy? Many scholars today would contend that social inequalities no longer have the same ability to undermine democracy as in the past. I would argue, however, that social equality still matters to democracy, both in theory and in practice. Democracy by definition should include a redistributive dimension.[3] As Jonathan Hartlyn describes in Chapter 6, political science is now moving toward an expanded conceptualization of democracy that acknowledges "important—though still not well-specified connections—from socioeconomic issues of inequality and the strength of civil society, to political democracy issues" (p. 127).

The belief that social inequality affects the *quality* of democratic governments to a greater extent than the *stability* of these states has been one reason that many scholars have been disinterested in social equality. The distinction between quality and stability is useful and necessary to keep in mind, but we must be careful not to exaggerate the difference. In certain cases, what might appear to be a degradation in the quality of democracy can actually be a degradation in the stability of democracy. Consider, for example, the question of crime rates on the scale found today not only in Brazil or South Africa, but in countries such as Argentina and Russia, which have traditionally had much better social indices and, until now, had seemed somewhat immune to these problems. A society's crime rate is related to its level of social inequality/poverty to some degree, even if the two phenomena do not correlate one-to-one. And high levels of crime can negatively affect both the quality and the stability of democracy. A democratic system that is unable to stop or prevent escalations in crime rates cannot be considered a "high quality" system. Furthermore, behind the façade of a seemingly stable democracy, civil well-being can be gravely threatened. Even the best-intentioned politicians may resort to repression or find themselves facing problems of corruption or police extortion when dealing with astronomical crime rates.[4]

Social inequalities, then, can undermine democratic governance, albeit indirectly. Through a sudden spike in the crime rate, a democracy can degrade abruptly. Once this deterioration passes the comfort level of a society's citizens, political stability can be cast in doubt. Over the long term, if inequality and other related societal tensions are able to continue uninterrupted, these tensions can erode the democratic rule of law. Furthermore, a sudden economic downturn, when widespread economic insecurities already exist, can produce social instabilities with sufficient strength to quickly affect the institutional stability of democracies.

Reducing Social Inequalities

The Role of the State

The decline in the importance of the traditional nation-state within the context of globalization is a white-hot issue in contemporary public debate. If in fact the power of the nation-state is declining, it will have wide-ranging implications for not only international relations, but also for domestic politics. The modern state has always been seen as the best environment for the efficient functioning of representative democracy. If observations about the diminishing power of the state are correct, the nation-state is disappearing as a territorial marker of political action at the same moment that the reach of democracy is widening. As Friedman observes, we are confronting the perverse paradox that millions of citizens are gaining the right to choose their leaders just when the choices are becoming irrelevant. These citizens are voting and making demands on their governments that remain unanswered, due to the fact that these governments are impotent to make effective public policy, particularly public policy targeted to reduce social inequalities.

For Faux and Mishel, this vision of the weakening of the nation-state has already come to pass: "What we have learned over the past two decades is that, in the real world, forced economic integration has led to a greater inequality of market incomes *and a declining ability to offset that inequality with safety nets and other public policies*" (2000:109, emphasis added). Chung-in Moon and Jae-jin Yang present a contrasting viewpoint in Chapter 7, on South Korea. They contend that neoliberal economic reforms have "served as a catalyst for the speedy transformation of [South Korea] into a welfare state" (p. 132). Steven Friedman and Theodore Lowi tend more toward the views of Faux and Mishel, although they are less pessimistic. They offer evaluations about what exactly can be done to reinvigorate the democratic state as redresser of social inequalities.

Friedman advocates "a stronger link between state and society [which] can be achieved only by strengthening democratic politics in general, and the representative function in particular" (p. 37). "Bringing politics back in" seems to be an apt summary of his position. Building upon his well-known analyses of government and public policy in the United States, Lowi suggests that "bringing politics back in" will do little to reduce inequality, and may well compound an already complicated problem (p. 47). Instead he argues for "bringing the state back in."[5] Going along with this idea is Joel Rocamora's scathing criticism of the "Washington consensus" in Chapter 4. Rocamora writes that richer industrialized countries demand fewer state interventions in the economy and insist that this is the way to develop "strong states," while what is often actually necessary "in many countries of the South, is to strengthen the government's capacity to intervene" (p. 85).

For most of the twentieth century, socialist and interventionist ideologies of varying shades saw the state as the instigator or promoter of social change. In fact, governments inspired by these ideologies had many opportunities to implement redistributive programs and the results were modest, to put it mildly. Latin America, in particular, has tried both austerity/gradualist programs and populist/revolutionary experiments in government, and today these can be seen as an impressive collection of failures, if the aim was to bring about a significant redistribution of income and wealth. One can argue that the results could have been even worse if they had opted for a model other than the import-substitution industrialization that predominated in the region. Ex post facto, however, neither the Mexican Revolution, with its strong intentions of restructuring the system from the ground up, nor Peronismo (grotesquely demagogic), whose fight against the rigid social stratification and aristocratic pretensions of the Argentine elite ought not to be underestimated, nor Brazilian Varguism, a little excessive in its initial use of fascist rhetoric that the left came to be seen as progressive from 1945 onward, nor the many left-wing military regimes of the hemisphere, like that of General Juan Velasco Alvarado in Peru or the Sandanista movement in Nicaragua—none of these experiments left unequivocally positive balances or models for action capable of inspiring the hearts and minds of people today. If there is to be one exception it might be the Cuban Revolution; but, at forty, even this movement seems to be ailing, especially now that it has lost the financial patronage of the former USSR. The revolution also looks incapable of ideologically reinvigorating itself, which it must do in order to make an orderly transition from a one-party system to a pluralistic democracy.

The historical evidence that the state always has had an important role to play in the economy is no doubt important, and the analytical proof (which Lowi offers in Chapter 3, building upon the work of Karl Polanyi) is that the market is not conceivable without a politico-state framework. Lowi's argument for "bringing the state back in" can be seen as a healthy ideological counterpoint to that which George Soros has called "market fundamentalism." In considering the statist argument, one must face the following two questions. First, to what degree have countries with a lot of experience in state-driven growth models, such as Brazil, been able effectively to reduce social inequalities? Second, in an era of globalization, can the state maintain sufficient capabilities and functions to formulate and implement in a centralized manner public policy relevant to the reduction of social inequalities, and do so with an advantage over private or mixed-source solutions?

The impact of the two points cannot be underestimated. As Lowi demonstrates, mainstream political science has diluted the role of the state in the assumed "political market" (that is, a play of pluralistic forces that work together in some rational manner to define the public good). But the revaluation of the state suggested by Lowi involves the risk of transforming the concept of the state into an analytic black hole, whose dense gravity consumes the ability to see how meaningful and autonomous political activity can continue. Under the mantel of "legal integrity" that Lowi views as an essential attribute of the state, we could unconsciously feel impelled to restore the rather naïve aspiration of the old German notion of *staatslehre:* the state as a "unit of decision and action." In sum, I turn again to Lowi: it is necessary to create a comparative accounting of the redistributive effects of diverse state-driven development models of the past century, conceptually elaborate upon them within the context of the globalized world that is forming before our eyes, and investigate the degree of both cohesion and autonomy that we can realistically expect from the actions of the state.

Class as an Agent of Social Change

The debate about class as a political agent has a long history. The reformers and revolutionaries of the nineteenth century nurtured an unbounded optimism in overcoming "false consciousness," or rather, the subordination of individual and utilitarian motives of the short term to the collective and altruistic objectives of the long term. They projected upon this issue the idea that everything that related to the nation-state was to be firmly placed within the framework of political struggle. Today, the question has to be examined in the context of the theoretical skepticism that predominates in thinking about the collective actions of class, the predominant perception of an erosion in the state's capabilities to effect social change through its policies, and in the more modest role played by the authors of public compensatory policies.

In fact, in the 102 years between the publication of Marx's *Communist Manifesto* and Marshall's "Citizenship and Social Class," the theoretical underpinnings that support the examination of class as a political agent did not change significantly. Marx envisioned that the proletariat would transform itself into a more cohesive revolutionary whole; Marshall did not go that far, but was optimistic about the potential of the working class to play a political role and assert a strong electoral presence. Philosophers since at least the eighteenth century (Hegel among them) have written about certain dilemmas inherent in collective action. A watershed work in this scholarship is that of Mancur Olson Jr. in *The Logic of Collective Action,* published for the first time in the mid-1960s. This work forced political scientists to revise the frequently inconsistent and ingenuous premises that they had relied upon to explain how individuals come together to act collectively as a group. Before Olson's writings, the predominant idea on the left was the historicist notion of the ripening of objective conditions, and that the proper progression of social struggles would transform false consciousness into class consciousness (and consequently into action). On the right, scholars were wedded, above all, to the theory of modernization, the idea that passivity and individual or clientalist conduct were traditional traits that inevitably would be superceded by the modern traits of activism and ideology. On all sides, scholars subscribed to the premise that sooner or later common interests would lead to common action. Under these assumptions and presuming that the main source of political action to be the nation-state, it was entirely logical to conclude that the destitute majority—or at least the working class—would become increasingly organized and would eventually change the world to reflect a more egalitarian vision, either through revolutionary means, as Marx believed, or through evolutionary reforms, as Marshall argued.

What we are witnessing today is a radical questioning of the assumptions about collective action outlined above. For every worker who joins a group and joins in collective action, we can easily identify dozens of others who seem to share common interests but who choose *not* to organize. When the individual feels that the costs of participation far exceed the benefits of joining, collective action becomes improbable. Whether the boundary for social inclusion is labeled "traditional" or "modern," the fact is that the individual impulse frequently works against the possibility of collective action. But this is not the only problem. When an individual chooses action over inaction, this does not always lead to *collective* action. Moreover, if the individual does choose collective action, it is not a given that he or she will choose *political* action—which is the crucial assumption of the theories discussed above. Thousands, even millions, of people the world over follow individual paths or choose to associate with highly organized collectives that are not political in nature, such as criminal groups (gangs or the Mafia) or drug distribution networks.

Lowi argues that multiclass alliances will not lead to the development of effective policies of social redress (see the passing reference on page 56), whereas Friedman and Xolela Mangcu contend the opposite in their chapters. Lowi just might be correct. If he is, the problem facing democracies grows much more complicated, since the old forms of class action—understood as autonomous action taken by the working class or the unwashed masses within the political context of the nation-state—are rapidly vanishing.

The sections above indicate just how complicated the problem of social inequality is. Solutions are neither obvious nor clear-cut. What is obvious, however, is that, at this turn of the century, neither the state-driven growth model practiced in Latin America and many other parts of the world for the greater part of the last century nor the market-friendly model that has begun to replace it have had very impressive results when it comes to global redistribution. If we are going to be able to analyze effectively why these policies have failed to remedy social inequalities and what alternative approaches might have better success, we must turn to comparative and interdisciplinary studies that go beyond the evaluations of specific social projects. The chapters that follow are a small step in this direction.

Notes

1. I am aware that poverty and social inequality are different concepts, but I treat them together in the present context because my primary focus is on countries in which both are severe—where the really destitute number in the millions and at the same time extreme inequalities exist in the distribution of income and wealth. I am also aware that social tensions have a variety of causes, not all of them tied to socioeconomic distribution. But it is important to understand the means by which social inequalities can be transformed into a threat to democracy.

2. I proposed a similar argument fifteen years ago in a work entitled "Brazil: Inequality Against Democracy," which has been included in various volumes on democracy in developing countries edited by Larry Diamond

(Lamounier 1989, 1995, and 1999; see also Lamounier 1997). Although that work focuses on an analysis of the Brazilian case, I think it can apply to a more general analysis because it does point out some reasons why democracy is essentially unstable and precarious in poor countries with aggregate and large inequalities in the distribution of income and wealth.

3. In my aforementioned article, "Brazil: Inequality Against Democracy," I put forward an argument about the importance that inequality plays in relation to democracy, not only in historico-empirical terms (the question of the determinants of the permanence of democracy) but also in conceptual and analytical terms. I try to delineate a minimalist conceptualization of the ideas of Joseph Schumpeter, while taking issue with the fairly celebrated 1971 study by Robert Dahl, *Polyarchy: Participation and Opposition*. Accepting the Schumpeterian view of democracy as a political subsystem of society, I challenge the model that attempts to understand the historical development of stable democracies (which Dahl calls polyarchies) without incorporating a reduction of social inequalities (which I call socioeconomic decentralization). I propose an alternative model that explicitly incorporates a redistributive dimension and a progressive "equalizing of conditions."

4. See Frühling and Tulchin (forthcoming).

5. See Rueschemeyer, Skocpol, and Evans (1985).

PART 1

THINKING ABOUT DEMOCRATIC GOVERNANCE

2

Democracy, Inequality, and the Reconstitution of Politics[1]

Steven Friedman

The global spread of formal democracy and market economics is beset by two related contradictions. Formal equality between citizens and the right to hold government accountable have never been so widespread; yet many new—and, perhaps, established—democracies find it more difficult to perform tasks expected of the democratic state, whether these are conceived, in T. H. Marshall's (1992) terms, as the extension of social citizenship to all, or, in more limited and "classical" terms, as the maintenance of public order sufficient to allow for free participation in public life. This first contradiction stems in large measure from the second—that while, at least until the financial crisis of the late 1990s, there seemed near-global consensus on the economic preconditions for growth and prosperity for most inhabitants of the globe, both seem as elusive as ever. The spread of formal democracy has been accompanied by increasing inequality both within and between countries (for data and details, see United Nations Development Program 1999:36–37, 39). This raises the uncomfortable possibility that the progress toward greater freedom and rights to participation that democracy's spread has promised may be halted as political liberty brings only straitened economic circumstances to most citizens.

To place this latter trend in perspective: increased inequality does not necessarily mean declining living standards and, viewed in a global perspective, it does not do so now. Although poverty remains ubiquitous in the South[2] and is also evident, although on a much smaller scale, in parts of the North, human living standards have been increasing as the gap between rich and poor has widened. But this is no necessary cause for complacency about democracy's material accompaniments—or its continued stability. Although the relationship between inequality and instability is less obvious than conventional wisdom holds, widening inequality could threaten social stability even amidst rising living standards as those at the bottom of the economic ladder compare their circumstances to those of the affluent, rather than to their own in the past. And, in at least some societies, one cause of widening inequality is a tendency for sections of the middle strata to lose economic ground, creating a class of "new poor." Since people whose standards decline are likely to be more discontented than those whose conditions remain much as they have been throughout their lives, this phenomenon too suggests that there are significant numbers of people for whom democracy's advent has coincided with economic causes for heightened discontent.

These realities raise important questions about democracy's nature and prospects for survival. If we accept that it is highly unlikely that citizens whose economic position has declined, either in absolute terms or relative to those of the affluent, are likely to have freely endorsed this development, and that democracy is meant, among other features, to provide a conduit through which citizens can express their interests and aspirations and see them acted upon by government, then there are significant numbers of citizens for whom democracy has failed to extend an opportunity to see their preferences translated into action by elected authorities. For them, "negative" freedom—from overt state coercion—has perhaps never been so pervasive. But democracy as "positive" freedom—the capacity of citizens to control public decisionmaking and to ensure policy outcomes consistent with the interests of majorities (which, of course, shift from issue to issue)—is absent.

The problem is not as new as it may seem. During the nineteenth century, thinkers assumed an innate contradiction between democracy and social inequality: on the left, Marx and Engels expected that universal suffrage would herald the victory of working-class power, while conservatives rejected universal adult franchise for precisely this reason.[3] Subsequent experience has shown that, contrary to these expectations, extending the vote to all did not herald the collapse of capitalism. One reason is that Marx's claim, in his letter to the *New York Tribune* of 25 August 1852 (cited in Lipset 1964), that the working class formed "the great majority of the population" proved inaccurate: as Przeworski (1987) has shown, nowhere did the proletariat as defined by Marxist theory constitute a majority, and in all cases, working-class parties were obliged to form alliances if they wished to win electoral power; this, of course, required compromise and a consequent modification of goals. Another reason, as Marshall suggested when he addressed this question, was that market economies made significant adjustments to accommodate the enfranchisement of workers.

So, while democracy did not end social inequality, as socialist visionaries had hoped, it substantially ameliorated it as workers and the poor used their vote to win improvements in their entitlements and living standards. Those who would argue that history demonstrates a compatibility or at least the likelihood of coexistence between universal political rights and social inequality ignore, therefore, the degree to which the extension of the former mitigated the latter: its failure to do so now is the key dimension that marks off the current spread of global democracy from its previous expansion within the countries of the industrialized North. Previously, expanded political rights did not generate an egalitarian utopia but did bring significant narrowing of the gap between rich and poor; their failure to do so now is, therefore, a novelty. Democracy has shown that it can survive in the context of continued, but narrowing, inequality; that does not necessarily mean that it has similar prospects if economic difference widens.

Evidence that, in parts of the globe, widening inequality is not received with passivity and approbation for parties that profess to offer a more egalitarian alternative to regularly win election, as is the trend in Eastern Europe. Their subsequent unwillingness or inability to introduce policies that do redress inequality suggests that current economic policy continuities do not stem from citizen consent but from new democratic polities' incapacity to respond to democratically expressed preferences.[4] This implies that democracy's resurgence has been achieved only at the expense of its hollowing out—the right to political choice seems to have been won only at the expense of having little about which to choose. Or, to put the same problem in another way, citizens in many new democracies have the right to choose but not to see their choices acted upon. The inability of democracies to address inequality also, of course, questions the assumption that democracy, by offering inequality's victims access to public decision-making, inevitably offers a surer route toward more equitable distribution of wealth than leftist authoritarianism.

Even if we accept that "hollowed out" democracy is better than none at all, because it does promise an end to politically sanctioned violence and other rights abuses, can new—and perhaps even established—democracies continue to exist alongside rising inequalities? For the present, citizens of new democracies do seem to have concluded that freedom is preferable to bondage, even if it widens the gulf between those who have and those who do not. But it is at least possible that this has much to do with recent memories of authoritarianism and that, if current trends in the distribution of resources, opportunities, and capabilities continue, or even if they are not significantly reversed, the next generation may find continued or growing inequality less tolerable than an authoritarianism that they have never experienced.

This possibility may be enhanced by the reality that inequality co-existed with stability in many parts of the world for centuries because deeply internalized notions of hierarchy sustained it. Inequality was held to be irremediable by government or collective effort—that some prospered and others did not seemed ordained by the natural order. But, while formal democracy certainly can be grafted onto deeply ingrained notions of hierarchy, democratization does rest on a notion of formal equality; this places ideological support for inequality under unprecedented stress, producing at least the possibility of growing aspirations for equality: it is, of course, this insight that inspired Marshall's assertion of an inevitable conflict between citizenship and class differentiation. If inequality is not addressed, citizens may increasingly come to question the degree to which egalitarian political values remain unrealized in society and economy. Population growth and increasing poverty may also enormously expand "the demand for discipline," internally or externally imposed, increasing the growth potential of fundamentalist and authoritarian movements. Within most national frontiers, populations are likely to become more heterogeneous, straining domestic and international governability and greatly expanding the potential for conflict.

A consequence of hollowed-out democracy is also a shortening of the reach of the state. In many societies, the relationship between citizenry and state becomes increasingly tenuous as putative citizens, faced with states that can neither offer the benefits nor impose the sanctions central to liberal democratic ideas of the state, opt out by choice or default, prompting warnings that chaos, not orderly democratic citizenship, may be the leitmotif of the twenty-first century.[5]

These considerations imply, at the very least, a need to move beyond much current scholarship on democracy to examine not only the cultural and institutional preconditions of democratic survival, but also the extent to which inequality threatens democracy. And, given the potentially corrosive effects of widening inequality on the social fabric, there is an equally pressing need to examine the latitude of democratic states to address inequality.

This chapter does not seek to offer definitive answers to these questions. It seeks rather to make a tentative contribution to understandings of the relationship between democracy and inequality and of the capacity of the former to redress the latter under current conditions. It is concerned above all to make a modest contribution to correcting perhaps the greatest contradiction of the current wave of democratization—that, as democracy has taken root to an unprecedented extent, classic democratic notions of politics and the political have been relegated to the margins of debate and of development and governance practice. It will, therefore, suggest that a renewed respect for, and normative commitment to, democratic *politics* lies at the heart of democracy's survival—and more particularly, the ability to manage and reduce inequality in the new century on which its health may depend.

Globalization: The Opiate of the Intellectuals?

Prevailing orthodoxy finds a simple explanation for the current predicament of the democratic state—globalization. The term has become pervasive: "Politicians and scholars, active citizens and passive spectators . . . all invoke its omnipresence and omnipotence when trying to make sense of the multitude of uncertainties which surround them" (Schmitter 1999:937). It may be used, depending on the perspective of the user, as a bogeyman to scare childlike interventionist states away from violating the new laissez-faire natural order, or as a left-wing expletive to explain any and every frustration of the socialist project. But, across the political spectrum, there is, with some notable exceptions (see, for example, Moon and Yang's Chapter 7, p. 135), wide agreement both that it exists and that it has sharply narrowed the options of states, bringing in its train the contradiction noted earlier: because the state's room to move has narrowed or (in the view of some students of globalization) collapsed entirely, authoritarianism is a less attractive option—but, for the same reason, democracy means an absence of overt coercion, not an opportunity to shape the public destiny.

But what is globalization, and what are its implications for the state? Clearly, changes in communications technology and the relative ease with which cultural artifacts now travel across national boundaries have important effects on intellectual life and popular culture. This has inevitable political and economic effects. But there are strong empirical grounds for suggesting that "globalization" is far more of an intellectual or cultural phenomenon than an economic process—both because the flow of ideas and symbols across borders is more significant than the journeys of goods and capital and because globalization's potency in thought (and therefore in policymaking) may be more real than its salience in economic and political life.

As Schmitter points out, this does not necessarily minimize its effects: "Globalization may not even exist in any material sense, but if enough people (and, especially, enough highly placed and resourceful people) believe that it is present and potent, then, it will produce a significant effect by anticipated reaction" (Schmitter 1999:937).

There is little doubt that the pervasive perception of globalization shapes economic and political responses across the planet. But if the phenomenon indeed does not "exist in any material sense" or if its existence is far less significant than current orthodoxy suggests, then the assumptions and policy decisions that it produces are, at least in principle, capable of reversal.

It is trite to point out that technological change has opened unprecedented possibilities for the movement of information and capital across national borders. But it has had no similar effect on the movement of goods, since the volume of international trade today is no greater than at the turn of the century (Rodrik 1997b): indeed, as Lowi points out in the present volume (p. 43), no less a mainstream source than *The Economist* has observed that, on measures such as share of foreign capital and domestic investment or cross-border flows of investment in relation to national output, "the world was more closely integrated before 1914 than it is now, in some cases much more so."

Nor, in purely numerical terms, has it generated cross-border movements of people greater than those at the beginning of the twentieth century (Krugman 1998a)—although cross-border migration, particularly by people culturally or racially different from the host country majority, has increased enough in the last few decades to demand a reassessment of Marshall's link between citizenship and entitlement, of which more later. Opportunities for the mobility of people with particular types of skills—inevitably to the advantage of the North at the expense of the South—may also have been enhanced, although this does hold some advantages for Southern countries in the form, for example, of repatriated remittances.

To deny that capital flows across borders hold implications for governments would be foolish since they appear to provide a far more accessible exit option for investors than in the past, so constraining the latitude for state intervention to impose undesired outcomes on investors. But whether, as enthusiastic management consultants regularly insist or leftist analysts repeatedly bemoan, this has reduced the nation-state to a quaint irrelevance[6] is another matter entirely.

Several important qualifications must be imposed on this image of a world in which footloose capitalists move their resources across boundaries in response to every real or imagined slight from the state. First, the size of capital flows, while substantial in the context of small Southern economies, is often grossly exaggerated: in 1993, the peak year of "emerging market" investment, only about 3 percent of Northern investment was diverted from domestic use; the entire post-1990 "boom" in this investment has diverted only about 0.5 percent of the North's capital to the South (Krugman 1998a:62–63). Even in the era of electronic capital movements, then, most investible resources stay at home or circulate within the North.

Second, the overblown claims of "pop internationalists" (Krugman 1998a) that the nation-state is fragmenting under the weight of globalization into myriad statelets is belied by the fact that the emergence of smaller political units out of nation-states has simply not happened outside Eastern Europe, where the trend is both limited and, in most cases, represents rather the reconstitution of political units that existed prior to the expansion of the Soviet empire: they are, therefore, related to the collapse of the Soviet Union rather than to the activities of hedge funds. In Africa, where the weakness of the state is surely most pronounced, and in which the proposition that current state boundaries are merely colonial administrative creations is decades-old, there has only been one major case of successful secession—Eritrea. However dysfunctional nation-states may be, their elites or citizens or both seem to cling to them tenaciously, if only for want of alternatives. Indeed, as Robert Dahl has recently suggested, "today, people in democratic countries may want more governmental action, not less, simply in order to counter the adverse effects of international markets" (1999:927).

Third, inequities in capital accumulation between states preceded cross-border capital flows and are not caused by them. Common sense suggests that before countries can become vulnerable to capital exports they need private businesses with significant capital to move abroad. The oft-lamented "marginalization" of sections of the globe—Africa primary among them—is, therefore, a consequence not of excessive penetration by global capital but of its opposite, the tendency for capital to avoid these regions and (more important, as we will see) of a lack of a domestic capital base sufficient to spur growth. Poor countries do, therefore, retain the option of seeking to build their domestic capital stocks, and if globalization has any economic effect at all, it lies in a denial of opportunity, not of sovereignty. Indeed, in some cases, the ability to move capital across boundaries can be a net plus for Southern countries, enabling them to benefit from the resources accumulated in their diasporas. Although the role of off-shore Chinese investment in mainland China's growth spurt is perhaps the best-known example, diasporas also play a significant role in transferring resources from the North to Africa, Latin America, the Caribbean, and Asian countries such as the Philippines and Bangladesh. And their propensity to do this stems not from the global cost-benefit calculations that the management consultants stress, but from intangibles such as family loyalties and continued identification with nation and state. Even in a "globalized" world—and across great distances—the call of kin and country continues to influence economic behavior.

Fourth, although middle-income countries such as Brazil and Korea are vulnerable to capital exports by domestic investors during times of economic stress, this capital tends to return once domestic prospects improve. In South Africa, by contrast, domestic capital that leaves tends not to return (Landman 1999). The difference between the two stems not from global capital flows in themselves but from differing relations between their domestic business classes and the state: while in the two first-named states, the owners of capital are fairly "rooted" in their domestic states, those in South Africa are not. So, while domestic investors' capacity to export capital may present its disaffected owners with options that were absent or more limited in the past, the degree to which these opportunities are exercised depends on intrastate politics: the nation-state and the manner in which it relates to owners remains, therefore, crucial. The alternatives to domestic investment may be more conspicuous and more lucrative now, but, even before the first offshore fund was invented, owners aggrieved by the political environment in which they operated retained the option of withholding or deferring investment.

Fifth, there is compelling evidence that direct foreign investment is not a cause but a consequence of growth in late economic developers (Rodrik 1997b). In other words, contrary to both globalization's passionate advocates and despairing detractors, countries' growth prospects do not depend, at least at the crucial initial stages, on their magnetism to foreign investment, but on their ability to induce its domestic equivalent. This explains the disappointment of African and Eastern European states which, having faithfully applied the prevailing proposed recipe for attracting foreign investment, discover to their dismay that the promised bounty fails to appear. The missing link is domestic growth, for which the role of the state—and the political environment more generally—in creating a conducive context remains crucial. And the requirements are much the same as they always were before global capital flows caught the imagination of intellectuals: administrative capacity, the ability to extract (reasonably voluntary) compliance from citizens, and the capacity to resolve conflict between competing interests. Individual states may operate in different terrain, but their capacities are arguably more, not less, important now than they were when capital's exit option was more limited.

Contrary to an orthodoxy that restricts the role of the state, particularly in the South, to creating an environment friendly to global capital, those that do chart growth paths do so by giving primacy to domestic constituencies and needs, rather than those of international investors. (This does not suggest any inherent conflict between domestic and international investor interests, and hence the need for a new protectionism; rather, it argues that, unless states build growth strategies on an accurate assessment of the domestic preconditions for growth, they will not achieve the initial "take off" that might later attract foreign capital).

But more is perhaps at stake, normatively and practically, than affording priority to domestic concerns. The issue may well be the self-definition of states that still seek a sustainable path to growth and reduced inequality. If globalization is indeed, as proposed here, primarily an intellectual and cultural phenomenon, then one of its tenets, again held by left and right, is that states, in order to maximize their citizens' welfare, are required to adopt a uniform self-image expressed in standardized recipes for growth. The argument advanced here questions this, suggesting that the effectiveness of responses is likely to depend less on the degree to which they implement a universal vision of the "internationally competitive" or "world class" state than on the extent to which states are able to frame responses that are appropriate to the particular, state-specific resources that are available to them and the contexts within which they function. Writing of democracy, rather than wealth creation, Guillermo O'Donnell has noted that, among Southern intellectuals, the "countries of the Northwest [are] admired for their long-enduring regimes and for their wealth, and because both things seemed to go together. . . . The Northwest was seen as the endpoint of a trajectory" (1996:46–47). Ironically, that trajectory is more likely to be realized if the strategies, policy agendas, and institutional forms of the South build on and respond to domestic specificities than if they seek to clone Northern approaches. Instead of asking how domestic contexts can be transformed into Northern forms, Southern states may be required to ask how the assets latent in the domestic environment can be harnessed to achieve the goals already realized in the North.

Finally, if we examine the evidence rather than popular mythology, theories of the decline of the state are less a description of a universal trend than an indictment of global interstate inequalities. The state's role in the economy has continued to grow in Organization for Economic Development and Cooperation countries into the 1990s, although in "developing countries" it has declined during the decade after steady growth since the 1960s (Tanzi and Shuknecht 1995). The straitened government-provided safety nets that survive the attenuation of the state in the North are often far in excess of those to which some Southern states can aspire (United Nations Development Program 1996:184). It is, therefore, in the affluent societies that the state plays a substantial and growing role. In the poorer ones, the state's role become attenuated—and diminished from a much smaller starting point. States are unable to fulfill the aspirations expressed in their laws and regulations, forced to play a far more limited role than they played in Thatcher's Britain or Reagan's United States. To the skeptical Southern intellectual, therefore, fashionable theories diagnosing the terminal decline of the state seem designed more to persuade poor nations not to aspire to that which affluent ones already have than to offer a plausible description of reality.

None of this should be particularly new: the role of Southern states—more specifically, those in East Asia—in inducing or inhibiting domestic investment and growth has been demonstrated by recent scholarship, which has stressed both the links between states and domestic business classes as well as the state's capacity to pursue a relatively autonomous agenda (Evans 1995). East Asian states are said to have mastered the prerequisites, while those in Latin America, Africa, and South Asia have failed to varying degrees. Although the Asian financial turmoil of the late 1990s forced an inevitable reassessment of these analyses, the recent troubles of East Asian economies do not gainsay the fact that they did achieve sustained growth and poverty reduction over several decades and that the role of the state in this trajectory was pivotal. Indeed, with the publication of the World Bank's 1997 *World Development Report* (1997a), the centrality of the state's role in growth (or its absence) has again entered the mainstream.

The evidence for the decline of the state is, therefore, unconvincing: despite the hyperbole, not only does it remain intact but its actions continue to determine, to a significant degree, whether societies prosper economically or stagnate. Nor do they do this merely by adjusting to the dictates of the global owners of capital: in principle, they retain significant leeway to set their own paths away from, or toward, growth.

The State as Normative Ideal

The state's role as an instrument of growth has, therefore, been rehabilitated. But its recuperation is at best partial for, even in literature reviving the importance of the state, it is seen as an instrumental means, not as a normative goal.

On the right, the idea of the state as, at best, a necessary evil, has deep roots: among its most articulate exponents is Robert Nozick (1977), who sees it only as "a protective agency" against force, theft, fraud, and the violation of contracts. Beyond that, theories such as

Mancur Olson's (1971) notion of "distributive coalitions" see states not as guardians of the public good but as instruments of powerful sectional interests hostile to the individual and the rational functioning of the market. On the left, a reaction to the authoritarianism of Soviet state socialism or the perceived tendency of the welfare state to reduce its beneficiaries to permanent dependence produced new enthusiasm for civil society, once seen by leftist thought as the terrain of inequality and domination, but lately viewed as an alternative repository of democracy and of public welfare, an arena in which citizens can free themselves not only from the shackles of the market but from those of the overbearing state (Keane 1988).

None of these theories denies the necessity of the state. Much of the right knows that its role in securing public order is crucial, much of the left that civil society has no meaning unless it is conceived of in relation to the state: to talk of a viable and effective civil society in the absence of an equivalent state is a contradiction, for it is the state that provides and enforces the legal framework from which the associations of civil society derive their freedom to associate and that arbitrates the competing claims within civil society; and it is from engagement with the state that civil society derives its rationale. But both are concerned to stress its limits: on the right, to confine it to providing a supportive framework to the free realm of contract, on the left to stress its limited capacity, as against social movements and citizens' associations, to offer emancipation. In both cases, liberty and social progress require that the state be curbed lest it extinguish market activity or free popular action in the public sphere. While, earlier in the century, the notion that control of the state was the key to action against poverty, inequality, or the denial of freedom stretched from Lenin to Marshall to Franklin D. Roosevelt, it is now seen, even in literature emphasizing its role in underpinning material progress, at best as a precondition for egalitarian or emancipatory action that occurs elsewhere.

In one sense, this stress on the limits of the state, despite its importance, is a crucial element of democratic theory. If democracy institutionalizes citizens' right to choose in the public sphere, it also requires that they enjoy the right to private space in which they are free to generate the independent initiative on which choice depends—for this reason, a democratic state is always limited by rules that limit its incursions into the private sphere.

But in another, the stress on the state as limited instrument ignores a crucial element of the democratic endeavor, for the state remains an independent prerequisite for the realization of democratic values and aspirations. If evidence is needed, it can be supplied in the negative by reference to a recent work by British conservative William Rees-Mogg that predicts, with undisguised enthusiasm, a future of rampant individualism in which the state will become irrelevant because all its classic functions, from personal security to education, will become the preserve of the private realm (Davidson and Rees-Mogg 1997). His normative framework will be rejected by democrats—just as it leads him to reject democracy. But the book is nevertheless largely accurate in its description of the likely features of a world without the democratic state: it is one in which the affluent live in heavily guarded fortresses, much of the rest of humanity in abject misery, a world far more redolent of that which Hobbes believed the state had been created to transcend than a new golden age. Unwittingly perhaps, it is a necessary antidote to contemporary democrats who exalt autonomous citizen action without recognizing the crucial role of the state in making such action possible.

It is perhaps no accident that, barring the work of political philosophers (Keane 1988; Barber 1998) that has little impact on the public-policy debate, enthusiasm for civil society as an implied alternative, rather than a supplement, to the state is applied primarily to Southern countries where the state is weakest. The suggestion that civil society is a better guarantor of liberty and equity than the state may, therefore, be more a despairing symptom of the malaise of many Southern new-democratic states than a pointer to a new-democratic direction. It may also be worth noting here that, while intellectuals and donor agencies exalt civil society in the South, it may be in decline in Northern democracies. Trade union membership in the Netherlands declined from 39 percent of the work force to 25 percent from 1978 to 1991, while that in the United States has halved in three decades (United Nations Development Program 1996:59). While that trend could be seen as a response to changes in work processes, Robert Putnam's (1995) finding that associational activity in the United States has declined, although hotly disputed, has claimed widespread attention. This does not, of course, imply that the state has somehow rendered Northern civil society redundant. But it does provide further reason for skepticism about current notions of civil society as an alternative to the state.

More important, civil society, for all its importance in providing a realm of citizen participation in public life, is by definition the arena of the partial interest. The state, by contrast, is the realm, at least in its ideal form, of the general good for, unlike civil-society associations, democratic states cannot explicitly reject the claims and concerns of, or deny participation in or the protection of their institutions to, any section of society. For those—and fortunately that means most of us—who believe that human interdependence and cooperation are as essential to the good society as individual liberty, the state represents an aspiration, a normative goal, even if its reach requires limitation. For without it, there is no public sphere and no cooperation, no common loyalties, no public deliberation and action. It is the state that makes possible the citizenship that Marshall's defense of the welfare state was concerned to enrich and endow with substance because, in its democratic form, it ensures the right to speak, to act in pursuit of public goals, and to decide. No wonder, then, that in the lives of most societies states continue to play a substantial role and that, where they do not, their erosion or collapse occurs despite despairing efforts to prevent it.

This proposed enthusiasm for the state must be qualified in one important way—one that has acquired new importance in the light of cross-border migration. Each state and the citizenship it bestows is available only to some: the notion of the state is at the same time inclusive and exclusionary, bestowing rights on those inside the political space it occupies just as it denies them to those outside it (unless the receiving state, in an act of generosity or expansive self-interest, decides to bestow them as a gift). This is important to consideration of the future of democracies, but particularly so if we are concerned with inequality's impact on democracy. Traditionally, measures employed by democratic states to address inequality were for citizens alone, as suggested by Marshall's concept of citizenship. In many cases, generous social policy regimes were achieved partly by erecting high barriers to entry (although in others—Latin American states such as Brazil and Argentina, or British dominions such as Australia and South Africa—European immigrants benefited from the barriers at the expense of indigenous people). If the (albeit exaggerated) idea of a state as a closed political community is now weakening, the benefits of statehood and citizenship could increasingly be possible only at the expense of ever-harsher measures to exclude noncitizens from the state.

The dilemma may yet prove painful to democracies. However, the challenge it presents is not to retreat from state and citizenship, but to confront the implications of seeking to extend them, either by rethinking the political and welfare implications of broadening the political communities that states express or by expanding the reach of interstate institutions and regulatory regimes. One important implication could well be the revision or erosion of the idea of "nation-state," not in the sense proposed by current theories of state collapse, but in a redefinition of the qualifications for participation in and protection by the state.[7] But the result may be less a redefinition of "state" as of "nation": change in the cultural composition of some states does not alter the reality that a democratic community is impossible without a state and that contemporary concern with protecting and sustaining democracy needs to be as preoccupied with the state as a vehicle for citizenship and democratic expression as with its limited role as a catalyst of economic activity—particularly in the South, where in many cases states still struggle to extend their reach over society, but also in those parts of the North in which declining participation rates signal the weakened appeal of the democratic state. Enriching and strengthening the state remain as important as continuing to limit it.

Politics as Necessity—and Aspiration

Two qualifications to the discussion thus far now require attention. The first is that current treatments of the role of the state in creating the preconditions for growth tend to emphasize government relations with business, not with other social groups. The other is that they stress its capacity to influence growth far more than its impact on inequality. Both limitations bear directly on our concern for democracy.

First, if, as some of the literature on the "developmental state" seems to imply, the state's role in triggering growth is essentially a matter of cementing relations with business alone—while effective antipoverty strategies were pursued, labor's exclusion from decisions is, in at least one case (Korea), said to have "[produced] militant workers" (Evans 1995:229)—the concerns expressed earlier about democracy's health and future seem to be underlined, since important interests and the majority of citizens are thus reduced to passive bystanders as owners and officials plot the course of economy and society.

It is important to stress here that, just as an approach that reduces economic progress to the diligent applications of particular policy recipes is likely to miss crucial dimensions, so too is one that seeks to compensate by locating it purely in the state-business relationship—and for similar reasons. An important antidote to this misreading is found in the work of Nobel Laureate Douglass North, whose work on economic history highlights the pivotal role not of economic policy recipes but institutions, understood as "the humanly devised constraints that structure political, economic and social interaction" (1991:97) and ideologies—or social understandings—in shaping societies' economic performance. In essence, North (1995) argues that economies are likely to grow if the institutions and ideologies that shape economic actors' behavior lower the cost of transacting; if economic strategies that have had particular effects in one institutional context—North's favorite example is privatization—are translated to another, they are, therefore, likely to have unintended consequences because they will be applied within a different institutional context. The idea that people do not act, in the marketplace as well as in other settings, purely as calculators of instrumental interest strikes an intuitive chord; it may also, when read together with, for example, recent work on extra-state economic activity in Africa (Simone 1994; McGaffey 1997; Tripp 1997), explain the sharp divide between economic policy intent and outcomes in some African and other Southern societies.

More important for our purpose, if institutions and ideas matter in the fate of economies, as the North insists that they do, then so too does politics. North himself formulates the link in a rather limited way: "The inability to have low cost specification of the attributes being exchanged and enforcement of agreements in economic markets is ultimately a function of the political markets of economies, because it is the polity that specifies the property rights and provides the instruments and resources to enforce contracts" (1995:10). Phrased in that way, the proposition might be endorsed by most economic technicians. But his focus on institutions and ideologies has more profound implications than North himself acknowledges here, for it is in the political realm that contending visions of the appropriate rules of "political, economic and social interaction" are proposed, debated, and translated into law and policy. The arena in which the preconditions for creating—as well as distributing—wealth is, therefore, the political. These insights on the preconditions of economic success suggest not merely that economics needs to take politics more seriously but that the contest of ideas and values (as well as interests) that we call politics may do far more to shape economic outcomes than price signals. And, since institutions and ideologies are shaped by, and shape the behavior of, a far wider range of individuals and interests than those who own businesses, it is the political life of entire societies, not simply government-business relationships, that creates or inhibits the preconditions for growth.

Second, if only government-business relations are relevant, prospects that democracies will address inequality then depend on the degree to which these two elites believe action against differentials to be in the interests of growth. Although in the East Asian development states they seem to have reached that conclusion (helped, if we follow North's hypothesis, by the prevailing institutions and understandings in their societies), there is no guarantee that they will do so elsewhere. And even if there were, action would then largely depend on the enlightened judgment of elites, and the degree to which a compelling case could be made to them that measures to address inequality are in their interests, not on the articulation of public interests and the consequent mediation between conflicting ones that are the essence of democratic politics.

If we put aside a sentimental attachment to idealized notions of democratic politics, why should that matter? Because current trends suggest that attempts to address inequality—and poverty—within this paradigm are not achieving results, even if they are measured in purely technical terms, because they ignore or misread the political.

An illustration can be found in current World Bank attempts to address poverty intellectually and in practical policy. The Bank, in keeping with much contemporary orthodoxy, has effectively depoliticized both poverty and inequality. In its continuing concern to devise ways of addressing the impact of economic change on the poor, its approach—in broad outline—is to set a poverty level of $1 per person a day and to define all those below it as the "poor," all above it as the "nonpoor" (see, e.g., World Bank 1996, 1997b). It then posits an inherent conflict of interest between the two, criticizing measures that reach the "nonpoor" as diversions of resources from the needy. Social policy formation becomes largely a technical exercise—admittedly demanding and sophisticated—whose chief aim is to devise instruments perfectly targeted to bypass the "nonpoor" as they reach the "poor."

An obvious quibble is that the standard is arbitrary and that measures that reach persons earning just above $1 a day may well be reaching those in dire need. A further objection, as another contribution in this volume argues, is that it reduces poverty purely to income, rather than embracing wider concepts such as Amartya Sen's notion of "capability poverty" (Mangcu: p. 95). But a further key weakness of this approach is that it almost inevitably excludes the possibility of democratic action against poverty, an outcome tacitly acknowledged by the Bank in early 1999, when it convened a meeting of scholars to advise it on why governments were not "pro-poor."

An examination of literature on the politics of social policy would quickly enlighten the Bank. There is, to be sure, evidence that elite attitudes do matter in determining whether societies will address poverty and inequality. In his study of the creation of welfare state systems in Western Europe and the United States, Abram de Swaan (1988) argues that a crucial element in societies' willingness to address poverty and inequality was the development among elites of a "social consciousness" whose elements are: an awareness of the interdependence of all social groups, a realization that elites bear some of the responsibility for the sufferings of the poor, and a belief that efficacious means of assisting the poor exist or might be created. But, as important as this stress on elite attitudes is, it leaves open the question of how elites might come to hold them. And the Bank's approach is almost guaranteed to ensure that they will not.

The effect of its approach is to separate off those on the bottom rung from the rest of society and to make poverty reduction purely a matter of enlightened technocratic concern. Because the poor are rarely able to organize themselves and are therefore forced to rely on alliances with other strata of society, egalitarian social policy tends to command political support in two circumstances. First, egalitarian social-policy application may be justified by criteria that elicit wide social consensus because they respond to norms that cross class and interest barriers. The expressed need to cater for Civil War veterans ensured a generous social policy regime in the postbellum United States, despite presumed American resistance to social spending, because it tapped into and built on widespread public support for those who had defended the Union (Skocpol and Katznelson 1996). Second, egalitarian social policy may be supported by a significant interest group—historically, organized labor—that is able to forge alliances with other interests that also stand to benefit from action against inequality. Contrary to some social-democratic romanticism, labor parties have always required the support of other interests to achieve their policy agendas (Esping-Andersen 1990; Przeworski 1987), suggesting that it is not only the unorganized poor who require alliances to realize redistributive policy agendas.

To be sure, not all labor-led welfare states redistribute to the poor. Latin American social policy, corresponding to Esping-Andersen's (1990) notion of the "conservative" welfare state has, in most cases, benefited labor and other organized strata at the expense of the poorest (de Souza 1996). In these cases, for a variety of reasons beyond the scope of this chapter, labor has become part of an alliance against rather than with the poor. But, while this argues against a romantic reliance on labor-led alliances in the current context—if labor is assumed to retain an ability to impact on politics that this analysis argues it now lacks—it strengthens the point that "pro-poor" policies are the outcome of alliances between the poor and other strata and that, where these are lacking, so too are social policies that advantage the poor.

Given these realities, a strategy and analysis that separates the poor from the rest of the society—and insists that their interests are in conflict with those of other groups—is certain to relegate their concerns to the peripheries, rendering democracies unable to address poverty or inequality, for two reasons. First, by creating an antagonism between the poor and other strata, it excludes the possibility of social consensus. Second and similarly, it eliminates the prospect of alliances between the poor and other, more organized and influential, groups. The only mystery attending the tendency of governments not to be "pro-poor" in these circumstances is that anyone should regard it as a mystery. Since the poor, because of their lack of resources and access to the political system, are usually the weakest and least influential group in society, the approach discussed here operates to exclude them from realistic prospects of policy influence. If further evidence were needed, the hostility toward welfare recipients in the United States, who are distinguished from the social mainstream by race and often gender as well as social class, provides a useful illustration.[8] Once alliances and political action are removed from the equation, the only champions of equality and action against poverty are the scholars and policy advisors, whose influence is hardly guaranteed and who, in any event, are as likely to oppose as to defend measures designed to address inequality. And alliances and common action are indeed excluded if an artificial antagonism is created between the interests of the poor and all other social strata.

As noted earlier, the belief of Marx and Engels that universal franchise would inevitably spell the end of class domination has been misplaced. But without—under nondemocratic conditions such as those that prevailed in most of the East Asian "developmental states"— a social consensus against severe inequalities or—under democratic conditions—either a similar consensus or political action by strata whose interests are compatible with those of inequality's victims, the prospect of sustained attempts to address inequality remain remote. The only prospect of effective action against social and economic disparities by democratic political systems lies in the revival of democratic politics itself.

That such a revival is needed is illustrated by prevailing development orthodoxy of which World Bank literature is again a useful exemplar. First, although the 1997 *World Development Report* indeed returned the state to the mainstream of the debate on the preconditions for growth for development, it did not do the same for democratic politics. Indeed, the only reference in a bulky document to representative democracy is a half-page passing reference in which its formal resurgence is noted without any serious attempt to discuss its implications; the discussion then passes to a topic more familiar to current development specialists—public participation techniques, which are designed to simulate (or perhaps bypass) rather then reinforce representative democracy.[9] More generally, representative democracy tends to be seen, in current Bank literature on economic adjustment, as an obstacle to appropriate policy rather than its pre-condition (see, e.g., Raczynski 1995).

Similar echoes can be found in much current development literature, which often seems willing to enthuse over any mode of public participation in decisions except formal democratic representation and contest. To be sure, current exaltation of civil society's role in development need not propose an alternative to democratic politics since, as implied earlier, civil society activity is meant to enrich, not replace, democratic political action (Keane 1988; Barber 1998). But civil-society delivery of development outcomes is routinely lauded as a more effective mode, and thus as an implied alternative, to that of the state, democratic or authoritarian. To cite two examples: in Sri Lanka, a change in state policy from direct housing delivery to citizen provision is said to have increased output several fold (Ali and Sirivardana 1996:221 ff); in Bolivia, religious nongovernmental organizations are reported to have achieved more effective schooling than state provision (World Bank 1997a:90). These empirical claims about particular development programs are not disputed. However, they tend to underpin an approach to development that sees the democratic state as an obstacle rather than an asset. This is open to challenge on practical as well as normative criteria once we move from the analysis of particular projects to society-wide challenges.

On the first score, action against inequality within civil society, whatever models it may establish, is inevitably limited in effect without the support of the state, which can, in principle, implement policy on a scale beyond most if not all civil-society organizations. The effect is likely to be action that may reduce poverty for its beneficiaries but is unlikely to address society-wide inequality because it is almost certain to reach only some of those in need.

More generally, these treatments ignore the degree to which politics can—and does—frustrate development plans and programs. On the micro level, there are countless examples in which political contests among the beneficiaries of development have frustrated development interventions, worsening the inequities they sought to cure (see Friedman 1993). On the macro level, the World Bank's lament at the absence of "pro-poor" governments may suffice to demonstrate the point; if it does not, empirical research indicating a strong correlation between societies' ability to resolve political conflict and their ability to raise living standards and address inequality should make it unequivocally (Rodrik 1999).

On the second score, civil society intervention that is not the outcome of a state policy and program is, by definition, beyond public political contest since civil society organizations are, with good reason, required to account only to their stakeholders, not to society as a whole. It may be no accident that, in practice, the exaltation of civil society in many Southern contexts has produced patronage rather than development, clientelism rather than democracy.[10] Analyses that emphasize both the effectiveness and representativeness of nonstate actors may thus hand control of resources to individuals and oligarchies who may limit democracy's reach and ensure that "development" becomes a source of patronage rather than equity. And this is possible because they remain beyond the political accountability that democratic states may not always guarantee, but which only they can offer because only they subject the allocation of resources and discussion of priorities to public contest, compromise, or coalition among *all* society's interests.

Emphases on "public participation" and "civil society" often also tend to ignore or suppress one of the key assumptions of democratic politics—the acknowledgment of difference not only as an intractable reality but as both a virtue that enriches society and as an injunction to tolerance and engagement. Ironically, the same literature that divides society starkly into the "poor" and "nonpoor" also assumes that there is a homogenous "public" (or "community") whose participation can be sought and secured. And, while political philosophers may claim to know better, much development literature tends to impute a similar homogeneity to "civil society." Since the inevitability of differences of interest and of value is not only an empirical reality but a normative precondition for democracy—if we all have the same interests, why bother to invent institutions to express difference and mediate between contending positions?—the effect is to deny the need for politics and so to hand over control of the public agenda to whichever interest is strong enough to dominate it (or, in some cases, to whoever's techniques currently conform to intellectual fashion). Whatever efficiencies that may yield, its result is unlikely to be either greater freedom or less inequality. And the inequities and suppression of weaker interests it brings in its train stem from its denial of politics.[11]

Similarly, much current enthusiasm among international financial institutions and development specialists for "good governance" as the precondition of democratic statecraft commits an error that, ironically, owes its provenance to Lenin—it reduces politics to administration (Polan 1984:58 ff). Public management technique, important as it undoubtedly is, is presented as an alternative rather than a supplement to democratic politics, which often then appears as an obstacle to, rather than the raison d'être for, effective government because it is not subject to the same managerial considerations.

The irony of democracy's current triumph, then, is that it seems to have been won at the expense of politics, understood as free contest between contending interests and visions within agreed rules that allow for the resolution of conflict in ways that guarantee the rights of the contending parties (and thus, of course, guard against differences being expressed in less benign ways). Although mainstream discussion of poverty and inequality usually pays lip service to democracy—sometimes with a suitable show of homage to nondemocratic "developmental states"—it is far more likely to be seen as a system that offers freedom *from* politics than as one that allows freedom for it. And, for that reason, politics as understood here is either presented as an unpleasant reality to be bypassed—or simply ignored. It is perhaps illustrative of the degree to which this represents the temper of the times that the dominant mode of political analysis—at least in the United States—at present is "rational choice theory," which seeks to understand politics through the (purported) rationality of economics and reduces normative political choices to instrumental calculations (see, e.g., Arrow 1963; Downs 1957; Olson 1971). North's work suggests strongly that the calculations assumed by rational-choice theorists do not govern most economic behavior (see, e.g., Denzau and North 1994)—particularly in contexts such as those in most Southern economies, where uncertainty prevails (North 1995); the claim that they determine political choices, relegating core determinants of preference and behavior such as identities and values to, at most, irrational interference with instrumental calculation, is even more untenable.[12]

But the argument presented here suggests that, if democracies are indeed to address inequality, they can do so only if democratic politics is nurtured and strengthened. Since differences of interest and value exist, and cannot be wished away by any amount of "good governance" or skilled public participation techniques, the effect of substituting technique for democratic contest is to frustrate precisely those goals that the architects of the new orthodoxy proclaim. Only those plans for stimulating growth and reducing inequalities that take politics into account are likely to be effective. But more is required: a realistic prospect of progress against inequality, and thus the strengthening of democracy, depends not solely on generating technically more sophisticated proposals but on a recognition that only political action, in which coalitions against inequality and poverty are built, and the strengthening and enriching of democratic institutions sufficiently to ensure that they are able to allow the conflicts generated by this action and these alliances to be resolved through politics, offer any prospect of allowing the freedom promised by democracy to translate also into greater social equity and human well-being that may, in a virtuous circle, also become a source of democratic strength.

The nature of those coalitions are, to be sure, less than clear. The classic Northern route of a labor-led redistributive coalition seems to be foreclosed by changes in the production process that are set to ensure greater informality in the labor market: the days in which large numbers of workers concentrated in factories provided a ready base for organization are gone. In Northern societies, labor in its traditional organizational form is likely to lack the numbers to lead an egalitarian coalition. In the South, while labor in some societies has made up in organization what it lacks in numbers when compared with the rural or informal poor, the reality that those in employment are better off than many others creates, as noted earlier, severe temptations for labor to seek gains at the expense of the poor. Identifying the sorts of coalitions that might pursue a new egalitarian politics is, therefore, a key intellectual challenge. But this does not alter the point argued here: that only new exercises in coalition building can ensure a politics in which democracy's redistributive promise may be translated into reality.

Reconstituting Politics—and the State

The intellectual—and practical—agenda proposed by this argument is a daunting one, and yet it may be essential if democracy is to endure, let alone to yield its promise of "positive" as well as "negative" freedom.

This chapter's argument may run counter to prevailing orthodoxies, but may well be little more than an attempt to resurrect some of the classic tenets of democratic theory in the face of the current assault against them (which is often now launched by democracy's proclaimed allies). But is the demand for robust democratic politics not utopian? Its theoretical attractiveness notwithstanding, the ideal of democratic politics as a free exchange within voluntary agreed rules open to all has been achieved rarely in "real existing" democracies. It may, therefore, be seen to represent as much of an unattainable albeit desirable ideal as one of its inspirations, Habermas's (1971) notion of a rational society in which all constraints to free dialogue are removed.

This objection can be answered by noting that the agenda proposed here is far more practical and attainable than Habermas's. The goal it suggests is not a society in which all constraints to politics for all are removed—an objective that probably is indeed unattainable. It is concerned only to propose an agenda for elected representatives and citizens concerned with strengthening democracy and reducing inequality that stresses goals such as political coalition building and the strengthening of democratic states as more appropriate concerns than technical and managerial formulae. But even this is no easy task, given the constraints, in those societies in which inequality is most prevalent, to political action by its victims (who, in contrast to an earlier period, rarely have access to the organizational possibilities and resources of factory workers) and to the strengthening of democratic states. A sober appraisal of these barriers could well lead to the conclusion that "negative" freedom represents the limits of the possible.

Yet it is not Utopia that is at stake, but the survival of democracy, certainly in those states where it has only recently taken root and perhaps also in those where it is more established. The danger may not be realization of the largely discredited conventional wisdom that social inequality leads to revolution, but the continuation of a trend already evident in parts of the South that helps to explain the already noted attenuated reach of many democratic states: because inequality places more and more citizens beyond the reach of the state, both because they cannot gain access to it and because it cannot reach them, democracy becomes so "hollowed out" that it loses much or all of its meaning as the gap between democratic state and society continues to widen. The inevitable result is then freedom and order for a few, subjugation to local power holders and insecurity for the many, even as the formal elements of democracy continue to be expressed, increasingly rhetorically, by the constitution.[13]

And, while an understanding of how that may be prevented still requires much scholarly work, the prospects of reconstituting politics and the democratic state sufficiently to prevent its abrogation by disuse may not be beyond us. To name but one possible pointer: the twentieth-century welfare state was built by coalitions between labor and other social interests; the prospects of a similar alliance between the unorganized poor and stronger social strata is less plausible because, unlike factory workers, those at the bottom of the current economic pile are far more diffuse and fragmented, greatly reducing prospects for organization and political action. But could it not be possible that, in some middle-income countries at least, the emergence of a class of "new poor" as a result of economic adjustment could present a twenty-first-century opportunity for an alliance between victims of inequality with the organizational and other resources to engage in democratic politics and those who currently lack it? If it did, its outcome would depend on the degree to which both political culture in the societies in which it emerged and the ability of democratic systems to respond appropriately to it ensure that it is channeled into a democratic framework rather than a new populist revolt: in many Southern states, where political participation is hardly automatic, it may, for example, require strategic vision by both political parties and candidates to identify groups with an interest in redistributive democratic politics and to seek to integrate them into democratic politics by seeking their support. The point is speculative, but at least suggests avenues for inquiry.

More generally, while an attempt to retrieve democratic politics could be obstructed by the incapacity of states, it could also become an antidote to their weakness. To argue for the reconstitution of classical ideas of the democratic state and society is not to suggest that this can be achieved in the same way as it was in the halcyon days of the welfare state that Marshall sought both to explain and to provide with a moral and theoretical underpinning. States' difficulty in achieving their goals, in the North as well as the South, has produced new thinking on the role of the democratic state—a genre that, despite significant differences of approach within it, sees the state less as a direct agent, more a catalyst: in the words of a fashionable book on governance, one that "steers" rather than "rows" (Osborne and Gaebler 1993).

In Southern states particularly, this new thinking is less practical than it seems. On the one hand, declining state capacity—in all societies—to undertake the heroic developmental and welfare projects of the past makes attractive the idea of a state that facilitates rather than directly delivers, in partnership with interests in society (but, in practice, more often than not with businesses). But there is no evidence that this project requires any less capacity than the more traditional one—at most, it requires a different sort of capacity than that of the previous delivery mode. To conclude effective partnerships that serve the general interest, states require the capacity to create a regulatory framework appropriate to their goals. They may also need a high degree of representative capacity to ensure that they accurately understand the needs of citizens, an ability to negotiate effectively in contexts in which the private partner is likely to command substantially more resources than the state, and the ability to monitor and enforce agreements so reached (Stacey 1997). This is clearly a substantial requirement for poorly capacitated states; without it, "steering" is likely to be a fashionable excuse for abrogating its responsibilities rather than a more sophisticated way of reconstituting the democratic state. The challenges facing many Southern states would seem even more intractable if Evans's argument is accepted that Southern states, if they are to generate economic growth, need to play four rather more demanding roles,[14] each of which requires far more substantial capacity.

And yet the problem may not be that intractable: serious as the "technical" constraints to newly democratic states in particular are, there is substantial evidence that the problem lies less in their failure to become states than to become democracies, at least sufficiently to render them capable of understanding and responding to the dynamics in, and the needs and demands of, the grass roots of their societies: if, as an important work argued some years ago, the problem lies in "weak states" attempting to govern "strong societies" (Migdal 1988), then only a stronger link between state and society might ensure that strong states govern stronger societies. This can be achieved only by strengthening democratic politics in general, and the representative function in particular. An example of a case in which a strong society does seem to have strengthened a weak state may be Peru, where mobilized citizen action is reported to have secured a property-rights system both more attuned to the needs of the poor and more functional to the operation of the state (World Bank 1997a: 101; de Soto 1989). But that, of course, requires a state responsive enough to react to citizens' demands and representative enough to hear them when they are expressed.

Similarly, if North is right to alert us to the role of institutions and ideologies in creating incentives—or merely lowering barriers—to engagement in economic activity (which, of course, is what lowering the costs of transacting ensures), then the absence or weakness of democratic politics may be perhaps the key constraint to economic progress in many Southern countries because it ensures a substantial gap between the assumptions of policymakers tutored in remedies framed in other institutional contexts and the means by which citizens at the grass roots understand and arrange their economic activity. Deeper representation and enhancement of grass-roots access to the political process are likely to do more to bridge the gap and, therefore, to make possible a closer alignment between economic forms and policies on the one hand and social understandings and arrangements on the other, than any number of "public participation" exercises.

The beginnings of an approach that may open the way to more effective states as well as revived democratic politics may, therefore, require a drastic departure from the prevailing orthodoxy, one that sees the route to the survival and strengthening of new democracies in the prioritizing of the representative function in particular and political democracy in general, not in management techniques and in their insulation from politics. After all, responsiveness and tolerance may be difficult, but they are arguably far more within the capacity of resource-poor societies than complex governance techniques. Similarly, the requirement that states, particularly those that preside over new democracies with limited resources, become vehicles of the latest fads in public management may be beyond them: the insistence that they listen to citizens, mediate between their conflicting claims, and then attempt to implement the outcomes may not be out of reach since these require capacities that are available in any society, whatever its level of technical expertise.

If the argument of this chapter is accepted, a new stress on representation, on the alliances that may make use of it, and, more broadly, on the democratic state as a repository of traditional democratic virtues rather than new management techniques is far more likely to yield effective states as well as a new flowering of democratic politics than the alternatives currently on offer.

Notes

1. This chapter attempts to build on a collaboration between the author and Bolivar Lamounier of the Economic, Social, and Political Studies Institute of São Paulo (IDESP), Brazil, which aims to establish a multicountry study of the issues raised here. I am grateful to Dr. Lamounier for inspiring some of the thinking—and providing some of the phrases—presented here. Needless to say, I take full responsibility for the argument (and the inevitable flaws) in this chapter.

2. The terms "South" and "North" are used here as equivalents for "Third World" and "First World" or "developing" and "developed" countries. This is, of course, the current intellectual fashion and has been justly criticized since the categorization is often geographically inaccurate. But their use does resolve some of the normative problems associated with the alternative terms and is continued here pending the emergence of more satisfactory labels.

3. For a citation of various sources, see Lipset (1964).

4. For new democracies' response to economic policy challenges, see Haggard and Kaufman (1995) and Perreira, Maravall, and Przeworski (1993).

5. For descriptions of the phenomenon in the African context see, for example, Simone (1995).

6. See, for example, Ohmae (1990, 1996) and Strange (1996). This prognosis has also recently been endorsed by no less an international icon than Vaclav Havel (1999).

7. For one attempt to retain but revise the notion of the state in the context of cross-border migration, see Benhabib (1999).

8. See, for example, Jencks (1992). Scholarly examples of the attack on welfare in the United States are provided by, among others, Murray (1984) and Tanner (1996).

9. For a discussion, in the South African context, of ways in which "participation" techniques substitute for, rather than supplement, representative democracy, see Friedman (1992, 1993).

10. In the African context, as one of the continent's most influential scholars has observed, many shack settlements "began with an emphasis on participation and ended up with a shacklord" (Mamdani 1995:295). See also White (1993).

11. For a classic expression of politics' indispensability as a vehicle for the institutionalization of tolerance, see Crick (1993). For a critique of

Marxism-Leninism's attempt to eliminate politics by asserting a putative proletarian interest as an alternative to political exchange and contest, see Polan (1984).

12. For an elaboration of this argument in a South African setting, see Friedman (1999).

13. For an analysis of the persistence of divergences between the universality of constitutions and the particularism of political practice in Latin America, see O' Donnell (1996).

14. The four are: "custodian" or regulator, "demiurge" or producer, "midwife" or aid to new forms of production, and "husband" or cajoler, and support to firms to meet new challenges (Evans 1995:13–15).

3

Progress and Poverty Revisited: Toward Construction of a Statist Third Way

Theodore J. Lowi

> It is both necessary and desirable that the government of a democratic people should be active and powerful; and our object should not be to render it weak or indolent, but solely to prevent if from abusing its aptitude and its strength.
> —De Tocqueville, *Democracy in America*

The central problem of this international project on governance has been stated as a search for "new approaches to the problem of addressing poverty and inequality." And the central question is posed as an urgent challenge: "In what ways can democracy and democratizing societies address [severe and growing social inequity] in the next decade and beyond?" It is a "struggle to find the capacity and political mechanisms to address this challenge." What this amounts to is virtually a minority protest against the answer to poverty and inequality that has already been given and is virtually hegemonic today: an economic theory of democracy.

Although our invitation is to engage in a struggle between the economics answer and a political answer, it will be the burden of this chapter to object to both. Two wrongs don't make a right. But the "third way" offered here will share nothing with and owe nothing to the Third Way offered by the likes of Clinton, Blair, and most of the other current G-7 heads of government. The third way between an economic theory of democracy and a political theory of democracy is not one of discovery but of construction.

Economic Theory Versus Political Theory

Economics as Ideology

Now that the Cold War is over, the question is not Who Won? but What Won? Although there may be other winners, the economists are

41

certainly correct that, so far, the big winner is capitalism, with its corporate structure and its private-market dynamics. So victorious has capitalism been that it has captured the terms of discourse, the manner of thought. The hegemony of economics has been a genuine paradigm shift.

All during the forty-year Cold War, the stated goals throughout the so-called free world were freedom over slavery, democracy over dictatorship, and human rights for all human beings. These are distinctly political goals, and the principal means for their pursuit—literally defining the national interest of the democratic countries—were equal rights for all to free speech, free elections, free inquiry, and free enterprise. But this has all been translated by the hegemonic paradigm into a single economic theory of democracy in which free enterprise is alone sufficient to produce all the other valued goals, including the equitable distribution of wealth.

This means that we have not come very far in the 120 years since the first epoch of globalization. In 1880, Henry George in *Progress and Poverty* was already questioning economics and its adequacy for addressing such problems as wealth distribution:

> The present century has been marked by a prodigious increase in wealth-producing power. . . . At the beginning of this marvelous era it was natural to expect, and it was expected that labor-saving inventions would lighten the toil and improve the conditions of the laborer. . . .
> Now, however, we are coming into collision with facts which there can be no mistaking. [Just as a community] advances in the scale of material progress . . . so does poverty take a darker aspect. . . . almshouses and prisons are as surely the marks of "material progress" as are costly dwellings, rich warehouses, and magnificent churches. . . . This fact—the great fact that poverty and all its concomitants show themselves in communities just as they develop into the conditions toward which material progress tends—proves that the social difficulties existing wherever a certain stage of progress has been reached, do not arise from local circumstances, but are, in some way or another, engendered by progress itself. (George 1948:3, 5, 7–8)

George was quick to recognize that the condition of the lowest class had in fact improved. But he questioned whether any of that improvement could be credited to the increased productive power—that is, to the ability of the lowest classes to improve their own conditions. George treated this as a moral issue, but of much more pressing concern was the instrumental, practical question of the social and political consequences:

This association of poverty with progress is the great enigma of our times . . . [and the] reaction must come. . . . *To educate men who must be condemned to poverty, is but to make them restive; to base on a state of most glaring social inequality political institutions under which men are theoretically equal, is to stand a pyramid on its apex.* (p. 10, emphasis added)

George dedicated most of the book to solving the problem of progress with poverty "by methods of political economy." This required that he concentrate on the debunking of "political economy, as at present taught" (p. 12). It was none other than the "classical economics" derived from Adam Smith's *Wealth of Nations,* and he called it a "pseudo-science." George goes to great lengths to debunk the most extreme statement of classical economic theory, that of Herbert Spencer, which sought to combine the ideal of a purely competitive economic system with a highly normative human version of Darwin's theory of evolution. This was the ultimate "dogma" comprising the "prevailing belief" as to the "law of human progress," including "the causes of the unequal distribution of wealth" (p. 478).

What George demonstrates for us is that an economic theory that recognizes no limit to its applicability is not science but ideology, or, as George put it, dogma. In effect, this is where we came in, and George is all the more applicable today because he was coping with first-era globalization. In its major 1997 world economic survey, England's important libertarian journal *The Economist* observed that "on several economic measures—such as the share of foreign capital and domestic investment, cross-border flows of investment in relation to national output, flows of people in relation to population—the world was more closely integrated before 1914 than it is now, in some cases much more so" (Crook 1997:37).

Another major indicator of "Globalization I" has been called imperialism, but it is nevertheless a major aspect of what we now call globalization. For example, between 1870 and 1898, Great Britain added 4 million square miles and 88 million people to its empire; France came into control of nearly the same amount of territory and 40 million new French subjects; Germany added a billion miles and 16 million people to its empire; Belgium added 900,000 square miles and about 9 million people to its national sovereignty (p. 37).

Globalization I is of special interest here because it confirmed a hypothesis drawn from the sociology of knowledge that Globalization II is in the process of confirming once again that every system of power tends to develop its own ideology, which rationalizes the government policies that sustain the system while legitimizing its place in the fundamental belief system of the society (see, e.g., Mannheim

1985). Anecdotal evidence does inform us that capitalism has brought down some authoritarian regimes and has enhanced democratic practices in others. But what of the numerous exceptional anecdotes, where rapid industrialization was antagonistic to democracy? And what of other instances in which capitalism has proved quite compatible with severely authoritarian regimes? The following is a warning from one of the *New York Times*'s most conservative columnists, the distinguished A.M. Rosenthal: "First, capitalism has shown itself flexible enough to have worked for the security of rulers, and the profit of investors, under governments based on fascism, religious fundamentalism, slavery, internal terrorism, apartheid, absolute monarchy, militarism—the whole nasty menu of non-democratic regimes" (1997:19). The point is that the free market does not make free all those who enter. Yet free-market ideology has spread around the world because it has support of the liberal philosophic tradition, it resides on a sacred property foundation, and, most important, it can account for all departures from its rational model.

Look first at their model. The economy is assumed to be a closed and self-generating, self-perfecting system that works through its own internal dynamics. As Wesley Mitchell put it not so long after Henry George, in his theory of business cycles, the recurrence of business cycles is a working out of an "inner mechanism" in which one phase of the cycle generates the next, with each period of the cycle containing the seeds that inevitably flower and produce the next phase. This is the modern translation of Adam Smith's "invisible hand" into an empirical phenomenon, a *visible* hand with working parts (reference to Wesley Mitchell in Hesion and Saardy 1969:603–608).

A closely connected ideological aspect of economics is the assumption of equilibrium, which leads George Soros to refer to economics ideology as "market fundamentalism."

> The global capitalist system is supported by an ideology rooted in the theory of perfect competition [where] markets tend toward equilibrium and the equilibrium position represents the most efficient allocation of resources. Any constraints on free competition interfere with the efficiency of the market mechanism; therefore they should be resisted. [I have] described this as laissez faire ideology but market fundamentalism is a better term [because it is] a belief in absolutes, a belief that every problem must have a solution. . . .
>
> [In the early 1950s, the idea that laissez faire] would stage a comeback seemed inconceivable. I believe that the revival of market fundamentalism can be explained only by faith in a magic quality ("the invisible hand").
>
> Market fundamentalism plays a crucial role in the global capitalist system. It provides the ideology that not only motivates many of

the most successful participants but also drives policy. (Soros 1998b: 126–128)

Another indication of the ideological nature of modern economic theory is its tendency to treat exogenous matters as sources of irrationality whenever predictions are not confirmed. As Soros puts it: "The insistence on exogenous shocks as a kind of *deus ex machina* to explain away the frequent reputation of economic theory . . . reminds me of the ingenious contrivances of spheres within spheres and divine forces that pre-Copernican astronomers used to explain the position of the planets instead of accepting that the earth moves around the sun" (p. 36).

Still another indication of its ideological nature is the tendency to assume the existence of the institutional framework within which the economic system works. As Henry George put it over 120 years ago, "This inquiry shows that differences in civilization are not due to differences in individuals, but rather to differences in social organization" (1948:xvi). In Globalization II, as in Globalization I, there has been a strong and dangerous tendency not only to assume away the political framework but to denigrate it as the primary source of irrationality in the economic world. This attitude was masterfully captured by one of the epigones of economic theory, President Ronald Reagan, in his most-quoted assertion that "government is not the solution, it is the problem." This attitude is at the back of most of the policies and virtually all of the theory of policies of deregulation, devolution, and decentralization. Ironically, the same attitude is shared by all too many political scientists. In the effort to make a science of politics, political science has been too quick to imitate economists in their stress on individual rationality, individual choice, individual competition. Treating politics as a decision process virtually requires the acceptance of an institutional framework as a given and thus to assume it away—or to bring it in conveniently to explain market failure.

Economic theory can be seen as coming neatly together as a normative system when it treats poverty and inequality the same way it treats bankruptcy and other market failures—these are the downside without which there cannot be an upside. There is merit to this point of view, though a danger when left as an untamed principle. Note how well the case is made by one of the contemporary world's greatest exponents of economic theory as ideology, George Gilder. First, "to lift . . . the incomes of less diligent groups . . . breaks the psychological link between effort and reward" (1981:88). Second, quoting a 1930s observation by Walter Lippmann, our system was based on an ideal that gave men "for the first time in human history a way of producing wealth in which the good fortune of others multiplied their own" (p. 8). And third, poverty and inequality *as a class* is only a statistical artifact: "The distribution appears permanent, and indeed, like the building, it will remain much the same year after year. But . . . people at the bottom will move up, and some at the top will [move down]" (pp. 11–12). Deliberate interference in this economic process of up and down, however well-intentioned, only produces net loss.

Democratic Theory as Ideology

We are hardly better off adopting a political-theory approach to poverty and inequality. Although democratic theory is fundamentally committed to political equality as a quintessential prerequisite, the process orientation of modern political theory in the science of politics actually militates against equality. It has trouble enough even with the very modest goal of equality of opportunity. At a minimum this means that we have to be very skeptical and guarded about any claims to significant contributions arising out of "bringing politics back in."

In looking to politics, people may be pinning their hopes on different understandings of that universe. Some may be taking a pluralist view. Others may be taking a populist view and will be speaking an entirely different language. Yet others will be coming from a partisan or party point of origin and will speak still another language.[1] But none of these offers an exit from the underlying commitment to process dynamics toward a substantive approach to poverty and inequality. Nor do they provide hope cumulatively. However, each deserves to be appreciated separately.

The pluralist solution. Pluralism reaches back all the way to Madison and shapes us all—whether as followers of the faith or as apostates. Madison saw, as many political scientists still see, politics as a competition among factions. Factions include what we now understand as interest groups, but to Madison they also included voting blocs in the legislature and caucuses and cabals among the nonelected—that is to say, any unit or combination of citizens "actuated by some common . . . interest, adverse to the rights of other citizens." Modern pluralists have dropped the last clause, "adverse to the rights of other citizens," and now accept the interest group—cleansed of the pejorative connotations of faction and pressure group—as a functioning and functional political entity, and in fact the primary unit of analysis in a pluralistic political science. For Madison, the cure for the "mischiefs of faction" was to encourage a great multiplicity of them so that it would be extremely difficult to combine into a majority-size faction and tyrannize the minority. In fact, the primary virtue of the Constitution for framer Madison was precisely that it would so "extend the sphere" of politics and so multiply the "variety of parties and interests," that a "majority of the whole" would be improbable. This process of forming factions and competition among factions was the Madisonian solution and to a very large extent the modern pluralist solution: As Madison put it, "The regulation of these various and interfering interests forms the principal task of modern legislation and involves the spirit of party and faction in the necessary and ordinary operations of government" (Madison 1961a:79). What he meant was that factions could be tolerated in government so long as competition among the many would neutralize them all. The pluralist view today is much the same, except that "regulation" becomes accommodation and equilibrium.

Pluralist theory has been stated here in its most simple, elemental, introductory textbook fashion, at the risk of boring needlessly the enlightened, in order to put the case as precisely as possible in the form that becomes the unarticulated major premise of those—enlightened or not—who have a pluralistic understanding or vision in mind when they recommend "bringing politics back in." There is beauty in a pluralist theory of politics that has been embraced at one time or another by virtually all political scientists because it recognizes an indivisible unit of action (the group); it can identify sufficient repetitive movement to constitute a process; it can be and often is wide open, public, transparent; and it does reach equilibrium, usually in inaction (the preferred Madisonian outcome) or stalemate (the same, but to those who want action and cannot get enough of it), or occasionally in actual public policy, which, because of the process, is usually accepted as consensual. Thus, the system is self-validating; it works, with equilibrium in inaction or action. And there are many who then impose David Easton's (1953) system on the whole process, with feedback following outcomes, and repetition back through inputs and "through-puts" to further inaction or action, making the whole process self-adjusting, self-perfecting, and self-fulfilling.[2]

It is neat enough to qualify as a science, albeit a nonquantifiable one, but there is almost nothing about pluralism, even if embraced and enhanced by a social movement, that can be brought directly to the service of poverty and inequality. First, there is a terrific class bias in pluralism. As Schattschneider put it over forty years ago, "The flaw in the pluralist heaven is that the heavenly chorus sings with an upper-class accent. Probably about 90 percent of the people cannot get into the [interest group] system" (1960:35).

And class bias is not the only problem. Most interest groups are "special interest" or "single-issue" groups. They are, as Madison said, held together "by some common impulse of passion, or of interest," and they overcome Olson's (1971) "free-rider" problem by maintaining passion toward the common interest and also by providing direct services to members. But the free-rider problem is not as great as Olson suggests, because, except for paying modest dues, members do not have to play much of a role unless the group begins to stray from the shared interest. Group action is left to the top leadership, which is narrowly oligarchic, and usually made up of those who formed the group in the first place. Granted, there are other types of groups. There are the large, federated, or "holding company" groups, so large that they approximate a whole class, of business, agriculture, or labor. They are still economic groups but are much broader than the typical special-interest group. Then there are the "public interest" groups, whose members are committed to public-policy goals in which they do not have a direct economic interest, such as Common Cause, League of Women Voters, and groups opposed to capital punishment or abortion, whose members are not likely to have any personal need for protection from the results of either. Groups of every category, including the more recent phenomenon of political action committees, all contribute to the consequences of pluralism—the good consequences envisioned by Madison and his descendants and the less-than-good consequences we will proceed to identify here.

First, pluralism has the upper-class bias identified earlier because it takes a lot of money and the command of a lot of political knowledge and social etiquette to work the pluralist system effectively. Access to the key players also takes time and experience. Some of the public-interest groups are organizations of middle- and upper-class people dedicated to "speaking for" the poor, but they are usually lacking in resources. Ironically, during their epoch of probably greatest effectiveness, the 1960s, many of these groups were actually financed by the philanthropic foundations whose resources had been drawn from the richest of all Americans. Meanwhile, groups that arise directly out of lower income and lower status strata tend to be local, church-affiliated, or neighborhood groups, for whom Washington, the tax code, the welfare system, and other means of effecting redistribution of wealth are extremely remote.

Obviously, not all of the economic interest groups are in principle antagonistic to the poor or to policies aimed at tilting the system toward the poor; but in practice these groups are forced by circumstance to be aloof and unconcerned about the poor. Their reason for being is the specific policies and agencies with the most direct potential impact on the members of their group, so that anything other than a momentary or sporadic association with some other type of interest can introduce considerable instability among the members.

This is why coalition formation is never easy or lasting. Moreover, redistributive policies create a type of politics quite different and quite antagonistic to the politics associated with regulatory policies and with promotional or public-works types of policies. Redistributive policies cut along class lines, and they almost always work through some larger aspect of the whole economic system, such as monetary policy and the interest rate or fiscal policy and the tax code. Those involve quite different government agencies, different technologies, different kinds of discourse than the everyday nuts-and-bolts issues of intellectual property rights, antitrust, food and drug regulation, environmental protection, or labor and civil-rights policies. Here again, even a momentary and temporary diversion from the regulatory or pork-barrel policy around which the group is organized toward a general interest or class issue of welfare or taxation can destabilize the membership of a group or can endanger the access it enjoys to the congressional committees and agencies that took so many years to cultivate.[3]

The interest-group process of the pluralist system is also a danger to the rule of law. As desirous as democracy is of an open, transparent political process in which competing groups balance each other for access and power, rule of law is a still higher priority, and groups, especially the ones with the most favorable access, prefer the very opposite, which I call policy-without-law. Policy-without-law can be defined as open-ended regulatory and public works (patronage) policies that permit and even encourage continuation of the pluralist/group process long after policies are adopted and handed over for implementation to the responsible agency or agencies in the executive branch. If the law governing the program is clear and has legal integrity, there is little room for bargaining over the decisions. If, on the other hand, the law is broad, vague, and open to interpretation, the political process continues, with agencies acting more like legislative committees making law than administrative agencies implementing law already made. It is probably true, especially during these past twenty years of Republican hegemony, that most interest groups share a belief with President Reagan that no government is best government. But their conduct betrays them. To most economic interest groups, a bad policy (open to bargaining) is most often better than no policy at all, because their member corporations and firms have the cover of regulation while being able to conduct their business relatively free of it. Consider, for example, the extraordinary merger movement during Globalization II in the context of U.S. antitrust law.

Again I risk boring the enlightened, but it is useful to articulate in some detail the unarticulated major premise of those who see solutions to wealth distribution in a pluralistic system. The group process is not self-correcting, self-perfecting, or teleologically oriented toward public interest or public goods. Like economic competition among corporations, political competition among groups does have many good yet unintended effects, as though by an invisible hand. But economic and political competition must be tamed. It must be tightly framed within an enlightened Constitution.

The populist solution. Populist democracy has an American pedigree as old as pluralism. If pluralism is the politics envisioned by the framers of the Constitution and is the "republic" Madison had in mind in *Federalist* 10, populism is surely the politics of the Articles of Confederation and of the anti-Federalists who, like Tom Paine, could be termed "radical democrats." This indeed is the position of the leading intellectual history of political science that identifies populism as the second of "two traditions of American political thought" (Seidelman 1985:ch. 1). I have taken some liberties with Seidelman's characterization of "Tradition I," which he calls "institutionalist," but only by stressing pluralism as the political-process dimension that most institutionalists assume, including Madison. Why else would Madison put his constitutionalism *and* his republicanism in the same masterful essay with his factional version of what we later came to call pluralism? My adaptation of the "radical democracy" of Seidelman's "Tradition II" is to update it as populism (pp. 5–7). Farmers in Western Massachusetts were giving voice to populism in their opposition to the ratification of the Constitution when they declared that it is "absolutely necessary that *the whole people* should be active in the matter of government" (p. 6, emphasis added).

Populist democracy is a real competitor to pluralist democracy in the United States. It is the political theory of the great history of social movements in America, just as pluralism is the political theory of mainstream interest-group processes. U.S. social movements have by and large been successful. They share little with social movements of Europe, which largely had a revolutionary bent—truly radical, a concept drawn from mathematics, which means getting at the roots and the foundations. U.S. social movements were not radical but reformist instead—using radical techniques but in order to redeem the regime, not to replace it.[4]

Populism haunts mainstream political science. It is clearly everyone's sentimental favorite, on the left and on the right, yet to political scientists, populism is flawed, and the key flaw is also its most outstanding virtue: its bonding to direct democracy. The movement for initiative and referendum in the early twentieth century is a moment of populist triumph, because it is the first great establishment of a

formal institution for direct democracy. A number of states, most no-
tably California, maintain initiative and referendum today as an important policymaking mechanism. But referendum methods of governing pretend away the extremely *non*-populist prereferendum stage,
during which a tiny oligarchy—far from the "whole people"—plans
and drafts the referendum provisions and spends multiples of millions of dollars on the campaign for its adoption. In other words,
most populist episodes of direct government are inspired and run by
a tiny vanguard—just as Lenin conceived of the leadership of the proletarian revolutionary movement. One of the leading theorists and
empiricists in the pluralist world of politics, David Truman, was hon-
est enough to admit that there was a "democratic mold" masking a
very tiny oligarchy in the inner life of interest groups (1962:129–
155).[5] This applies all the more to populist episodes of democracy,
whether referendum campaigns or genuine social movements.

The populist response to this critique is, quite properly, that the
popular sentiment is a necessary condition for the social movements
and for the referendums that are responsible for major institutional
and policy changes in U.S. history, especially in the twentieth century.
And populism has in fact had a tremendous boost with the rise of the
new institution of public opinion as measured by random-sample surveys. Elections have to a large extent been displaced by preelection
polling of the sentiments of everyone, nonvoters as well. Congress
and state legislatures are deeply influenced by survey results of attitudes on major public-policy issues. And presidents are so involved in
dialogues with national samples and small focus groups that the
"plebiscitary presidency" has become an important characterization
of the office of president in our time. Although public-opinion surveys can be great debunkers of claims made about what "the people"
want, sample survey results drive the media of mass communication
and both feed and expand the influence of the people taken as a
whole. But here is another case of a strength of populism that is also
a great weakness: Of all the forms of conviction, belief, and knowledge, the opinion has to be the weakest of bases of judgment and
choice. Nevertheless, populism lives, in the new institution of polling.

There is indeed strong warrant for warnings against the embrace
of populism to address poverty and inequality. Even a "consolidated
democracy" with extensive public education about the facts and the
dangers regarding progress with poverty can produce more mischief
than results. Leaving aside the thin and superficial opinion as the
basis for making political judgments, there is a still more flimsy public basis for public choice: One of the earliest discoveries of national
sample surveys was the widespread distribution of ignorance, with

greater ignorance and lower political participation and weaker "sense of political efficacy" as one moves down the level of formal education. Political scientists have tried to put the best possible face on these findings, but ignorance, especially since it is highly related to degree of formal education, means that those with the biggest stake in addressing poverty and inequality are the least likely to express themselves politically and are thus the least likely to be mobilized by that vanguard of middle- and upper-class intellectuals ready to commit their all to the cause of reducing the gap between rich and poor. Thus does democracy quickly become paternalistic oligarchy; and thus does the chance diminish that populism can produce genuine results when addressing poverty and inequality.

But even a fully mobilized populace that has drawn in a significant number of the poor will not necessarily be able to address the kind of wealth and status redistributions that would be required to begin making significant change in the tremendous gap between rich and poor. What seems to happen is that genuine populism, even if it mobilized all classes of U.S. citizens to engage in direct government, would lack the capacity to focus precisely on genuine redistributive policies. That is, when populism is truly "the people," it is not a mobilized lower class adverse to the interests of the upper class—as would be the case with a genuine, mobilized proletariat. This is why U.S. social movements have had their greatest impact on social, cultural, and moral causes rather than purely class or economic causes: abolition of slavery, "the great school wars," child labor (whose main opposition came in fact from the parents of laboring children!), prohibition, suffrage, and, more recently, anticommunism, antiabortion, antievolution in the schools, and school prayer. The labor movement was an organized class and had some success in changing the rules determining who shall be poor, but the organized-labor movement never truly addressed the lower class. I have been unable to find the source of this quote, but there is a worthwhile comment attributed to Bernard Shaw that trade unionism is the capitalism of the proletariat.[6]

Although one would still have to look to populism as a more hopeful politics to encourage and consolidate for a run against poverty and inequality, there are here again reasons to be apprehensive if not downright pessimistic. Take, for example, the 1930s, when Depression conditions provided unusual provocation for mobilization of the poor, swollen to unprecedented numbers, and class consciousness by those suddenly rendered poor. As we shall see, the results in public policy were only barely redistributive, and, more important, almost nothing was done to change the rules governing who shall be poor.

One moderately redistributive policy adopted by Franklin Roosevelt was prompt devaluation, which, in boosting inflation, may have helped some debtors. Public-works programs provided decent hourly wages for a few hundred thousand poor and unemployed. Some help went to subsistence farmers, through loans for home and capital improvements and to convert some tenancy into ownership. The 1935 Revenue Act boosted the surtax on the highest levels of personal income, and both personal and corporate incomes were put on a graduated tax basis. However, these were significantly counterbalanced by neutral and regressive measures. Many changes in the 1935 Revenue Act softened its redistributive effect until the war taxes of the 1940s, and no more than 5 percent of the population was even required to file an income tax return until 1943, when withholding was put into effect (Pollack 1996:60–66). The payroll tax for Social Security contributions was and still is a highly regressive tax. Food prices were artificially boosted by the vast price support program. Social Security was set up for the seniors but only if they had been employed prior to retirement; women were included only if they had been fully employed or were widows of working "independent men." Fair Labor Standards Act provisions for minimum wages and maximum hours, plus improved standards of working conditions, were designed to exclude service occupations and agricultural workers, which meant exclusion of most low-wage female and African-American male and female employees (and Mexican Americans, Native Americans, Philippino Americans, and Asian Americans). And since no civil-rights protections accompanied the agriculture price support and farm/home improvement loan programs, African-American subsistence farmers were excluded by practice if not intent.[7]

A brief look beyond the New Deal is less cloudy, but with only a few more rays of sunshine. Federal personal and corporate income taxation became progressively more progressive. Needs-based welfare was established, even for single women with children who had never been in the work force. For a while, between 1973 and 1996, such welfare was treated as an entitlement. Civil-rights laws remedied much of the social bias in formally neutral programs. As a consequence, the gap between the top quintile and the bottom quintile of personal and family incomes actually shrank between 1944 and 1960 and remained the same without widening between 1960 and 1980, after which it began once again to widen.

But even the moderately redistributive period of U.S. policy, in particular the most progressive 1960s, was hardly a product of populist dynamics. Some of the progress was driven by race, which, though a potent social movement between roughly 1956 and 1970, was very much a race/civil-rights movement that did not even move its rhetoric from "black power" to "green power" until the early 1970s. In fact, the decade of greatest progress against poverty and inequality, the 1960s, reveals an important truth about the entire phenomenon in the United States: *lower-class advances in public policy cannot be significantly expanded unless they are linked to advances for the middle classes.* It was no coincidence that Medicare for formerly stably employed seniors was adopted the same year (1965) that Medicaid was adopted to cover the structurally unemployed and in large part the unemployable. Even the significantly enhanced graduations of the income-tax structure were accompanied by dynamic and creative uses of tax incentives for investment that basically gave the lie to the formally extremely steep steps in the upper tax brackets.

In sum, there was at best modest evidence of real redistributive policy, and what there was of it was driven only in smallest part by class-grounded populist politics. Progress was aided by race politics, but it was aided all the more by war, whose concessions to the poor were largely the homage vice pays to virtue for all the "canon fodder" provided by the lower classes. And it was focused and driven largely by "alienated intellectuals" who, in articulating the terms of the policy debate and dramatizing the debt owed the poor and the dangers of not recognizing it, were engaging in a kind of "paternalistic populism." And even with the significant progress that was made in confronting poverty, not much was done at all about inequality.

We should stop here and make a proper distinction between the two.[8] *Poverty* is an empirical phenomenon whose reference is to *who is poor,* thus limited to the actual distribution of wealth and the identification of a conventional cutting point that is derived from some consensual criterion about the cost of the basic necessities. *Inequality* is a far more normative concept, and it is to be defined in terms of the references made two or three times in this section: inequality is derived from rules—formal and customary—that literally determine *who shall be poor.*[9] Policies concerned with inequality are therefore policies that are concerned with making or changing the rules that determine who shall *not* be poor. It is impossible to define precisely what is meant by equality, but it is not difficult to deal with degrees of inequality, by examining the types of persons who lack access to the possession of goods, status, and other things of value in the society. Capitalism in an industrial society would, other things being equal, tend to produce a broad layer or class of poverty whose composition would be close to random. All poverty is cruel, but becomes socially bearable if it is objective, mechanical, and random. But when a disproportionate number of any social category is present or absent from the poverty class, then we confront not poverty but inequality. The result may be called prejudice, but prejudice is nothing unless it is expressed in rules that can implement the prejudice in the real socioeconomic world. When these inequalities are recognized as the outcome of rules, we then can develop a policy focus, for rules are human contrivances that can be changed, replaced by other rules. Civil-rights laws replaced some of the old rules, albeit not so many. Secondary-education reform may have changed a few. Clearly the GI Bill and other higher-education reforms changed some rules. Populism has not had a great record of changing the rules of inequality because some of the time populist politics exist to *prevent* change in the rules. Therefore, many of the important changes in the rules of inequality, just as is true of the rules protecting civil liberties, are the result of the "paternalistic populism" referred to above.[10]

Party Democracy as a Solution

For a number of decades from the mid-nineteenth century into the twentieth century—thought by many to be the golden age of party democracy—party democracy was the widely recognized vision of politics. With its elevation into a major theory of democracy, party democracy stands as probably the single greatest contribution of political science to the grand tradition of political theory. As Schattschneider put it in his classic *Party Government,*

> It should be stated flatly at the outset that this volume is devoted to the thesis that the political parties created democracy and that modern democracy is unthinkable save in terms of the parties. . . . The parties are not therefore merely appendages of modern government; they are in the center of it and play a determinative and creative role in it. (Schattschneider 1942:1)

Party, not populism, is responsible for making numbers the sine qua non of democracy. In the process, citizenship was validated as a political force, and parties have provided the prime channel of access to political power for upwardly mobile members of the working classes. One of the major reasons why political machines were so detested in the major U.S. cities was that all of them were influenced by their working-class constituents and many of them were literally controlled by proletarians and "ex-plebes."[11] Political parties democratized the presidency, made Congress and the state legislatures the most creative lawmaking representative assemblies in the history of the world, and in general made leadership selection the most open and transparent process in history. And there is more.

The question here, however, is whether party politics offers a more promising approach to the problem of poverty or inequality. The answer seems to be no. And as with pluralism and populism, this pessimistic estimation is based upon the strengths and virtues of the party system, not its flaws. The focus here is only on the U.S. two-party system; things could be different with three or four important parties, but that is purely academic.

Our first consideration is that U.S. parties are not class parties and never have been. This makes them inherently limited in any sustained discourse and debate on policies to change the distribution or to change the rules. Historically, U.S. parties have functioned virtually to the contrary, blunting rather than sharpening class cleavages and class consciousness about those cleavages. Both major parties have made strong appeals to working-class and poor voters, and both parties have legitimate claims on the gratitude of the lower classes for some accomplishments in the public policies and programs of days gone by. Although the Republican Party has the reputation of being the capitalist party run by corporate interests and country-club respectability, it is also the party of abolition and was for a long time the party with the welcome mat out for new, lower-class immigrants. The Democratic Party was at the same time a southern party and remained so until the New Deal. In fact, the Democratic Party of the late nineteenth century was a nativist, *anti*-immigration party. At its 1896 presidential nomination convention, it adopted a platform that urged restriction of European "pauper" immigration and in general favored laws providing protection from foreign workers. The Republicans distinguished themselves from the Democrats by favoring "cultural pluralism." Tariffs were supported as protection against foreign *goods* but foreign *workers* were welcomed. In a campaign speech in Pittsburgh, Republican candidate William McKinley sounded like a chip off the Statue of Liberty:

> The equality of all . . . lies at the basis of popular government. It emphasizes the American spirit. Here are working men . . . the native born and the naturalized citizen—all equal in privilege and power before the law. . . . Here is a striking protest against the unworthy effort on the part of those who would divide our citizens into classes. (Mink 1986:139–140)[12]

Later the Democratic Party became the party of unions and in a sense the working class, but by the 1930s, the union movement had cooled down into a bunch of organized trade-union interest groups, in a sense confirming the Shavian quip about trade unions being the capitalism of the proletariat. The National Labor Relations Act was, for example, not truly *labor* law but labor *union* law. Labor was part of the New Deal coalition, one of a combination of highly contradictory units and groups; and the policies adopted by the New Deal were essentially by-products of keeping the coalition together. What was redistribution was largely accidental. The same can be said of the Republican national coalition that replaced the New Deal coalition in the 1980s: yes, this capitalist party became the home of the Christian Right, but of course the millions of conservative Christians included a very high proportion of working-class and ex-working-class evangelicals and fundamentalists. Thus, since both parties have been open to all classes, there is no way either party could in the past or can now develop a genuine redistributive message.

This characterization is in no way intended to denigrate either of the two major political parties. It is intended to confirm what should be obvious, that the two parties are inherently limited when it comes to addressing the most fundamental aspects of poverty or inequality.

The second consideration follows directly from the first, that class politics is all the more blunted by the much more dynamic cultural forces of the political parties: race, nationality, religion, and geographic region. Messages along these lines have always been sheer poetry for political parties. But parties are not in any way a melting pot. They are social conglomerates, and the messages to these components, along ethnic and racial lines in particular, reinforce those identifications long after the original basis for that type of consciousness has passed.

All of this makes the two major parties by nature conservative—not so much ideologically conservative but sociologically conservative, to the extent that their normal functions and their conventional messages all serve to reinforce existing social cleavages, to legitimize those cleavages and yet not to mobilize any one set of them against another. Parties are also politically and constitutionally conservative in the same sense. It is not that the two parties have an ideology that embraces and rationalizes federalism; it is that parties are themselves creatures of the federal system and reinforce federalism in virtually everything they do. U.S. political parties are truly organized from the bottom up. Virtually every unit of government in the United States within which some kind of election for some kind of public office takes place will have in it a party committee of one or both of the major political parties. The purpose of that party committee is to organize and implement the electoral process, and in the process of doing that getting its own nominees elected. Now, in our day not all of these local electoral districts are as important as they used to be, but still, the tradition and the very fiber of political parties is their district-by-district structure. In this sense, it is in the nature of political parties to think locally, even when their policy orientations are national or even international. Does that make them parochial? That varies with the individual. Even George W. Bush, whose father spent his life in foreign-policy matters, seemed a total parochial on the great global issues of the day until the terrorist attacks of September 11, 2001. But they are quick learners, and it may well be that the "national interest" is to be discovered in the boondocks.

Where does all this get us in the matter at hand? To be brutally brief, the tendency of U.S. party politics in governance is institutional conservatism—what I have elsewhere referred to more academically as "the constituent function," which is literally concerned with the makeup of government and command of its processes, not its ends. There is great virtue in this, but, as in any tragedy, it has the weaknesses of its own particular strengths. Even though there are discernible differences of ideology and policy between the two parties, they are not programmatic parties. As a consequence, party politics in the United States is no better suited to address poverty and inequality than are the two alternative forms of politics. A select few illustrations will be offered.

The first example is also the most important, because it deals with the role the two parties played in constituting the "welfare revolution" of 1935, which goes on to shape most of the rest of social policy at the ensuing half century. The late Morton Grodzins, no raving left-wing radical, gave us the leading analysis of the influence of parties on the U.S. system, which produced in all the New Deal legislation what was for him a totally unwarranted role for the state governments. Grodzins was especially struck by the role of the parties in redistributive policies, where "there existed compelling reasons for establishing [the] programs without state participation" (Grodzins 1960:994).[13] The one New Deal program to be singled out by Grodzins for special emphasis was the Social Security Act of 1935. Even while the national government was expanding and the Constitution was being expanded by the Supreme Court to validate a national presence in U.S. society, the political parties were engaged in a "silent conspiracy" to keep the eighteenth-century constitutional structure.[14] As the Social Security legislation was going through Congress, many controversial issues had to be confronted; but one fundamental issue had been settled without debate at the outset: Social Security would be federal, not national. Grodzins provides numerous other examples of policies in which the spirit of party determined a structure of "state sharing," indicating that members of Congress on both sides of the aisle were more concerned over the role of the states than they were over the fact that their actions were creating not only a welfare state but a "new American state" (pp. 980 ff; see also Witte 1962). And, more to our point here, Suzanne Mettler demonstrates that decentralization of implementation of national policies to the states meant that not only institutional conservatism but also profound, indeed radical, social conservatism was implanted—which meant keeping classes, genders, and races in their established places. This social conservatism was the tacit contract essential to keeping the South in the New Deal coalition; it was also comfortable for the Northern liberals, who put party first (Mettler 1998).

The federal bias is a clear line running through almost all redistributive legislation ("social policy") from the New Deal through the last phase of policy activism, ending around 1973. But the ultimate expression comes in the 1990s with the penultimate effort to dismantle the New Deal. There has been a bipartisan reform movement to federalize social policy still further, with the profoundly conservative social consequences that could have been (and were) predicted. It is not a paradox that a bipartisan majority left virtually all of the New Deal programs of the 1960s and even of the 1930s on the statute books. Politically and substantively, the ultimate goals of constitutional and social conservatism in the 1980s and 1990s could be accomplished by decentralization through federalization.

The most significant recent illustration is the welfare reform of 1996, the Personal Responsibility and Work Opportunity Act (popularly referred to as the Personal Responsibility Act [PRA]). Generated by the Republicans and made a key part of their "Contract with America," which produced the Republican electoral triumph of 1994 and the potent Gingrich Congress of 1995, it was picked up, ultimately sponsored by, and credited to President Clinton and his "New Democratic" party. Whatever it did to meet the promises of the Republican campaign of 1994, it also met the needs of President Clinton's 1992 campaign promise "to end welfare as we know it." PRA was the culmination of thirty years of bipartisan, I repeat, bipartisan efforts to repeal "welfare entitlements," taking away the government's assurance that "desperate economic circumstances will not deteriorate into abject destitution." The 1996 law explicitly terminated entitlements under welfare programs across the entire nation, and it also added a number of national standards that required all the states to test eligibility not only on a needs standard alone but also on a moral standard (Mink 1998:6). But most of the major changes in the PRA came as a result of provisions in the PRA that decentralized implementation of welfare to the states, permitting the states to use their discretion in how to carry out the established and the new national standards for the eligibility of unmarried women and mothers for public assistance. It is this decentralization that returned the poor, especially impoverished women, to the status quo before 1935, when welfare and local police functions were tied closely together. Decentralization to the states was the bipartisan dimension cutting through all the changes PRA brought to more than half a century of welfare policy.

Welfare policy combines with many other areas of public policy to confirm not only the distinct rightward turn in the United States,[15] but also the two-party preference for federalization for its own sake. Yet—and no irony is intended—the downsizing of the national government in favor of the state governments actually confirms ever more strongly the "role of the state" in this free society and free economy. The states collectively are a major part of "the state" in the traditional European sense of the word. The states are *state* in the European sense, and the Founding Fathers were very much aware of this. They chose "state" as the name of the second level of government in a federal system in full awareness of the European understanding of the state as the source of sovereignty—that is, coercive—power. It is strange and wonderful how many U.S. citizens think that state government meets Rousseau's ideal of governing according to the General Will, in which a government-of-the-people has imposed state coercions on themselves and therefore is not coercive at all. Having established now that state governments are not only coercive governments but are the source of most of the relevant policies that do directly and coercively affect the economy, we can now try to find a way to address poverty and inequality in a way that theories of economic or political democracy cannot.

Bringing in the State: Taming Politics and Markets

Social scientists have grown so committed to "systems"—for all the analytic power that comes from closure around an agreed-upon set of factors—that they tend to embrace the system as the truth. This has led to the treacherous conclusion that the system is self-correcting and self-perfecting in the real world. Such theories become the worst kind of ideology because of their defense mechanisms, warning us that any intervention, any artificial, deliberate, willful effort to improve upon the workings of the system will only make things worse.

My purpose here is to break through the barriers of these well-established economic and political theories to find ways to address the chronic problems of market freedom and political freedom without undermining either. To do this, the state not only has to be brought in as the source of authoritative action but as the framework that facilitates spontaneous economic and political competition and also tames or harnesses them toward social goals—alleviating poverty and inequality—that history has proved they are incapable of dealing with by their own spontaneous devices. This amounts to a modernization of Madisonian republicanism and Smithian free enterprise while remaining loyal to both. As for Madison, pitting ambition against ambition was a solution to the mischiefs of selfish interests, *not a form of government*. Political competition provided for limits on the use of governmental power that went beyond mere parchment guarantees. This is in large part what Madison meant in *Federalist* 51 when he said, "You must first enable the government to control the governed; and in the next place oblige it to control itself" (Madison 1961b:322). Thus, politics was conceived as a process to limit government; but government was conceived as a process to limit politics. And, since the Constitution provided that Congress (that is, the national government) was to have power "to regulate Commerce with foreign nations, and among the several States . . . [and] to make all Laws which shall be necessary and proper for carrying into Execution the foregoing Powers," there is no way economic life was to be considered so separate from political or social life that it was to be free from government or politics.

On the basis of these clarifications, this statist construction will be grounded on seven actual assumptions *real players have to make* before taking their goods or services out of their cave in order to compose a market with other real players. To the social scientist, these assumptions are not a logical point-of-origin or a fictional "original position" that philosophers use to initiate an argument about the nature of the good life or justice or right or the state of nature. These assumptions are about real things; they are practical expectations about institutionalized practices that are outside the market and must be recognized as prior to the market—or if not, homo economicus *stays home*. From a sociologist's or a political scientist's standpoint, these would be called "functional prerequisites." From a psychological standpoint, these might be called presuppositions. Either way, it must be emphasized once again that (1) all of these prerequisites or assumptions are in play before the game begins; (2) none of them is produced by markets in response to demands; and (3) none of these is produced by any one or a combination of the three political processes for their own time and circumstance.

The seven prerequisites identified and discussed here are fundamental. But I do not pretend to have identified all of the prerequisites and presuppositions that must precede a market economy.[16] Brief treatment is sufficient; each will be obvious, once stated.

1. *Provisions for law and order.* Predictability in human affairs obviously precedes everything else. Risk itself is a probability statement about the extent of danger in an otherwise orderly environment. Although market regularities may often contribute to social order, markets cannot exist in the first place without it. And the social order is more than the order imposed by military means, important as that is. It requires what Max Weber called "calculable law"; as he observed, "the royal 'cheap justice' with its remissions by royal grace introduced continual disturbances into the calculations of economic life" (1992:277).

2. *Provisions for property.* Property is a legal fiction. It is a synthesis word for all the laws against trespass. Through this process, law renders highly probable that we can enjoy real dominion over that which we claim as our own. "The market" can come only after the risks of property ownership itself have been close to eliminated.

3. *Provisions for contract enforcement.* It is impossible to imagine transactions today without contracts. And it is also close to impossible to imagine contracts without virtually absolute assurance that some source of authority *outside* the market and *prior* to the market will make breach of contract more expensive than observance. Some needy economic ideologues will respond that contract enforcement is a matter of "private" or civil law dealt with by courts. But courts are very much "the state"; court orders, including decisions regarding breach of contract, are backed by just as much coercive power as any other authoritative state decision. All outside the market.

4. *Provisions for exchange.* Although contract is at the very center of any modern conception of exchange, there are still other matters that lie behind contract, making contract itself possible. In brief, there has to be an agreed-upon language by which contracts are written, and there has to be an agreed-upon set of terms for the specific goods or services to be exchanged by the contract. This means *standardization*. Standardization is of two kinds: the *legal* language and the specific *technical* or *substantive* language. Both precede the contract and thus precede the market. Here again, some will object with the response that most standardization in contracts, especially the technical or substantive standardization, is actually done voluntarily by the main players in a given industry, or by their organized trade associations. It is true that most of this paraphernalia of contracts is privately developed by those who have the biggest stake in the production, distribution, and use of the matters dealt with in the contract. But as soon as a participant disregards a standard by selling something as "short staple cotton" or "porcelain enamel" in violation of a trade association

standard, this will be enforced in courts and will then become "public policy" just as certainly as if adopted by the legislature.

5. *Provisions for social overhead capital.* Social overhead capital is an old-fashioned term for what is now called "public goods." Virtually everyone, including Adam Smith, would agree that the media of exchange, transportation, and communication would be examples of functions that must come before markets and cannot be readily provided from within the normal workings of the market. Time and technology can transform an existing public good into a normal marketed commodity. But in any epoch there will be some functions that individual market players cannot provide for themselves without providing them free for others. There is, according to Hume, an inherent *dis*incentive for one or more neighbors to empty the nearby swamp when they are aware that "free riders" can enjoy the result without paying (see, of course, Olson 1971:33).

6. *Provisions for meeting the requirements of work.* There is a wise old saying that in order to work, capitalists need inducements and workers need punishments. Creation of a large working class required compulsion backed by vagrancy laws, debtor prisons, and other forms of forced labor (Polanyi 1957:chs. 7, 8). Apprenticeships for skilled labor were subsidized but also legally enforced. Universal compulsory education has rendered many traditional work provisions unnecessary, but every epoch will find appropriate means of getting people to work. Frances Fox Piven and Richard A. Cloward in their important book, *Regulating the Poor* (1971) were reviving an almost forgotten historic commonplace that welfare systems were always part of social control systems and police functions whose rewards and punishments were all related to the work ethic.

7. *Provisions for the allocation of responsibility for injury and dependency.* Although conquest and the imposition of law and order eliminate the most violent interferences with the establishment and maintenance of markets, that still leaves a vast source of interference, most particularly in highly developed market economies, in the uncountable number of unintended consequences following from vigorous and lawful economic endeavor. No sane person would enter a market conscientiously if all responsibility for their initiative were personal and if there were no limit to that responsibility as their products or services pass through the economy. Tort law is one of the prominent examples in most capitalist environments, in which adjudication establishes responsibility. But there are other provisions for allocating responsibility for injury, including the principle of the corporation itself. One of the most valuable incentives for organizing economic activity in a

corporation is that the liability of the participants is limited to their share in the ownership of the corporation and does not extend to any other property or valuables they hold.

Poverty, Inequality, and the State:
Taming Markets and Politics

Where We Are and How We Got Here

The most compelling conclusion arising from the foregoing analysis is that in the real world there is no such thing as an economy. There is only *political* economy. The functional prerequisites of the market economy were shown to have been met entirely or in large part by deliberate, institutionalized government activity, originating in what we in the United States would call public policies. Some policies have been in operation for so long that they are not recognized as deliberate contrivances developed by courts or adopted by legislatures or heads of state and their cabinets. But that is the case. Markets have always been shaped and tamed by some kind of governmental framework.

At first blush, this tends to confirm Marx's thesis that capitalism is a system imposed through the state by ruling interests. But it is far closer to the truth to propose that capitalism did not need to be imposed, only facilitated.

The analysis also confirms the view of most political scientists that the political process, far from being an epiphenomenon, actually does produce, through government, many of the fundamental decisions that shape the economy and the society. But that, too, falls short of the truth. Political processes do make a difference but only *through government*. At any specific cross section of time, the political process plays virtually no direct role in shaping the political economy. Moreover, very few public policies are truly fundamental to markets. Fundamental national policies in particular are about as rare as constitutional amendments and indeed may require a constitutional amendment to validate the authority to shape the economy. Since 1792 (after adoption of the first ten amendments), only two amendments had any direct effect on the activity or the framework of the economy: the Thirteenth Amendment, which freed the slaves without compensation, and the Sixteenth Amendment, which authorized Congress to impose taxes on incomes. (One might add the Eighteenth Amendment, the prohibition of the manufacture, sale, or transportation of alcohol, but it was adopted in 1919 and repealed in 1933.) The only other major paradigmatic act that can be said to have been produced by the political process in a given moment in time would be the decisions made by the Supreme Court in 1937, one line of decisions validating the power of Congress to regulate commerce down to the level of the plant itself, and the other line culminating with the decision to validate Congress' power to finance basically redistributive policies.[17] But all of that constitutional authority granted to the national government did not produce anything year by year that appreciably altered the structure of markets that had been in place all along. The most important modern additions to the way in which governments meet the functional prerequisites of the market—that is, the most important change the political process (through government) produced this century to shape the market and capitalism—was probably the graduated income tax as set in place in the 1930s and the withholding system of collecting those taxes set in place in the 1940s.[18]

Another very important and pregnant conclusion to be drawn from this analysis is that virtually all of the policies in the United States that have met the functional prerequisites of the market in the United States were provided by state legislatures, not by Congress and the national government. Despite all of the ideological noise of the past twenty years about how the national government has grown at the expense of the states, and how the national government is responsible for all of the so-called interventions into the private economy, there are still no national property laws, still no national corporate laws, still no national contract laws or education laws or laws controlling entry into the professions. Even the power to adopt laws regulating bankruptcy, a power reserved to the national government, has been left largely to the states. Because the national government did so very little toward the creation and structuring of capitalism and the market, an impression was given that the economy was free and independent and that its processes provided all of the structure necessary for its own perfection. Thus U.S. citizens could develop the myth and the ideology of the "free market," and developed a science of economics on this basis, without making equivalent progress toward *political* economy. The term "political economy" has crept back into the vocabulary in recent years, but it is largely in the hands of the rational-choice subdivision of political science, which is classical economics played out on the political process but with far less finesse than that of economists. But we need to reclaim traditional political economy, making it once again the basis of a *state-centered* science of government.

Where Do We Go From Here?

Ideas have consequences. To address poverty and inequality in a constructive way for this epoch it was necessary to break the grip of theories on practice. The most important theoretical barrier to progress *against* poverty has for at least twenty years been economic theory. This is not the first time economic theory served as ideological guardian of private interests against state theory and public policy. What has triggered it into hegemony at least three times since the industrial revolution was the threat or prospect of globalization in one form or another. The first was at the time of its origin in the late eighteenth century, with the physiocrats in Europe and Adam Smith in England, when it became the compelling argument against mercantilism, the source of barriers to what globalization there was at that time. And as though to demonstrate that the emerging economic liberalism would be compatible with almost any regime, the physiocrats, according to Sabine, "were content with absolute monarchy if it would follow an enlightened economic policy" (1950:568). This was followed and built upon by Smith "and a generation of English writers [with] a kind of social Newtonianism which regarded institutions and their history as scientifically irrelevant [and] . . . economics and government [as] mutually independent" (p. 686). This led Polanyi to assert that "social not technical invention was the intellectual mainspring of the Industrial Revolution. . . . The discovery of economics was an astounding revelation which hastened greatly the transformation of society and the establishment of a market system" (1957:119).

Laissez-faire economics made its second coming for Globalization I, during the latter half of the nineteenth century. In fact this was the period when it came to be called "classical economics," and when it became clothed with a broad developmental ideology of natural social betterment called Social Darwinism. Its third coming is still with us, because it is once again so compatible with economic expansion, in Globalization II.

There can be no restoration of deliberate social experimentation through government until the spell of economic theory, operating as an all-encompassing social theory, is broken. This has nothing to do with genuine scientific economic theory. The goal is to shrink economic theory back into the smaller sandbox of its applied mathematics, equations, and models. Good science must always know and continually recognize the limits of its own applicability.

For similar reasons, political-process thinking and the three leading U.S. political theories built on process also had to be confronted, because commitment to politics as process put them to a large extent in the same boat with classical economics—the more so as political science began to draw directly from economics in general and rational choice in particular. In their hands, government, especially democratic government, becomes a tabula rasa onto which the results of competition, agitation, and election in the "private sector" are inscribed on the tablets of government as public policy.

Even the concept of "public policy" itself is an expression of the problem. Public policy is to be found only in the English language, and is a synonym for law, statute, rule, edict, ordinance. Policy became the reference of preference most probably because it is a good euphemism. It sounds less authoritative, less unilateral, less permanent, and more reciprocal, human, temporary, and accommodating than the traditional formulations of, for instance, law. In other words, government decisions and actions are treated as a logical and empirical extension of the political process. It is no wonder that the laws adopted by—or rather the statutes passed in—Congress are drafted in such a way as to leave almost entirely open the rule of law in back of the policy, so that political participation can continue uninterrupted throughout the implementation process. I have elsewhere, beginning more than thirty years ago, referred to this as "policy-without-law," to help convey the argument that most laws in the participatory environment are almost totally lacking in legal integrity. This is really a modern version of Max Weber's formulation quoted earlier about "cheap justice"—which can be interpreted to mean the intervention of government on a highly personal, essentially arbitrary basis. The whole quote is worth repeating: "Its remissions by royal grace introduced continual disturbances into the calculations of economic life" (1992:277). Now to restate it for the argument here: *arbitrariness and lack of ability to predict the law is much more demoralizing and discouraging than the actual coerciveness of the law itself.* Virtually all of the laws meeting the prerequisites of the market outlined above are coercive. The whole point and purpose of laws meeting prerequisites is to make them so coercive that those involved in the activity can predict so much more readily the other people's behavior.

Why blame process? Process untamed can destroy virtually all respect (analytically, but also normatively) for the *substance* of policy. What kinds of laws is the process producing? What are they for? What impact are they intended to have? To ask those questions is to make jurisprudence a central if not *the* central component of the language of politics and public policy.

But here's the rub: to do that is to bring the state back in. The democratic state is and must be the end product of the democratic political process, but that process has to be guided and limited (tamed) by the fundamental requirement of a good state: the rule of law. Within the political economy, this means that the political process should not be permitted to produce an outcome with the status of law unless that law embodies a rule that can become part of the *structure* of the economy whose implementation *as policy* can be predicted and therefore adjusted to as just another part of the fixed economic environment. Good news or bad news—Organization of Petroleum Exporting Countries' oil price increases, embargoes, twenty-four-hour stock markets, the Internet, the end of the Cold War—the change can be figured in as part of the "cost of doing business" as long as it is not capricious, arbitrary, individualized, or prejudicially distributed.

Yet there is and ought to be a human dimension of laws that have clear legal integrity and are strictly and consistently implemented. This human dimension is our knowledge that in a democracy all law, all policy, is an experiment. A law is an effort to control some aspect of the future; that's why is must be authoritative and coercive. We may know fairly well the specified aspect of the future we want; there may be overwhelming consensus about it. But getting there is not only uncertain; there is rarely consensus about the particular rules, the particular techniques, and the particular methods of government to get there. The rhetoric employed in the political process to get a majority—forget consensus—can alas give the impression that the policy chosen is "the one best way" and that it deserves a place in the pantheon of public policy for generations to come. That rhetoric violates the spirit of democracy, for in a democracy, everything, including democracy itself, is an experiment. And since the jury is still out on democratic government, its policies must also be seen as defendants awaiting judgment.

In this context, we do not need term limits on representatives, because it takes a long time to learn the ways of government and politics. *But there ought to be term limits on the policies and programs they adopt.* A ten-year limit should be imposed on every statute, and as the end of its tenure approaches, the experience with the policy or program should be brought back into the political process, before the jury. If the experiment has been a disappointment, let the policy/program die. If it deserves a second term, it should not merely be validated; all of its ten years of use, and all decisions implementing it, should be codified; and the provisions and standards in the organic law should be clarified so that it serves even better as a structural and predictable part of the market framework. State legislatures often codify longstanding laws; the U.S. Congress rarely does.[19]

If we appreciated the policies of the state as an experiment rather than a permanent fixture or as a mere outcome of a political process, we could be a great deal more precise and authoritative in the formulation and more direct and authoritative in the implementation of policies, knowing that redemption for a failed experiment is never very far away.[20] If "democratic government" is a magnificent oxymoron, why can't "temporary permanence" or "reformable structure" or "experimental rules" be accepted as good oxymorons too?

With that reassurance, we can turn back to a state-centered approach with some relaxed optimism. We might even enjoy the suspense as the experiments play out, even if the rules embodied in the policy are tough and expensive. We could begin the consideration of an experimental approach to the state with one more reference to the seven prerequisites identified above. This is a troubling but very promising linkage: *a state that can make a market economy can unmake it.*

With that in mind, I conclude with a few proposals that hold out promise for useful experimentation in the problem areas of poverty and inequality. There could be no better time to do this, because we are looking at these problems in a prosperous era. Even so, the proposals are made simply to round out the analysis, not with any expectations of adoption.

1. In this first experiment, we confront a genuine conundrum when we ask public policy to deal effectively with poverty or with inequality, because it has been demonstrated that the collective decisionmaking of a democracy cannot produce logically consistent and cumulative decisions. Kenneth Arrow won the Nobel economics award for his demonstration of the impossibility of logical social choice, and this has provided philosophic grounds for a policy-of-no-policy (Arrow 1963). Permit me to reduce Arrow's impossibility axiom to a more practical level of abstraction: a highly competitive market is the enemy of good citizenship. That shocking proposition is simply another way of saying what every laissez-faire ideologue espouses as a great virtue: Competition will reduce prices toward marginal cost. If that is so, and there is no reason to believe it isn't, then no individual competitors can choose out of the goodness of their hearts to raise wages or to improve their work environment or recycle their waste products, because the added cost would force them out of the market. There is of course a second barrier to citizenship, the theory of "public goods," which holds that even where competition is irrelevant, any neighbor wanting to do a good thing, such as draining the swamp, would have a disincentive to do so because all the other neighbors could enjoy the result without paying for it.

One answer that could very well make some headway toward alleviating poverty would be a genuine, professional minimum wage pegged to 120–130 percent of the poverty line; uniformly applied and universally enforced, that would keep all the competitors on an equal plane or playing field, thus allowing them to be the good and responsible citizens they would choose to be if their generosity did not force them out of the market. Would the minimum wage increase unemployment in the process of improving the conditions of some? Unlikely, especially in the prosperous times we have assumed. But compare that to the predictable, immense costs of not doing anything. Soon there will be such production capacity in the world that, for example, 80 million cars a year will be produced. Either the United States has to continue being the "buyer of last resort," or a lot more people in the world will have to buy a lot more cars. Henry Ford recognized this in 1929, when he raised wages to $5 a day ($2 over the prevailing wage). Years later, Ford's nemesis Walter Reuther discovered the same principle: "You will never build an auto industry with bicycle wages."[21] Luxury purchasing was once thought to be the driving force behind a prosperous, competitive economy (e.g., Weber 1992:170–171). Mass consumption is now the answer, and producers are doomed to having to worry about adequate consumer power. We may in fact learn in our experiment that the minimum wage will not work in any form or that it has not worked because it was not universal enough or generous enough. In ten years we would be able to make better policy, to make the minimum wage *more* generous, or close down the experiment altogether and try something else.

2. Since even a successful minimum wage can do no more than keep a larger percentage of people above the poverty line, there would remain large numbers of minorities who cannot get jobs no matter what the wage is. Changing the rules of inequality requires much more positive investment than in a mere minimum wage. More investment in the secondary and primary schools has probably helped a bit, but this is already an experiment whose modest success is called by many a failure (see, e.g., Traub 2000:52). But what has failed? Maybe it is not the schools that are failing but the policy or principle behind schooling. Up to now, in the United States at least, the policy has been schooling-as-a-right, and that is the experiment that has failed. So, let us experiment with a different policy, of schooling-as-an-*obligation* imposed by law. In the United States, school attendance is an obligation very much like the draft. In fact, universal compulsory schooling is the single largest coercive intervention by the state in the history of democracy—maybe in the history of the world. In the United States, this obligation has on occasion been tested for its constitutionality, and the Supreme Court in its most recent review, in 1972, revalidated compulsory schooling as a "compelling interest" and therefore a proper and constitutional exercise of "state police power." Police power indeed. And the Court cited two and only two reasons why this exercise of police power was justified: first, "education

is necessary to prepare citizens to participate effectively and intelligently in our open political system " and second, "education prepares individuals to be self-reliant and self-sufficient participants in society."[22]

On with the experiment. As with draftees, put pupils on salary. Each pupil would be on contract, paid for each day's attendance and paid additionally for each phase of the term completed—perhaps still more as grades improve. Payment of course goes to parents or guardians, partly because pupils are minors, and partly because parents ought to be paid for their own role in meeting the contract. Here is an attack on poverty but also an attack that changes the rules of inequality, first by enabling all students to attend and second by giving them experience in the very important middle-class value of making contracts and meeting the conditions of contracts. There is another middle-class value involved here: the salary in the contract provides incentives rather than punishments to work. An experiment with no guarantee of success, but what is ever guaranteed?

3. Poverty is not only a matter of minority inequality, it has also been highly gendered. One of the unspoken but systematic rules of inequality is that home work has no economic value. Thus, those closest to destitution and those most responsible for preventing the delinquency that produces so much of the crime and social disorder, unmarried mothers, are left to their own devices. Experiment: put them on salary. Monetize home work. Home work is denigrated because it has never been given market value. And bear in mind, except for addicted mothers, the biological mother, even if quite poor and uneducated, is a far better caregiver than a foster or an institutional home, and cheaper, even in the short run, not to speak of the long run. If the schooling experiment were also in place, and the mother is thus sharing the salary of her school-age children, we have a double whammy here, because we are meeting the needs of proper upbringing and we are also meeting in the best possible way the work requirements of the 1996 PRA. Since stealth weaponry is almost certainly going to be proved a failed experiment in the defense policy area, we could divert those savings—along with the savings of closed child-care institutions and foster programs—so that we would hardly have to raise taxes at all to put home work on wages.[23]

4. This experiment begins with a premise that ought not to be so startling: Poverty and degradation of the environment are very bad for society; but they are costly only for the rich—for the poor they are very valuable. Thus, for purposes of this policy experiment, I will call

poverty and environmental degradation *negative capital* (Keller, Lowi, and Gendlin 2000). It is negative because its value lies in its absence; it is capital because those who can afford to pay for its absence are willing to pay a lot.

We can begin this policy experiment as we ended the experiment with salaries for home work: by commoditizing poverty, drug taking, delinquency, crime, and environmental degradation in all its forms. As Milton Friedman asked at the very beginning of the environmental-protection movement, "How much pollution can we afford?" Expand on that. We can make some good guesses from the cost of controls and damage and remediation how much all of this is worth. We could begin by counting half the 2 million souls in U.S. prisons who would not be there if they and their parents had had some wealth and some work. A few trillion dollars on a world scale could make an immense difference in the domestic gap between rich and poor and also an even more dramatic difference in the gap between rich countries and poor countries, which make the cost of this experiment with redistribution pale into insignificance compared to the cost of wars that inevitably arise out of maldistribution.

I am elsewhere participating in an exploration of negative capital and can already report that there are reasonable methods for investments in poor people and poor countries by rich individuals, rich corporations, and rich countries that have promise for acceptable levels of pay-off (Keller, Lowi, and Gendlin 2000). There is an undoubted, proven willingness on the part of the wealthy to pay limitlessly for security, through taxes and through private security guards, sentinels, alarms, dogs, compounds, suburbanization, and so on. And one is hearing no complaints against the steep rise in new government expenditures for larger armed services to fight at least two wars at a time, and for more money for police, satellite and computer surveillance, antiterrorism, border checks, and ethnic profiling. All this accompanies globalization and spectacular economic growth. Just as poverty seems to accompany progress, so does great vulnerability accompany great power.

If progress with poverty and power with vulnerability are tragedies and not paradoxes, then they can be addressed and alleviated by public policy. Democracy is in peril if we require solutions. The test of democratic government is appropriate and constant coping, not irrefutable success. The democratic state as a series of policy experiments is part of the democratic experience in the making. Even if we cannot equalize the benefits, let us do our best to democratize the costs.

Notes

1. Rational choice, a more recent discourse, is either another view or may be considered a meta-view cutting into and informing the other three. But this adds nothing to classical economics as science or ideology.

2. A longer version of this critique will be found in Lowi (1969).

3. For more on the different politics that develop out of different types of policy, see Lowi (1985).

4. For more elaborate treatments of these matters, see Lowi (1971:chs. 1, 2; 1976:ch. 16).

5. Truman relies on the famous book of Robert Michels to support his contention that interest groups, including major trade unions, are oligarchic throughout the world of democratic politics. See Michels (1949:14).

6. Daniel Bell (1960) also uses it in his celebrated *The End of Ideology*, but he does not cite the source.

7. For coverage of these various rules that determined what categories of people shall remain poor, see Mettler (1998:ch. 1) and Mink (1995).

8. This passage is drawn from a somewhat longer treatment in Lowi (1976:672–682).

9. We could complicate this argument by adding to our definition of inequality the rules that determine who shall be detested, who shall be spat upon, and who shall be hidden from view. But in a society where money is valued so greatly as a symbol of worth as well as a mark of wealth, "poor" is an adequate focus.

10. These latter examples of policies that changed the rules of inequality actually did more to change the rules determining who shall be *middle class* rather than who shall be poor. That is a form of progress, but not the form of concern here. For more on this latter point, see Wilson (1978).

11. For an enlightening history of this relationship between machines and the proletariat, one that is especially instructive because it is not about the famous Tammany Hall, see the history of nineteenth-century New Haven in Dahl (1961).

12. This paragraph is based on Mink (1986:134–142).

13. A Grodzins generalization is worth quoting: "The parties became a chief avenue for the achievement of decentralized government. But governmental (here formal constitutional) factors are partially responsible for the manner in which parties are structured. So government 'causes' the form of party; party 'causes' the form of government" (1960:994).

14. This passage is drawn from my use of the Grodzins argument, in Lowi (1975).

15. For a more extensive argument on the rightward movement associated with globalization, see Lowi (1998).

16. For another approach, with additional anthropological and sociological "antecedents" to the market, see Polanyi (1957:chs.3–6, 8).

17. The first litigation culminated in *NLRB v. Jones & Laughlin Steel Corp.*, 301 U.S. 1 (1937); the second culminated in *Helvering v. Davis*, 301 U.S. 619 (1937), and *Stewart Machine Co. v. Davis*, 301 U.S. 548 (1937).

18. There is a lesson in this also, which will return in the final section, that changes that governments make in the political economy, even when opposed by the prevailing interests of the day, quickly become part of the structure of

the economy and are quickly adjusted to by the players in the economy. But that holds true only so long as the policies adopted embody a set of rules that are clear enough to become a regular and habitual part of the structure. Laws that are left open and vague and subject to all kinds of interpretation and day-to-day bargaining are the types of government actions that are corrosive and counterproductive.

19. To my knowledge, this proposal for a general "tenure-of-statutes" act was first made in my *The End of Liberalism* in 1969 (pp. 309–310). Common Cause later adopted it and gave it a far better title, Sunset Law. Former Supreme Court Justice William O. Douglas reports in his autobiography, and there is no reason to doubt his claim, that he "told FDR over and over again that every agency he created should be abolished in 10 years," and that "he should insert in the basic charter of the agency a provision for its termination" (1974:297). But there is no public record of such a proposal until mine in Lowi (1969).

20. The Supreme Court itself tried a version of this in 1935, when it held the important National Industrial Recovery Act unconstitutional on the grounds that it had delegated too much authority to the executive branch and to private trade associations and had not accompanied this broad delegation of lawmaking with appropriate standards for guiding decisions (*Panama Refining Co. v. Ryan*, 293 U.S. 388 [1935] and *Schechter Poultry Corp. v. U.S.*, 295 U.S. 495 [1935]). The so-called Schechter rule was so widely and systematically disregarded after 1935 that it was effectively reversed by disuse. It has been applied to one or two unimportant cases in recent years, but no serious effort to subject policies and programs to fundamental review for legal integrity has been made. This sort of thing should, in any event, come from the legislature, and instead of putting budgetary caps on programs, the legislature should put legal and term-limit caps on them.

21. The quote and the general statement of the problem is from Greider (1997:111–115, 390).

22. *Wisconsin v. Yoder,* 406 U.S. 208 (1972).

23. Compare with Mink (1998:ch. 5), which provides the foundations for this experiment.

4

A Clash of Ideologies: International Capitalism and the State in the Wake of the Asian Crisis

Joel Rocamora

When the histories of the last years of the twentieth century are written, the Asian financial crisis will be seen as a watershed in state and market discourse. The ideological triumphalism of the Washington consensus is over, an unwilling and unwitting victim of what started as Asian but quickly became a global crisis. It is too early to say what will replace it, if anything. What is clear is that the ideological retreat of the state in the face of the ideological onslaught of the market is over.

The retreat of the state as an ideology in public discourse began with the governments of Ronald Reagan and Margaret Thatcher in the 1980s. Riding a wave of dissatisfaction with the U.S. and English states, respectively, Reagan and Thatcher came to power and set in motion almost two decades of conservative ideological ascendancy. The collapse of the Soviet Union and Eastern European socialist states gave further strength to antistate elements in the political discourse. Already under pressure from Reaganism and Thatcherism, people who continued to believe in the possibilities of state-led socialism now found themselves adrift without an ideological paddle. The collapse of the USSR was particularly disorienting because, for all of the criticism of the USSR by socialists everywhere, the USSR established the ideological yardstick for Marxist-Leninist socialism.

The post–Cold War period coincided with the resumption of large capital flows from developed to underdeveloped countries (after years of capital flight in the wake of the 1980s debt crises) and the start of a rapid growth of capital markets. By the second half of the 1990s, daily monetary transactions counted in the trillions of dollars, less than 10 percent of which were connected with actual exchanges of goods and services. More than half of these financial flows were within Asia.

This fast-paced, high-gloss "casino capitalism" was accompanied by the catchword of the 1990s: "globalization." Endowed with limitless powers and possibilities by its proponents and enemies alike, globalization was supposed to be turning the world into one seamless market. In the process, globalization would triumph over all of its enemies—primary among them, the state, the new manifestation of the "evil empire." Its subjects would welcome it, because one of the qualities of globalization that made it irresistible (apart from the spread of McDonald's and the Spice Girls) was its efficiency in allocating its multifarious benefits. And globalization's membership requirement was simple: open capital accounts.

This is the world that came crashing down with the Asian financial crisis. The sense of limitless power that accompanied the helter-skelter growth of capital markets in the early 1990s is gone. Despite attempts by the still considerable number of its promoters in securities companies and business magazines, it has become rather difficult to claim that the market is the most efficient allocator of capital. The cutting edge of globalization is, if not finished altogether, considerably blunted.

The Disappearance of the State: Real or Imagined?

In recent years, the idea that globalization has eroded state power has taken hold in both scholarly and political circles. Some have even argued that the nation-state will soon cease to be a meaningful concept. Linda Weiss has written of this trend in the social sciences, terming it "state denial."

> Wherever we look in the social sciences, the state is being weakened, hollowed out, carved up, toppled or buried . . . This [era of "state denial"] may well be more intense and encompassing than ever before, for the state is being killed off not so much by the appearance of new perspectives, but by the emergence of allegedly new tendencies in the world at large—from social movements and democratization . . . to the globalization of markets. (1998:2)

This trend of "state denial" is problematic for several reasons—first and foremost being that its claims are entirely misguided. Several scholars, including Weiss, have pointed out that, rather than being weakened, states have been strengthened by globalization in many ways. For example, Dani Rodrik's research shows that globalization has led to a larger role for the state: "The small, highly open European economies like Austria, the Netherlands, and Sweden have large governments in part as a result of their attempts to minimize the social impact of openness to the international economy" (1997a:21,25).

And Weiss writes, "Far from becoming an anachronism, state capability has today become an important advantage in international competition." She defines state capability here as "the ability of policy-making authorities to pursue domestic adjustment strategies that, in cooperation with organized economic groups upgrade or transform the industrial economy" (1998:5). The state's capacity in this sense depends not on its ability to "coerce" compliance to its policies but on the depth and breadth of its ties with society. Peter Evans argues that states that are more effective in achieving their economic reform goals tend to be not merely sufficiently autonomous to formulate their own goals, but also sufficiently embedded in particular industrial networks to implement them: "It is an autonomy embedded in a concrete set of social ties which bind the state to society and provide institutionalized channels for the continual negotiation and renegotiation of goals and policies" (1992:162).

Far from converging around a point of "incapacity" as a result of globalization, state capacity continues to vary greatly from one country to another. While underdeveloped countries tend to have weaker state capacity, there is great variation among underdeveloped countries as there is among developed countries. This variation has roots in the kind of capitalism developed in each country and the country's institutional history. The United States, for example, has highly developed skills in international economic "diplomacy" (some call it arm twisting), but the pervasive homelessness in the United States attests to the limited capacity for social policy.

Furthermore, rather than globalization curtailing state action, the reverse is true. The actions of nation-states have shaped globalization. As Weiss argues,

> Globalization . . . is often misunderstood as something imposed by microprocesses, such as the revolution in information technology. A number of sophisticated studies, however, have begun to attribute global economic change to the actions of state authorities as they have set about responding to domestic economic crisis precipitated, in turn, by a series of external shocks, by U.S. financial deregulation to support extraordinary levels of deficit financing, and ultimately by prolonged world recession. (1998:11)

The points raised by Weiss's analysis help to explain many elements of the skeptical and fearful view of globalization from the South: first, that globalization does not just happen but is pushed, often with severe economic and political sanctions; second, that it is the United States and the international financial institutions it dominates, the International Monetary Fund (IMF) and the World Bank, that are most avid in pushing globalization. (While other European and Organization for Economic Cooperation and Development [OECD] countries support one or another element of the globalization conundrum, it is fundamentally a U.S.-UK political project); and third, that if it is the United States and other countries of the North who are pushing, it is mainly countries in the South who are being pushed.

It is not so much that the state has "disappeared" as it has deliberately been pushed out of political discourse. When you are trying to get a government to give up a set of powers, say over macroeconomic policy, it helps to be able to say "don't feel put upon," everyone else has lost, or is going to lose, the same powers. Being able to claim a general phenomenon helps to mask the interests behind a particular policy advocacy. If, as I suspect, the political conditions behind the extraordinarily powerful antistate thrust of neoliberalism have been blunted by the recent worldwide financial crisis, it should now be easier to look more closely at the actual situation.

The Asian Economic Crisis and the Death of the Washington Consensus

What happened in the Asian economic crisis is well known. In Thailand, Indonesia, South Korea, Malaysia, and to a lesser degree, the Philippines, banks were allowed to pile up unhedged dollar loans that made them vulnerable to sudden, large currency devaluations. These banks took advantage of often large interest-rate differentials between foreign-currency (more often than not, U.S. dollars) interest rates and local-currency interest rates. Banks did not hedge their dollar loans because they believed that their governments would maintain policies that kept exchange rates stable.

The same policies tended to push banks toward lending to real estate developers, stock market players, and other speculative investors. Inflated by increasing amounts of foreign funds, real estate and stock market "bubbles" arose. These bubbles were highly susceptible to developments that interrupted the steady increase in asset prices. In 1997, a real estate glut in Bangkok made it difficult for developers to pay their loans and in turn made it difficult for local banks to pay their foreign loans. The bubble that was the fast-growing, loan-financed Thai economy burst. As foreign fund managers pulled their funds out en masse, investors in nearby countries quickly followed.

What started out as a banking crisis turned currency crisis quickly metastasized into generalized economic disaster throughout Asia.

With massive devaluations, even well-managed banks and corporations suddenly found themselves unable to pay their dollar loans. Overambitious, adventurous banks now became ultraconservative in their lending. Panicky governments raised interest rates in a vain attempt to dcfcnd local currencies but put loans beyond the reach of many businesses. Many companies closed or retrenched heavily, suddenly putting millions of people out of work. Weak demand then added to this already poisonous cocktail to push economies into deep recession.

Most of the decisions that led to the crisis were made in the private sphere, but these decisions were not made in a policy vacuum. Government policies created incentives and disincentives that shaped private-sector decisions. The most important of these policies was financial liberalization. Reviewing the literature on balance-of-payments and banking crises over a twenty-five-year period (1970–1995), Manuel Montes writes that "financial liberalization appears to play a significant role in explaining the probability of a banking crisis preceded by a private lending boom. In turn, a banking crisis helps to predict a currency crisis" (1998:8–9).

Another set of policies was geared toward attracting capital flows. Governments were pressured into running up budget surpluses and central banks were pressured into keeping the monetary stock within narrow parameters to maintain low inflation and high interest rates. Local currency to pay for large inflows of dollars was sterilized to keep exchange rates stable and local currencies steadily appreciating. It should be remembered that all these policies were recommended by the IMF and other international financial institutions and by a steady drumbeat of neoliberal propaganda in the media and in academic circles.

While we cannot say that the IMF wanted weak financial-sector regulatory mechanisms, in the heyday of "emerging markets" rhetoric in the first half of the 1990s, regulation was a poor cousin to liberalization. It is only now that IMF Deputy Director Stanley Fischer can say, "The opening of countries' capital accounts should be handled prudently. This means neither a return to pervasive capital controls, nor a rush to full, immediate liberalization, regardless of the risks: the need is for properly sequenced and careful liberalization." The IMF apparently does not recognize its responsibility for imprudent liberalization, however, because Fischer then goes on to propose that "to encourage the orderly liberalization of the capital account, the IMF is at work on an amendment of its charter that will make the liberalization of capital movements a purpose of the Fund" (1998:15).

Western Responses to the Crisis

Western media coverage has targeted the Asian newly industrialized countries (NIC) model of close government-business coordination, termed "crony capitalism," as the source of the crisis. By pinpointing state involvement in the business sector as the cause of the crisis, the crony-capitalism explanation follows neoliberal, antistate logic. Under crony capitalism, it is asserted, corruption is endemic. Although corruption is indeed widespread in much of Asia, this is not because of the development state model, as crony capitalism suggests. In fact, the countries most associated with this model, such as Japan, South Korea, and Taiwan, have lower levels of corruption when compared to Southeast Asia.

This is not to say that corruption was not one of the main contributing factors to the Asian economic crisis. It was. Authoritarian governments took advantage of the opportunities opened up by capital-accounts liberalization and easy "emerging markets" funds to further family and other particularistic interests, in the process making their economies vulnerable to "emerging markets" volatility. Suharto provides the grossest example of this proposition, but there are many other examples in the region. Many of the financial houses that ran up the tens of billions of unhedged U.S.-dollar loans that sank the Thai economy were owned or run by cronies of former prime minister Chaovalit and other politicians. In the Philippines and Malaysia, ruling parties became the main avenues for business deals on large infrastructure, privatization, and other megaprojects. What these examples show, however, is that corruption combined with financial liberalization, not the strong economic role of the state, are at the root of the crisis.

The neoliberal view of the state and crony-capitalism as the causes of the Asian crisis shaped Western responses to the crisis. Comments by Deputy U.S. Treasury Secretary Lawrence H. Summers reflect the prevailing logic: "Reforms are less about changing the short-term policy mix than they are about changing the long-term institutional environment. . . . Reforms of the role of government have sought, not merely an end to those public interventions directly contributing to the crisis, but fundamental change in what government is expected to do." For good measure, it is also about "opening the economy to foreign participation and competition with sweeping trade and financial sector liberalization" (1998:12).

This logic, however, is flawed, supported more by ideology than factual evidence. In contrast to the Third World debt crisis of the 1980s, which was brought on by public-sector debt, the Asian crisis of the 1990s is a crisis of the private sector. In the 1980s, principally in Latin America, national economies were plagued by balance-of-payments crises, budget deficits, and high inflation, much of this linked to government profligacy. Asian governments in the 1990s, on the other hand, went into crisis with balanced, often surplus budgets, low inflation rates, and high levels of national savings and investment. Governments maintained what economists call "good fundamentals."

What failed in Asia was the market, not government. As the World Bank's chief economist in 1998 in Helsinki, Joseph Stiglitz spoke of market weaknesses, stating that "financial markets do not do a good job of selecting the most productive recipients of funds or of monitoring the use of funds and must be controlled" (Bullard 1998:41). George Soros, understandably not a hard-line critic of financial markets, also admitted that "financial markets, far from tending towards equilibrium, are inherently unstable. A boom/bust sequence can easily spiral out of control, knocking over one economy after another" (1998a:2).

Identifying the locus of the Asian crisis is a crucial issue because it lies at the root of the debate on the IMF formula for dealing with the crisis. The components of the formula all call for actions in the public sphere: central banks raising interest rates to prevent speculation on the local currency, governments cutting subsidies and other expenditures to keep inflation low, legislatures passing yet more liberalization and privatization laws to entice foreign investors to come back. IMF critics contend that this formula is geared toward solving a 1980s-type crisis of the public sector, not the market crisis of the 1990s.

The IMF approach does indeed raise some serious questions. First, as has been well documented, the IMF's strategy in Asia following the crisis did not have the intended positive economic impacts. Indonesia provides an excellent example. "As the crisis erupted, Indonesia carried out classic, adjustment policies of tight credit and higher interest rates that exacerbated the weakness in the banking system. The impact of credit constriction on the real sector is to reduce expected profits in companies and the banking system. These abetted further attacks on the equity and other asset markets, worsening the performance of the rupiah. The worsening rupiah further weakened the economy's prospects and encouraged investment withdrawals" (Montes 1998:5–6).

Second, IMF policies in Asia raise the political question of who pays for economic rescue efforts, both directly and indirectly. High-flying bankers may be having difficulty making payments on their condominium loans and BMWs, but IMF austerity measures, tighter monetary and budget parameters, and high interest rates hit smaller businesses and poorer segments of the population harder. Montes points out that crises such as occurred in Asia "have always tended to be resolved by using taxpayer resources and through higher unemployment and lower growth so that the costs have been borne mostly by those whose incomes are not based on asset holding" (1998:7).

Financial bailouts also create a moral hazard. The existence of a number of guarantees on bank transactions, national and international alike, lessens the risks from lending and contributes to debt crisis, both on public debt as in the 1980s or private debt as in the Asian crisis. If bankers believe that governments will bail them out, they are not likely to exercise much care in their lending decisions. Furthermore, if banks, local bank borrowers, and foreign lenders get bailed out with public funds at a time when social service budgets are being squeezed, the political outcry is likely to be deafening.

Why then, given the above drawbacks, would the IMF pursue such flawed policies? Only power politics can provide an explanation. U.S. companies have a strong interest in Southeast Asia; they want to gain fuller access to Southeast Asian markets, which have historically been some of the most protected in the world (Bello 1997:45). The IMF's structural-adjustment policies, which encourage liberalization and deregulation, cater to these corporate interests.

Not-So-Strange Bedfellows: Democratization and International Capitalism

The rhetoric of globalization has gone hand in hand with discussion of democratization and governance. The Asian economic crisis has given Western institutions a new justification to pressure Asian governments to democratize. The West's focus on democratization and governance, however, deserves a closer look. How is the West defining democratization and governance and what is its motivation?

Democracy and "Asian Values"

In many international forums, Asian leaders, most important former Singapore prime minister Lee Kuan Yew and Malaysian prime minister Mahathir Mohammad, have spoken out against pressure on Asian governments to democratize and to observe internationally recognized human-rights norms. These pressures, they say, serve Western political and economic interests, and seek to impose political norms that are alien to Asian culture. Asian culture is communal, they contend, in contrast to the individualistic culture of the West. Where democracy in the West emphasizes limits on government in favor of individual rights, Asians give greater weight to the government as the repository of community interests. Lee Kuan Yew calls Western-style democracy too undisciplined; it fails to curb individualistic selfishness and to organize society for community goals. Citizens must be willing to give up individual rights in exchange for faster economic growth.

Critics of this school of thought say that it is merely an ideological justification for authoritarianism. Indeed, the most vocal proponents of "Asian values" ran authoritarian states. Suharto's Indonesia was a dictatorship with a repressive military apparatus that touched all levels of society. And both Singapore and Malaysia have internal security laws that are used to suppress opposition.

Certainly, authoritarianism is intolerable, and efforts to reduce corruption and increase accountability in public decisionmaking are important. However, the Asian values argument has some merit in so far as it questions the narrow Western definition of democracy. The kind of democracy that is being pushed by the North is very specific. It is formal, constitutional, Western-style democracy. It is a form of democracy that separates politics from the structures of power in the economy. Ideologically, it is very much linked to neoliberal antistatism. Harking back to Lockean theory, but with a more modern Thatcherite patina, democracy here is understood simply as "less government."

In its academic garb, the argument is that "political democracy per se is a goal worthy of achievement, even at the expense of foregoing alternative paths that would seem to promise more immediate returns in terms of socialisation [social reform]" (O'Donnell and Schmitter 1986:13–14). In more direct, political terms, the same argument might be restated as "OK, you can have democracy, but only if you leave the economy alone." This view represents a crucial condition for foreign investors, assuring relatively free entry and exit and the least possible intervention in profit making while in-country.

Democratization, Western-Style

The governance and democratization discourse cannot be understood outside of the interests and agendas of international capitalism and the national and multinational public institutions that support these interests. The leaders of the current discourse on democratization are multilateral institutions (such as the World Bank and the OECD) and Western governments (led by the United States). Western Europeans have pushed human-rights issues for a long time, but have only recently entered into the democratization and governance discourse, following the lead of the World Bank and the U.S.

government. Among multilateral banks, the Asian Development Bank is a latecomer.

The acceleration of Western penetration of the economies of the South has increased Western pressure on governments of the South to democratize. To facilitate this thrust, specific elements in the Western conception of liberal democracy have been pushed, particularly an antistate bias and free-market ideology. Trade and other forms of liberalization have been packaged as democratization. Since governments are corrupt and inefficient, the argument goes, democracy can be advanced only if many of the economic functions of government are privatized or turned over to the market.

The most important reason for problematizing the governance and democratization discourse is that it is being pushed by international capitalism: by multilateral institutions such as the World Bank and the governments of advanced capitalist countries led by the United States. After supporting authoritarian regimes throughout the world (from Somoza to Marcos to Mobutu) for decades, why has international capitalism now begun to support democracy? (Robinson 1996). Furthermore, if globalization is the current stage of the expansion of capitalist relations into countries of the South, what is it about the particulars of this expansion that makes democratization the preferred political strategy of international capitalism? Is it the antistate aspect of neoliberalism? Does movement away from authoritarian states in the South mean weaker governments? Or is international capitalism mainly interested in moving against protectionist, nationalist, ruling-class factions, enabling modernizing elites to come to power and make way for the expansion of capitalist relations into new economic areas?

It is no accident that the intensification of Western demands for democratization go hand-in-hand with demands for trade liberalization, privatization, and other forms of deregulation. The Western push for democratization can be read as part of the process of opening up the South for Northern investment and trade.

Western democratization efforts have sought to shift the power structure within a country away from elites that were part of the old authoritarian regime and toward a new class of elites more supportive of free trade. Authoritarian governments in the South have tended to be controlled by elite groups based in agro-exports or in manufacturing built up during the heyday of import-substitution industrialization in the 1950s and 1960s. The "modernizing" elites in these countries are in the financial sector or in import-dependent nontraditional exports. These "democratizing" elites, not surprisingly, are also the class factions most needed by international capital as local partners in the ongoing acceleration of globalization.

The governance and democratization discourse's focus on transparency might also be understood as relating to capitalist interests. The velocity of international capital flows is such that fund managers require up-to-the-minute data on monetary and fiscal accounts. Authoritarian governments—usually accompanied by cozy relationships between government officials and their business clients—often must hide or doctor this kind of data.[1]

The end of the Cold War enabled the West to pursue these strategies. With the collapse of the USSR and the socialist bloc, one of the major reasons for Western support for authoritarian regimes in the South disappeared. To make way for accelerated entry of goods and services, most importantly financial services, protectionist and authoritarian regimes have had to be removed or forced to democratize. Furthermore, the removal of socialism as an alternative to capitalism has given the West's push for democratization an added sense of legitimacy. This new justification is expressed in its most extreme form by Fukuyama's "end of history" conceit, which claims that Western-style liberal democracy is the final goal of political evolution.

But does movement away from authoritarian governments in the South mean weaker government? Why, then, is the antiauthoritarian thrust of Western pressure accompanied by governance programs meant to strengthen government capacity? This paradox exists if we look only at the ideology of Western-style democratization. If we look at the process from the vantage point of the requirements of international capitalism, the contradiction disappears. The antistate thrust of neoliberalism with respect to the Third World does not so much seek to weaken Third World governments overall as it does to limit government involvement in the economy. Neoliberal economies actually require governments strong enough to create conditions that allow markets to operate effectively.

Governments in the South, whether authoritarian or not, tend to have limited governmental capacity. For foreign business, this creates problems in both the political and economic realms. Weak governments have weak capacity to assure political stability, a major requirement of investors. At a minimum, governments have to have a monopoly over the legitimate uses of violence to assure peace and order and end armed challenges to the government.

The Philippine state does not possess even the basic legal or administrative capacity to institute the laissez-faire model advocated by the United States and the large multilateral institutions—the IMF and the World Bank. The tremendous increase in state administrative functions that historically has been required for the development of laissez-faire is well beyond the country's reach (Polanyi 1994). Overwhelmed by the myriad particularistic demands of powerful oligarchic interests, the Philippine state is unable to provide anything approximating the "political and procedural predictability" necessary for the development of more advanced forms of capitalism" (Hutchcroft 1993: 580–581).

Two current concerns of Northern governance programs in the South, decentralization and anticorruption, can also be understood best from the vantage point of foreign investors. Decentralization programs need not be seen as necessarily weakening central governments if they strengthen the capacity of local government units to implement central government programs. This is particularly true for government economic services such as infrastructure. In the same vein, corruption is seen as an added "cost" for investors that distorts local factor markets.

The IMF and Democracy

There is another dimension to the issue of democracy and the Asian crisis that is seldom mentioned in media reports: the role of the IMF. There is a lot of controversy over the economic wisdom of "conditionalities" linked to IMF rescue packages. Where the politics of the IMF role is raised, however, it is often in a positive light. IMF pressure on Suharto comes off as the IMF pushing for democracy in Indonesia. In fact, I would argue that the political impact of the IMF role is distinctly antidemocratic.

Macroeconomic policy is one of the most important areas of policy in government because it affects everyone in the country. In a democracy, setting the framework of macroeconomic policy should be the subject of wide-ranging discussion. In countries under the IMF thumb, this area of policy is closed off to the public. The IMF demands transparency of everyone except itself: accountability where it cannot be made accountable because it does not belong to the polities it intervenes in.

Martin Feldstein, professor of economics at Harvard University, president of the National Bureau of Economic Research, and former adviser to U.S. president Ronald Reagan, is very critical of the IMF:

> The Fund should not use the opportunity of countries being "down and out" to override national political processes or impose economic changes that however helpful they may be . . . are the proper responsibility of the country's own political system . . . a nation's desperate need for short-term financial help does not give the IMF the moral right to substitute its technical judgments for the outcomes of the nation's political process. (Bullard 1998:41)

The Fund has also been attacked for its intellectual arrogance in applying the same solution, regardless of the problem, and for applying bilateral agreements to solve a regional problem. A main problem is the belief that economists use almost exclusively simplistic accounting methods, leading to the situation where "economists would fly into a country, look at and attempt to verify these data, and make macroeconomic recommendations for policy reforms, all in the space of a couple of weeks" (Bullard 1998:42).

Imposing macroeconomic policy would already be a problem if there was agreement on what these policies should be. In this case, disagreement cuts across ideological lines, uniting the strangest economist bedfellows. It would be one thing if the IMF record of economic management were spotless. In Indonesia, "rather than restoring confidence . . . the IMF directive to close down sixteen insolvent banks caused panic, precipitating a run on two-thirds of the country's banks, further weakening the financial sector and eroding faith in the economy. The Fund itself admitted as much in an internal memo which was reported in the *New York Times* in mid-January" (Bullard 1998:12).

"Criticizing the solutions imposed by the IMF in no way implies an uncritical endorsement of 'Asian' capitalism," Bullard insists. "The political and economic development models in these countries have brought some overall improvements in health, education, and living standards. But the cost has been high in terms of sharpening the divide between rich and poor, environmental exploitation and loss of community control over natural resources, and growth without economic democracy or expansion of political participation" (1998:2). "Domestic" interests face one standard, while "foreign" interests face another. Whereas domestic firms are abandoned to free-market forces—the IMF refused to bail out financial institutions in Indonesia and Thailand, for example—foreign investors "are given enhanced rights to ownership, the possibility to convert debt to equity in struggling Asian enterprises and the chance of picking up others at bargain basement prices, thanks to changes in foreign ownership rules included in IMF packages" (p. 41).

Concluding Thoughts

In the previous pages, I have spoken much about ideology and the use of ideology to mask reality. I have argued that international capitalists and their supporters have used neoliberal ideology to push for specific policies that support their interests. By taking this ideological approach, they have tried to disguise their interests as general principles. My analysis has sought to "unmask" these interests and show how neoliberal ideology has no empirical basis.

The Asian crisis has made this task easier, because it has publicly revealed the flaws in the neoliberal approach. International capitalism, embodied by the IMF, pursued policies in the wake of the Asian crisis that were clearly not effective in resolving the crisis. Propositions about inflation, government budgets, monetary parameters, and other economic policy issues were not espoused with the power of theory or empirical evidence, but rather with the economic and political power of developed-country governments pushing specific agendas. By pursuing such wrong-headed policies, the IMF revealed itself to be an entity driven by particular interests, rather than realities.

The task that I have begun here—the task of unmasking the ideological propositions that have driven policy discourse in recent years—has been undertaken with an understanding that this debate must go beyond texts. We have to enter arenas that economists and even political scientists are loathe to enter—the arenas of power and power agendas, of national interests and the clash of these interests. We will not necessarily resolve these debates, but we might at least shed enough light on the issues to assist our leaders in making decisions, decisions that will affect all of us.

Note

1. This point was suggested to me by John Gershman.

PART 2

CASE STUDIES

5

Toward a New Approach to Welfare Policy in South Africa: Building Assets in Poor Communities

Xolela Mangcu

In his famous book *Citizenship and Social Class,* the British sociologist T. H. Marshall (1950) divided the evolution of modern citizenship into three stages, each defined by a specific set of rights. First came the development of civil rights, such as freedom of speech, freedom of religion, and property rights, in the eighteenth century. The second period came in the nineteenth century with the extension of political rights through representative democracy. The third period, in the twentieth century, was characterized by the extension of social rights that guaranteed a minimum standard of living.

According to Skocpol (1995), the modern welfare state originated in Europe during the latter half of the nineteenth century with pension and social-insurance schemes for the needy. Even though the idea of a public family goes back to Swedish leader Per Albin Hansson's concept of the *folkhem* (people's home) in the 1920s, the vast elaboration of the welfare system through the state came after World War II. In fact, the term "welfare state" originated with the British Labour Party's efforts to integrate all of its social assistance programs into a coherent social policy (Wolfe 1989). The growing role of the state in social welfare became official orthodoxy throughout the 1950s and 1960s, even in the United States, which saw the growth of welfare throughout the 1960s—with the enormous expansion of Aid to Families with Dependent Children, the major form of public assistance to poor families—and 1970s (Skocpol 1995).

Central to Marshall's conception of social rights were two interrelated concepts—the equalization of incomes and the equalization of status. Marshall's linkage of incomes to status was based on an old civic-republican idea that poverty impeded its victims from being effective citizens—an idea that goes back to Plato, Aristotle, Machiavelli, and Rousseau. It is also an idea that was used by conservative philosophers such as Edmund Burke to say that the poor were not adequately equipped to engage in rational political discourse because of their desperate passions (King and Waldron 1988).

My concern here is that income-based welfare programs have historically been used to define and marginalize the poor outside a common citizenship. Marshall himself noted how Britain's Poor Law of 1834 "treated the claims of the poor, not as an integrated part of the rights of the citizen, but as an alternative to them—as claims that could be met only if the claimants ceased to be citizens in any true sense of the word"; he further noted that "the stigma which clung to poor relief expressed the deep feelings of a people who understood that those who accepted must cross the road that separated the community of citizens from the outcast company of the destitute" (1950: 80). Welfare has continued to carry such a stigma for poor and particularly minority and immigrant communities in the United States, Britain, and other European countries where there have been rollbacks to welfare provision.

One of the few places where income transfers and citizenship seem to have been pursued successfully through social policy are Scandinavian countries such as Sweden. That is because, first, the income transfers "were coordinated with Keynesian strategies of macroeconomic management and then targeted interventions in labor markets" (Skocpol 1995:12). High labor-force participation rates meant that more people contributed to the fiscus than took away from it; and for those people outside the labor force, the system provided training opportunities that connected them to the labor market. Esping-Andersen argues that "a Pareto optimal welfare state of the future might very well be one that shifts the accent of social citizenship from its present preoccupation with income maintenance toward a menu of rights to lifelong education and qualification. A major problem with postwar welfare states is that they pursued 'equal opportunity' more through income maintenance than through labor supply management . . . a social investment type of welfare state might therefore opt for some degree of targeted human capital guarantees" (1996:260). Over and above coordination with the labor market, social policy in places such as Sweden provided broad-based, cross-class benefits, which meant that they had political support.

In recent years there have also been attempts to rethink welfare policy from an asset-based perspective. The argument here is that building individual and community assets does more to enhance individual citizenship than do income transfers. However, the building of assets implies public policies that would allow people to save and invest their resources. Such mechanisms already exist for middle- and upper-income earners in the form of retirement annuities and tax deductions for mortgage interest and property taxes. But these institutional mechanisms do not exist for poor people because they do not earn enough or own taxable properties. The question is whether there can be welfare policies that would allow poor people to accumulate savings that would in turn make them asset owners.

After a brief survey of the literature on asset-based development, this chapter specifically explores the possibilities for an asset-building approach to welfare in South Africa. At present the South African government is proposing an income grant for the poor and unemployed as an antipoverty mechanism. My argument is that such a strategy is unlikely to be effective in reducing poverty unless it is coordinated with community development and job-creation strategies.

From Income-Based to Asset-Based Welfare

In *Assets and the Poor,* Sherraden (1991) makes a distinction between assets and incomes, and outlines their respective strengths and weaknesses in the fight against poverty: incomes are consumed on a daily or monthly basis, assets are passed on from generation to generation and become the basis for long-term planning within families. Sherraden argues that individual and family development are not based on receiving and spending incomes but on accummulating savings and investing over time. Moreover, Sherraden argues, "people think and behave differently when they are accumulating assets, and the world responds to them differently" (1991:148). Assets, for example, can be used as collateral when families take out loans, whether for children's education or other kinds of investments; thus, asset inequalities set in one generation can set the pattern of social relations for several generations to come. Chambers argues that poor households become poorer through loss of assets. In times of crisis the poor often have to mortgage whatever capital assets they have: "Where these events entail debts at high interest rates or loss of productive wealth, they can have ratchet effects, like movements down past a cog which are difficult to reverse, making poor people permanently poorer" (1983:114–115).

According to Ford Foundation executive and sociologist Melvin Oliver, the focus on income disparities in U.S. social policy has shielded from view the greater inequalities in asset ownership not only between the rich and the poor, but also between blacks and whites: "Middle-class blacks, for example, earn seventy cents for every dollar of wealth held by middle-class whites but they possess only

fifteen cents for every dollar of wealth held by middle-class whites"
(Oliver and Shapiro 1997:7). As a result, white children tend to have
more assets and therefore better and varied life options than black
children, whose parents are more dependent on monthly incomes.
Even educated, middle-class blacks often do not possess assets comparable to those of their white counterparts.

Oliver joined the Ford Foundation with the specific purpose of
pursuing an agenda of asset building in poor communities. The foundation, for instance, sponsors "Individual Development Accounts" in
poor neighborhoods in which, for example, a family could make annual deposits of $500 or more into a nontaxable, interest-bearing ed-
ucational development account that would be matched by government and/or other donor agencies. Similar accounts could be
opened for setting up businesses or saving for home ownership. As
mentioned above, middle-income earners already have institutionalized savings that allow them to build up long-term assets. This means
that even though personal savings are low for all U.S. citizens, the
middle and upper classes are able to build long-term assets without
taking anything away from their incomes—they are able to consume
and save at the same time.

Unger and West (1998) have suggested reform of the tax system
so that the poor can keep more of their money through mechanisms
such as a tax deduction for savings. In the United States, home mortgage deductions, which are in effect a major subsidy of the middle
class, far exceed welfare payments to the poor. Oliver points out that
home ownership represents the biggest component in the wealth
portfolio of most U.S. citizens, especially among those with modest
incomes. Moreover, the value of the average house has outstripped inflation, thereby providing stable appreciation of wealth over time.
The fact that most of this property accumulation was among whites, as
a result of deliberate public policies that specifically prohibited property ownership by African Americans in the rush of post–World War II
suburbanization, contributed a great deal to the racialized asset disparities that dominate life in the United States to this day. It is for these
reasons that the scholars and foundation executives mentioned above
have been calling for institutionalized savings for the poor as well.

However, the problem is that many of the working poor earn too
little to save money and too much to qualify for welfare. Many poor
people simply opt out of the labor market to join the welfare rolls,
which enables them to get a whole range of government benefits. The
United States is now moving toward a "workfare" system under which
people must work to qualify for their welfare benefits. In some states,
such as Wisconsin, this has led to dramatic increases in the number of

people taken off the welfare rolls. However, since workfare jobs pay very low wages they still do not adequately address the issue of asset building for poor people. So, in addition to linking work and benefits, strategies are needed that allow people to build their own assets.

Social Policy and Community Development

Rethinking income-based social welfare would of necessity require dramatic shifts in our understanding of poverty and development. In their book *India: Social and Economic Opportunity*, economists Dreze and Sen argue that poverty is not just a matter of income deprivation:

> Poverty of a life, in this view, lies not merely in the impoverished state in which the person actually lives, but also in the lack of real opportunity . . . to choose other types of living. Even the relevance of low incomes, meagre possessions, and other aspects of what are standardly seen as economic poverty relates ultimately to their role in curtailing capabilities (that is their role in severely restricting the choices people have to lead valuable and valued lives). Poverty is thus ultimately a matter of capability deprivation. (1995:11)

The authors conclude that the success of development programs must ultimately be judged in terms of their capacity to expand people's choices in the long term—one of the advantages of asset ownership. The issue of choice can be problematic, because setting up asset accounts for specific purposes might restrict people's choices. But it could also be argued that there is a much broader way of looking at choice: for example, if savings are for expenditure on education, the longer term benefits are in the choices that education opens up for the recipients of asset-building grants.

Although the attack on welfare has generally come from right-wing quarters, there has been growing concern among community activists about the debilitating political effects of welfare programs on individuals and communities. Activists working with poor families and children are advocating for comprehensive community-based initiatives that target individuals and families in communities in which the schools or the police or the health systems do not work properly. Unless those systems are reformed, income transfers become economically unsustainable and politically unpopular. In what may at first seem like a return to the concept of the people's home in civil society, community organizations around the world are experimenting with community-based approaches to social policy. If government agencies also start exploring civic-based, collective approaches to how people care for each other and educate their children, this might alleviate the negative experiences of welfare recipients and be a basis for collective organizing for economic development.

The world is full of examples of the poorest of the poor transforming their communities through collective efforts. From Oakland in California to Navrongo in northern Ghana, community-based organizations have been able to turn around infant mortality rates in their neighborhoods. The Chatham-Savannah Youth Authority in the United States has played a leading role in creating safety nets for poor people in the wake of federal rollbacks in welfare provisions. Its director, Otis Johnson, argues that they are working to restore the original idea of institutions as mechanisms to meet the needs of the people. The Barefoot College in Tilonia, northern India, is one of the preeminent examples of the extremely poor working collectively to deal with issues of health, education, and environmental protection in their communities. The Chipko movement in India is also one of the best examples of community mobilization to protect the natural resources that are a source of meaning and livelihood for the poor. After successfully resisting the cutting down of forests by multinational companies and obtaining a twenty-five-year ban on commercial logging in India, Chipko now manages one of the largest eco-development programs in the nation. The result has been an impressive reforestation of the denuded slopes that were once the cause of endless natural disasters. Chipko became the inspiration for other community-based environmental movements in India, including the famous Narmada Bachao Andolan—a movement started by villagers to oppose the construction of dams on the Narmada in the state of Gujarat. Movement leaders argued that the dams would displace 400,000 families, disrupt the social ecosystem of the region, and submerge tens of thousands of hectares of agricultural and forest land (Mangcu 1998).

Faith institutions have become the basis of community economic development in places such as New York and are often the last institutions to remain after all others have left. Community development corporations have been another succesful resource in the United States. Although these corporations began by building houses, they have in recent years begun to focus on the social networks and value systems necessary for long-term economic development. They realize that development is not just about bricks and mortar and that it has to occur within a context of strengthened communities. Boston's Dudley Street Neighborhood Initiative (DSNI) is an excellent example of asset building within a community-building context. The DSNI initiative arose out of a protest movement against waste dumping in

Boston's predominantly black and minority community of Roxbury. DSNI organized for and became the first community organization in the United States to obtain the power of eminent domain. After a protracted period of fund raising and community organizing, DSNI used the neighborhood's intrinsic assets—proximity to downtown and highways, a local economy of $60 million, and community cohesiveness—to revive this area of Boston.

In addition to this civic focus, community-based welfare organizations are also engaged in efforts to transform social service delivery systems so they can be more empowering of the poor. Dreze and Sen attribute much of the progress in social policy in places such as India to the role of community organizations:

> The role of public activism in influencing government policy can be particularly important in promoting the positive functions of government. . . . These positive functions include the provision of basic public services such as health care, child immunization, primary education, social security, environmental protection and rural infrastructure. The vigilance and involvement of the public can be quite crucial not only in ensuring an adequate expansion of these essential services but also in monitoring their functioning. (1995:89)

Naturally, then, a community-based asset approach to social development, as many of the cases cited above demonstrate, will require strong community institutions and leadership skills. What makes poor people particularly vulnerable to the vagaries of poverty is not just a lack of incomes; the absence of supportive environments and institutions leads to despair. For instance, homelessness in a major urban center is likely to be more devastating than in a closely knit rural community. Explaining the impact of market capitalism on famines in India, the economic historian Karl Polanyi once wrote that "while under the old regime of feudalism and of the village community, noblesse oblige, clan solidarity and regulation of the corn market checked famines, under the rule of the market the people could not be prevented from starving according to the rules of the game." He then concluded that "the catastrophe of the native community is a direct result of the rapid and violent disruption of the basic institutions of the victim" (1944:159–160). If Polanyi was right in linking the experience of poverty to the communal infrastructure of the community, then it is only logical that poverty-alleviation programs and social policy also pay closer attention to the role of collective assets. Communities that have strong social networks not only cushion the poor from the vagaries of poverty; those networks and relationships can be used to grow businesses.

Building Cross-Class Coalitions for Welfare

A serious problem with the traditional income-based approach to poverty is the ghettoization of the poor by cash programs directed exclusively at them without the support of the middle classes. And when the popular mood changes among the powerful sectors—as happened with welfare in the United States under Bill Clinton—welfare can be readily and summarily dispensed with. Thus some scholars point to the vital importance of making linkages with middle-class constituencies in the fight against poverty. Clavel (1996) argues, for instance, that relatively isolated movements oriented toward the poor must grow into more diverse coalitions oriented toward both poor and middle-class constituencies. This creates a broad base from which to capture administrative and political institutions that can in turn be used to support and sustain those coalitions and their agendas. Earlier in this volume, Ted Lowi makes a similar point about the critical importance of coalition building in generating broad-based support for anti-poverty strategies: "Lower class advances in public policy cannot be significantly expanded unless they are linked to advances for middle classes"(p. 54). He argues that support for medical aid for the poor was made easy by the fact that it was preceded by Medicare for formerly employed middle-class constituencies. Similarly, the idea of building assets strikes a chord with most people, rich and poor. From a strategic political perspective, asset building has a greater chance of gaining the support of other sectors of society than a program of income transfers. Powerful business constituencies might find the language of asset building more inviting than that of redistribution, even if both terms describe the same activity (for example, land reform).

The South African Case:
The Jobs Crisis and the Welfare Response

The great paradox of the South African transition to democracy is the growing economic insecurity and joblessness among those who expected the most from freedom's promise. Labor analysts attribute the job attrition to long-term structural shifts from primary goods production to service industries. For example, agriculture and mining's share of GDP declined from 18.6 percent in 1970 to 11.9 percent in 1997, and between 1970 and 1995 the demand for labor in agriculture and mining declined by 50 percent and 30 percent, respectively. These long-term trends have been exacerbated by the loss of a million jobs over the past ten years. These losses are not likely to subside anytime soon; on the contrary, hundreds of thousands of jobs are on the line in different sectors: energy (90,000), textiles (28,000), construction (30,000). An additional 300,000 jobs are expected to be lost as the public sector downsizes over the next five years.

Although a great deal has been said about how the economy will ultimately reabsorb these people, the fact is that the translation between economic growth and job creation is tenuous at best—hence the term "jobless growth." Most of the displaced workers do not have the skills to join the service sector, where most jobs are now being created: between 1970 and 1995, demand for financial and business services increased by 200 percent. Seventy percent of South Africa's unemployed are unskilled and are mostly in the forty-four to fifty-five age group. Many of them will simply become the lost generation of the new South Africa. Not surprisingly, the brunt of the job losses will be borne by African workers, for whom—between 1970 and 1995—demand declined by 4 percent, while that for all other groups increased by at least 45 percent. According to Bhorat (1999) it is primarily African and colored workers who will experience a nonincreasing demand for their services while white and Asian workers are likely to be in greater demand. That is economic jargon for saying the economy has no use for unskilled African and colored workers.

Imagining a Different Social-Policy Response

South Africa's social-assistance programs are currently limited to a few categorical grants, such as child grants, disability grants, and old-age pensions. Any poor and unemployed person over the age of six and under sixty who does not suffer from a disability is excluded from the social-assistance system. This basically excludes all victims of the layoffs mentioned above—the very people whose employability is at risk because of skills deficits. Not only do the payments for unemployment insurance take a long time to pay out, the benefits also often run out before people can get new jobs, if they do at all. The government's response to the growing job losses and the inadequacy of the social-assistance system has been a proposal to establish a basic income grant for the poor and unemployed.

What is the alternative? In my view, what is needed in South Africa is not a system that will cement poor people into a status from which they will not be able to escape for generations to come, but a productivist, asset-based approach to welfare that focuses on building people's long-term self-reliance and independence. Bowles and Gintis (1996) argue that it may be very hard to redistribute through a tax-and-transfer system because after-tax profits are still a significant factor in the considerations of investors. They also argue that Keynesian demand-side redistribution no longer has the same impact on output and employment because producers are now oriented toward international markets. Hence they propose a shift away from what they call productivity dampening, demand-side redistribution to a productivity-enhancing strategy based on the redistribution of assets whose productive use will boost international competitiveness. For example, a shift of ownership in a firm from capitalist owners to a workers' co-operative, or of a residential property from the landlord to tenants, will improve productivity because of the stake that the workers and the tenants will then have in their newly acquired assets: "Workers' interests are now to save and to invest in a way that protects or enhances the value of their asset" (1996:318).

Although I am sympathetic to Bowles and Gintis's focus on the redistribution of assets, I think they may underestimate the importance of domestic demand conditions and overstate the importance of international demand conditions, especially for poor countries. In a poor country such as South Africa, a great deal of demand is for basic infrastructure services. According to Samson et al. (2000), income transfers to the poor shift aggregate demand toward labor-intensive industries such as agriculture, especially small-scale agriculture: for example, poor people can use grants to purchase food from peasant farmers and thereby boost their regional rural economies—which could fuel additional job creation within those economies. A case therefore exists for providing some sort of income redistribution through active labor-market and tax policies, even if this is tied to the asset-building strategies that Bowles and Gintis advocate. The obvious difference between the South African response and the productivist Scandinavian approach is that the labor market was an integral part of welfare in Scandinavia: in Sweden welfare was based on high labor-participation rates; in South Africa, low labor-participation rates prevail.

Given the failure of the formal economy to generate jobs, the government could undertake a productivist approach to welfare through public works and community-development programs to absorb many of the unskilled laborers shed by the private economy. Unemployed people in each community could participate in programs identified by the community itself in return for monthly incomes. However, mechanisms would still have to be devised to allow the working poor to save. An asset-development fund could be established to provide matching grants for the working poor to build up savings or for groups that wish to start joint economic development projects. Each individual or group would have a nontaxable, interest-bearing savings account for specified asset-building purposes into which the government would deposit its share; they would also be exempt from income taxes through an earned-income tax credit.

A targeted income grant might still be necessary for those who are indigent or clearly incapable of participating in such efforts. Although genuine concern has been expressed that this would stigmatize the poor and lock them in a poverty trap, this would be a problem only if the income grant were adopted as it is now proposed—that is, as a substitute for job creation. But if the grant is for those clearly incapable of doing anything for themselves, it might gain sympathy in the broader political community.

And here it is important to note that the scourge of HIV/AIDS is going to increase the number of people who can do absolutely nothing for themselves and yet need to be taken care of through the social-welfare and health systems. The productivity challenges are therefore not simply limited to the unskilled segment of the labor force but also to the skilled and educated. Unless some drastic measures are successfully implemented, the HIV/AIDS pandemic is going to compound an already dire skills situation. An important caveat to the call for a productivist approach to welfare is a recognition of the drop in productivity that will take place as skilled people die of AIDS-related diseases.

The only alternative to a targeted welfare grant is a universal grant that would be reclaimed from the upper-income groups through the tax system. The problem is that the cost for such a universal grant has been estimated to be at least R28 billion, without factoring in administrative costs. One can say with certainty that such a proposal would not pass muster in the present political and economic climate; this is where Bowles and Gintis's argument about the dangers of a tax and transfer system become real for investors. But before we dismiss the universal grant, it is quite possible that if we factor in the large numbers of people coming onto the welfare rolls because of HIV/AIDS, then the differences in cost may not be that high. Moreover, HIV/AIDS is a disease that affects not only the poor. A universal welfare proposal that includes middle-class individuals could still be politically viable.

Greater attention also has to be given to the role of civil-society networks in the provision of care for needy people. An individualized system of monetary grants may not be adequate for the kind of communal, emotional sustenance that people need. Bowles and Gintis argue for grants to nonprofit organizations that have traditionally provided this kind of "caring labor" without being compensated. This kind of caring labor will be even be more pressing with the growing number of people suffering from HIV/AIDS. As it is, hospitals are now releasing HIV/AIDS patients to their homes where they can die in the comfort of their families.

Ardington and Lund (1995) also argue that it is important that social grants meant for specific groups of people not be seen as alternatives to public works but as complementary to them. The criticism of public-works programs is that they are low paying and also produce only temporary jobs. But according to some specialists it is not always the case that public works have only short-term benefits. According to Twala and McCutcheon (1999), public works depend on long-term planning that includes technical and management training. These are portable skills that can be taken from one project to another. Although a specific project such as building a bridge will come to an end, there will be continuing needs for roads and bridges in places such as South Africa: "Through the establishment of local associations, poor people are able to plan improvements in their community, negotiate with local authorities for a greater share of investment resources and learn to organize construction and projects" (p. 22).

Egypt has attempted to compensate for the social consequences of its Economic Reform and Structural Adjustment Program by establishing a Social Fund for Development. The fund includes a public-works program aimed at improving basic services and infrastructure in low-income communities. The program creates short-term jobs by providing funding for community-based, labor-intensive construction projects and long-term employment by providing training in the management and operation of infrastructure projects. However, further investigation into the operation of public works and social funds is warranted, since evidence of their ability to reduce poverty and unemployment is mixed (Tendler 1999).

Questions still remain about the ability of poor people to save when there are so many demands on their limited incomes. But the poor have demonstrated that they are just as able to defer gratification in order to send their children to school or provide support in other ways using limited old-age pension money. That same generous spirit and forward-looking perspective can be used to build long-term savings for future generations. Matching grants could come from a variety of sources, including the national department of welfare, local economic development funds, the Business Trust, and other donor funding. The problem in South Africa is that so many development institutions and initiatives are not coordinated with each other in any way—each is doing its own thing. What is needed is a single national authority tasked with fighting poverty as part of a national development strategy. South Africa's social-welfare efforts cannot be sustainable unless they are tied to a national development program—something that is still missing on the political agenda.

6

Democracy and Consolidation in Contemporary Latin America: Current Thinking and Future Challenges[1]

Jonathan Hartlyn

Latin America is currently undergoing profound economic and political transformations. Economically, it is the most unequal region in the world, and its patterns of inequality were exacerbated during the 1980s and only modestly improved in some countries during the 1990s as most countries in the region underwent dramatic market-oriented economic reforms. Politically, the democratic transitions of the recent past have affected the largest number of countries in the region's entire history. Yet, the result to date has disappointed those who expected a rapid transition from democratic transition to democratic consolidation, while confounding others who expected that recurring economic crises and sustained inequalities would inevitably result in a pendular swing back to authoritarian rule. Indeed, as detailed in the first section below, the resulting pattern for Latin America has been one not of sustained movement toward unrestricted political democracies, but of many countries oscillating around mixed kinds of modestly or marginally democratic regimes, with some improving and others deteriorating.

Building on older debates with regard to conceptualizing democracy, confrontation with this empirical reality has led to further debates about how to understand the nature of political democracy in the region and regarding the concept of (and the prospects for) democratic consolidation. Drawing on the work of various authors, in a second section below I identify an expanded conceptualization both of political democracy and of democratic consolidation and indicate that what follows from this is logically a consideration of a multiplicity of components required for consolidation of political democracy, beyond those that might be viewed as tightly linked to procedural elements of democracy at the regime level. The most helpful analyses, in my view, are those that delimit these components to those focused particularly on the state, its relationship to civil society and its impact on relations within it.

This selective review of the literature is employed both to underscore frustrations with a narrowly electoral unidimensional classification of the region's contemporary democracies and highlight the value of moving beyond it, in order for scholars to best grapple analytically with key issues confronting these countries. As I argue in a third section, from this review one can extract elements crucial for the establishment of a comprehensive framework within which to understand the contemporary challenges to democracy in the region. Many of the components identified as central for consolidating liberal democracy evolved in the industrialized democracies in a more gradual, sequential manner. This is now not possible for Latin American countries, even as the consequences of their own particular historical evolution and contemporary challenges must be considered. Thus, as the apparent persistence in many countries of electoral democracies with illiberal tendencies has continued, explanations have tended to shift away from more proximate domestic factors such as the mode of transition. Instead, explanations focus more on the historical legacy of the evolution of structural and institutional factors, particularly related to the state and the rule of law. They also consider the variegated consequences of globalization, particularly those associated with three issues: international rejection of outright reversion to authoritarianism; socioeconomic tensions and associated political effects generated by globalization; and transnational influences expanding global understandings of what democracy is. The concluding section provides a brief summary and explores pessimistic and optimistic scenarios one might plausibly imagine for the region.

Unexpected Patterns

During the past seventy years in Latin America, one can observe two historical cycles with regard to democracy (considered at least in the minimalist sense of electoral democracy): one from the late 1920s to the late 1950s (with a subcycle in the late 1940s) and another from the late 1950s to the late 1980s and continuing to the present. Each began with a predominance of civilian regimes, many of which succumbed to military rule only to return subsequently to rule by civilians, though the number of countries involved was greater in the more recent period. Prior to the 1990s, the most auspicious moment for democracy in the region occurred in the late 1950s and early 1960s. The pendulum swung sharply back in the 1960s in the aftermath of the Cuban Revolution and this time the nature of dictatorship changed in qualitative terms. Between 1962 and 1964 eight military takeovers occurred, and these were followed by many more in the subsequent decade. Military coups in Brazil, Argentina, Peru, Chile, and Uruguay inaugurated bureaucratic authoritarian or other military regimes that sought to rebuild the institutional order, either in direct response to threats from the left or in an attempt to preempt that threat. During the 1970s, depending on the year, there were from twelve to sixteen authoritarian governments in Latin America, most of them intent on modernizing and transforming their societies by excluding not only the old politicians but the citizenry as well.[2]

Then, in the 1980s, in the throes of the worst economic crisis since the 1929 Depression, the most dramatic political reversal took place on the continent since the 1930s. During the period 1988–1991, for the first time in the history of the continent, presidential elections were held in every single country except for Cuba, although some of the electoral processes were problematic.[3] Political democracy, although limited and constrained even in terms of a minimalist conception of this definition in several countries, appeared triumphant on the continent as the last decade of the century began. This shift in the region ran parallel to a broader international trend toward democracy. The number of states that the Freedom House annual survey rated as "free" (an approximation of political democracy), grew from forty-two in 1972 to fifty-two in 1980 to sixty-five in 1990 to eighty-one in 1997 (Diamond 1999:26).[4] At the same time, simplistic renditions of an "end of history" argument suggested that international legitimation of democracy also presaged its consolidation.

However, there are reasons to believe that optimism about this latest "democratic wave" must be tempered, both worldwide and in Latin America. As the number of states rated as "free" grew, so did the total number of countries, such that the percentage of free countries first fell from 41.5 percent in 1991 to 37.9 percent in 1993 before increasing to 42.4 percent in 1997; in turn, the percentage of partly free countries in those years fell from 35.5 percent to 33.2 percent to 29.8 percent, respectively.[5]

In Latin America, Freedom House measures during the period from 1980 to 1999 also provide an indication of a more mixed record that is first one of considerable progress, then of partial retrogression, followed by slight improvement (see Table 6.1).[6] Transitions to democracy in the late 1970s and the 1980s in the region are evident by the increase from three countries rated "free" (with added scores between 2 and 5) in 1977 to six in 1980 to eleven in 1985 and 1988. By 1990, though the number of countries rated "free" declined slightly to ten, the number of countries in the categories just below (scores of 6 or 7) jumped from one to seven; indeed, 1990 also had the lowest (most democratic) mean score (5.9) reported in Table 6.1 during the time period from 1977 to 1999. The average "Polity IV" measures reported in Table 6.1 suggest a similar overall pattern of dramatic improvement followed by a leveling off at a less than fully democratic level, even if with slightly more progress during the 1990s than indicated by the Freedom House scores.

These indicators help us to understand why scholars of the region have been straining to come up with descriptive "adjectives" (see Collier and Levitsky 1997) to highlight the reality of democracies with deficiencies, as the vast majority of these regimes have not moved smoothly to an equilibrium point high on the democracy scale. Although neither the two indices nor country specialists may well concur on the placement of individual countries in a given year, two trends appear clear from this imperfect exercise. One is that there has been considerable movement in year-to-year scores indicating political systems in flux; another is that by the end of the 1990s, there was an oscillating convergence around more mixed kinds of modestly or marginally democratic regimes.

Movement in Freedom House year-to-year scores can be observed in Table 6.1. As the table highlights, the pattern is one of apparent retrogression from 1990 to 1995 (decline in the mean score for the region from 5.9 to 6.8), and then of partial and uneven improvement from 1995 to 1999 (mean score of about 6.3). The only two countries that consistently scored between 2 and 4 during the 1990 to 1999 time period were Costa Rica and Uruguay, and Chile and Panama were the only countries that consistently scored at least a 5 during this time period. Two others, El Salvador and Mexico, showed improvement during this period. In turn, Brazil, Colombia, Peru, and Venezuela experienced some decline. And a larger group of seven countries, according to these indicators, experienced decline and then at least some improvement: Argentina, Bolivia, the Dominican Republic, Ecuador, Guatemala, Honduras, and Nicaragua. Paraguay reflected no change in its status as a semidemocracy, and Cuba and Haiti both remained below the score of 7 during this time period. In other words, during the 1990–1999 period, there was considerable movement in the democratic status of these countries as measured by these indicators.

According to Freedom House, average scores also remained relatively low on the democracy scale. The combined scores for political rights and civil liberties for the four years 1996–1999 have been averaged and countries ranked by them in Table 6.2. Once again, the table illustrates how Costa Rica and Uruguay stand apart from other

Table 6.1 Summary Freedom House and Democracy Scores for Latin America, Selected Years

Scores	1977	1980	1985	1988	1990	1995	1996	1997	1998	1999
Free (2–4)	2	3	5	6	6	3	3	4	3	5
Free (5)	1	3	6	5	4	3	4	5	8	4
Partly Free (6–7)	2	3	1	1	7	7	10	7	6	6
Total	5	9	12	12	17	13	17	16	17	15
Mean FH score (n=20)	9.1	8.1	6.7	6.5	5.9	6.8	6.3	6.3	6.2	6.3
*Mean Pol IV score (n=20)	12.0	10.3	8.1	7.8	6.0	5.8	5.4	5.4	5.4	5.7

Source: Freedom House and Polity IV data sets.
Notes: FH = Freedom House; Pol IV = Polity IV.

Table 6.2 Latin American Countries, Average Scores, 1996–1999

Average score	Countries (lower average scores first; then alphabetical)	
	Freedom House Indicators	Polity IV Democracy Score
Liberal democracy (2–3)	Costa Rica; Uruguay	Costa Rica; Uruguay
Between liberal and electoral democracy (3.01–5)	Bolivia, Chile; Panama	Bolivia; Ecuador, Panama; Nicaragua; Brazil, Dominican Republic; Chile, Venezuela; Guatemala
Electoral democracy (5.01–6)	Argentina, El Salvador; Dominican Republic, Ecuador, Honduras; Nicaragua, Venezuela	Colombia; Argentina, El Salvador; Haiti
Electoral democracy (6.01–7)	Brazil; Guatemala, Mexico, Paraguay	Paraguay; Honduras
Electoral democracy (7.01–8)	Colombia	Mexico
Between electoralist and authoritarian (8.01–9)	Peru	
Authoritarian (>9.01)	Haiti; Cuba	Peru; Cuba

Source: Freedom House and Polity IV data sets.
Notes: Cutoff points based on Freedom House combined political rights and civil liberties indicators (ranging from a combined high, more democratic, score of 2, to a low of 14). Polity IV scores, which range from a high, more democratic, score of 10, to a low of 0, were standardized to Freedom House range and reversed in sign.

countries in the region—as liberal democracies (to be defined below). Three others, Bolivia, Chile, and Panama, have average scores that might place them as between liberal and electoral democracy. The bulk of Latin American countries are clustered in the next two categories, on the boundary between the "free" and "partly free" categories: eleven of the region's twenty countries have average scores between 5 and 7. Below these are found Colombia, and, even lower, Peru. Even during this four-year period, fourteen countries had some change in scores, three quite sharp. As Table 6.2 indicates, employing the Polity Democracy scores, countries in the region tended to have somewhat higher overall average scores, though Costa Rica and Uruguay continued to stand apart. And, within the Polity data set, fourteen of these countries had some change in scores during this time period, three of them quite substantially so.

This overall pattern both of transition away from authoritarian rule combined with partial and uneven movement toward unrestricted democracy, although not without historical precedent for many of the countries in the region, has demanded scholarly attention because of its unprecedented regional scope, sustained nature, and (for some) distance from initial more hopeful expectations. In a search for understanding, scholarly attention has increasingly focused on the contrast between the broader historical context and evolution of Latin American and current Western European democracies in a context of expanded understandings of democracy and expectations about what it should deliver. One result has been a renewed debate around key concepts.

Re-Elaborated Concepts and Multiple Components

Contemporary trends of democracy in Latin America have led to renewed debates both about how to conceptualize political democracy and about the meaning and utility of the concept of democratic consolidation. They have helped force a rejection of an evolutionary view from transition to consolidation and have also highlighted inextricable ties between the two concepts. A once standard view in the comparative literature, which has increasingly been called into question, is that to determine if democratic consolidation has occurred in a particular country, "it is necessary first to ascertain whether the country's new political regime is fully democratic, and then to determine whether that democracy is consolidated" (Gunther, Diamandouros, and Puhle 1996:152). In contexts of clear and sharply delineated transitions from unmistakably authoritarian to "fully" democratic regimes, this may be a reasonable strategy.[7] For, implicit in this notion, as Felipe Agüero has noted, is that democracy was attained first, at which time a process of consolidation would begin, and that therefore "the democratic nature of post-transition regimes ceased to be problematic" (Agüero 1998:9).

However, as the previous section has demonstrated, Latin America in the 1990s is better characterized by the unexpected reality of what one might term the unconsolidated persistence through time of regimes and states that are variably but rarely strongly democratic. In at least one case, Chile, there appears to be a regime that *is* consolidated, but with constraints regarding its democratic nature. As countries in the region have not clearly evolved from a transition to (unproblematic) democracy to a consolidation of this democracy, scholarly attention has shifted to ask about the connections between the kind of democracy a country maintains, the likelihood of its persistence, and whether it can be "deepened." This has led to inextricable links across the conceptual debates around political democracy, consolidation of democracy, and the "deepening" or improving of democracy.

Let us look first briefly at debates surrounding the appropriate conceptualization of political democracy. Among some scholars there has been a gradual trend toward accepting a more expansive—if still largely procedural—conceptualization of political democracy. In their acute analysis, Collier and Levitsky (1997) clarify the critique of electoralist conceptions as well as an emerging consensus around an "expanded procedural minimum" definition of political democracy (which builds on Dahl's influential formulation in *Polyarchy* [1971]). Drawing from literature on Latin American cases, they also highlight the extent to which analysts have generated "diminished subtypes" from these conceptions.

Thus, for a substantial group of scholars, there has been a continued acceptance of the value of a conceptualization of political democracy focused on procedural issues rather than substantive outcomes and which does not conflate democracy with social and economic dimensions. At the same time, there have been fruitful debates regarding how to expand beyond the limits of narrow types of procedural conceptualizations.[8] These debates have led scholars to pay much more attention to a broader set of institutions and factors than those simply associated with free elections. These include a coherent state, effective and democratic accountability and rule of law, and civilian control over the military, sometimes as part of their conceptualization of political democracy and other times in their analysis of democratic consolidation. For example, Larry Diamond draws a distinction between electoral democracy, intermediate conceptions, and liberal democracy, which extends beyond both of the former.[9] Liberal democracy requires, first, the absence of reserved domains of power for the military or other actors not accountable to the electorate, directly or indirectly. Second, in addition to the vertical accountability of rulers to the ruled (secured mainly through elections), it requires the horizontal accountability of officeholders to one another; this constrains executive power and so helps protect constitutionalism, legality, and the deliberative process.[10] Third, it encompasses extensive provisions for political and civic pluralism as well as for individual and group freedoms—of belief, opinion, discussion, speech, publication, assembly, demonstration, and petition—so that contending interests and values may be expressed and compete through ongoing processes of articulation and representation, beyond periodic elections. Freedom and pluralism, in turn, can be secured only when legal rules are applied fairly, consistently, and predictably across equivalent cases, irrespective of the class, status, or power of those subject to the rules. Under a true rule of law, all citizens have political and legal equality, and the state and its agents are themselves subject to the law (for more on the relationships between democracy and the rule of law, see O'Donnell [1999]). Thus, liberal democracy understood in this way extends beyond the political regime to consider elements of the state as well. This makes explicit what was present by assumption in several earlier procedural conceptualizations of democracy based on the European experiences with democracy.

Similarly, there have been debates surrounding the concept of democratic consolidation. Based on a fourfold regime classification similar to Diamond's (authoritarianism, electoral democracy, liberal democracy, and advanced democracy that has achieved certain socioeconomic objectives), Schedler (1998) has pointed out that "democratic consolidation" may be considered as deterring a negative outcome (preventing democratic breakdown to authoritarianism or preventing democratic erosion from liberal to electoral democracy), as a process that enables a more positive outcome (completing democracy by moving from electoral to liberal democracy or deepening democracy from electoral or liberal democracy to advanced democracy), or in terms of organizing liberal democracy's "partial regimes." Yet another reaction has been to eschew the term for various reasons, replacing it as the main "dependent variable" with one or more alternative terms in ways that sometimes replicate discussions around consolidation while avoiding potential teleological implications of the term. In the end, even though scholarly consensus on the meaning or usefulness of "democratic consolidation" is unlikely, I believe one can identify a partial conceptual convergence around what I term (borrowing from Collier and Levitsky [1997]) an expanded academic conception of the term (or others similar to it) that is useful in analyzing contemporary trends of democratization in Latin America.

Those who rely on more minimalist procedural conceptions of democracy (typically electoral democracy or some variant) and compare countries in the region to their past, especially their most immediate past, tend to end up with more positive overall evaluations. They emphasize particularly that these democracies have persisted and have survived, more of them for a longer period of time, than in any previous period of Latin America's history, "in the face of daunting challenges and what initially seemed to be long odds" (Mainwaring 1999b:102; cf. Agüero 1998:4–8). For most countries in the region, a principal contemporary challenge to democracy has been economic. Yet, contrary to past experience, with the exceptions of Haiti, Peru, and Ecuador, severe economic crisis during the 1980s and 1990s has not been associated with breakdown, even as many countries have been able to enact far-reaching market-oriented reforms.[11] Furthermore, in this most recent "wave" of democratization, several Latin American countries—including Paraguay and many in Central America—have experienced either their first or their most sustained experience with democracy, even if limited. Indeed, for nearly all the countries in the region, their longest uninterrupted period of democracy is the one that began for them in the late 1970s or the 1980s (the exceptions are Chile and Uruguay). Yet, typically even scholars who provide these more positive assessments recognize the limitations and shortcomings of democracy in the region; one way they do so is by shifting their object of study from political democracy or democratic consolidation to elected regimes and their endurance or survival (e.g., Mainwaring 1999b:102, 106).[12]

Not surprisingly, those scholars who do focus on democracy incorporating such elements as respect for democratic procedures and basic human rights and civilian control over the armed forces and compare the regimes in Latin America to more established democracies in other regions, have a less sanguine prognosis. For example, Huber, Rueschemeyer, and Stephens (1997) present a three-part classification of democracy as formal, participatory, and social, in which the latter types presume by definition all elements of the former one(s) plus first additional elements related to full participation across all social groups and then to greater socioeconomic equality in outcomes. They present three key causal factors related to the balance of class power, the state and state-society relations, and transnational structures of power, and conclude that Latin America in the recent period overall has made only modest advances in formal democracy while facing "mounting obstacles" in terms of participatory, much less social, democracy (p. 337).[13] And, building on the concept of "liberal democracy" mentioned earlier in this chapter, Diamond discusses the "[h]ollow, illiberal, poorly institutionalized democracy" of Latin America and other third-wave democracies (1999: 31–49, quote on 49).

An alternative approach is developed in some of O'Donnell's articles. In these, he begins by accepting a more limited conceptualization of political democracy as polyarchy. However, he then establishes a new distinction between countries that satisfy these minimal criteria yet do not possess other characteristics linked to state institutions and accountability issues associated with what he terms representative democracies (1994) or formally institutionalized polyarchies (1996a), concepts that closely approximate liberal democracies as discussed above. Countries that satisfy only the minimal criteria may nevertheless endure as democracies, though of a diminished type: in O'Donnell's nomenclature, as delegative democracies or as informally institutionalized polyarchies, in which deficiencies at the conceptual level of the state set them apart from other types of democracies.

There is of course no necessary link between different conceptions of political democracy and use (or acceptance) of the term democratic consolidation. Yet, typically, scholars who conceive of democracy in minimalist terms as electoral democracies are more likely to dismiss consolidation as an unimportant or meaningless concept (e.g., Przeworski et al. 2000:101–103), or to consider consolidation as simple persistence through time. For example, Gasiorowski and Power (1998) argue that consolidation, rather than implying simply the survival or the persistence of a democratic regime, implies "that qualitative changes have occurred in the country's political institutions and practices that make breakdown unlikely—though not impossible—in the future" (1998:5, web version). However, in order to generate sufficient comparable data across countries, when it came time to operationalize the concept for their quantitative analysis they ultimately relied on regime indicators that did not really reflect whether qualitative changes exist or not: surviving a second election, or surviving an electoral alternation in power, or simply democratic persistence for twelve years or more. As a consequence, a relatively larger number of Latin American country cases were deemed to be consolidated than would be by area scholars or based on other types of indicators. For example, based on their second criterion, Latin American countries that were considered consolidated in the 1990s included Argentina, Bolivia, Brazil, Colombia, Costa Rica, the Dominican Republic, Peru (until 1992), Uruguay, and Venezuela.

In turn, those whose conception of democracy is closer to liberal democracy tend to have a more stringent (or expanded) view of what is required for consolidation or formal institutionalization. Yet, developing clear benchmarks to determine the existence of qualitative changes in institutions and practices has turned out to be difficult; similarly, in part due to perceived strong feedback mechanisms, scholars have not always clearly disentangled benchmarks or defining elements from causal factors from consequences of consolidation. Linz and Stepan, for example, define a consolidated democracy as "a political situation in which, in a phrase, democracy has become 'the only game in town'" (1996:5), and provide behavioral, attitudinal, and (partially overlapping) constitutional benchmarks for this phrase. However, they then go beyond their initial benchmarks to present "five interacting arenas" that they argue must be present for consolidated democracy to exist, placing them even more distant from a minimalist conception of either democracy or consolidation.[14] In this way, while they begin with a fairly standard procedural definition of political democracy, the shift in analytical attention to what is required for consolidation to exist vastly expands the factors considered necessary for the realization of a "consolidated democracy." They note that "no modern polity can become democratically consolidated unless it is first a state," and then focus on five crucial arenas necessary for democratic consolidation. They argue that three of them, "a lively and independent civil society, a political society with sufficient autonomy and a working consensus about procedures of governance, and constitutionalism and a rule of law . . . *are virtually definitional prerequisites of a consolidated democracy,*" while underscoring the importance as well of the other two, a functioning state apparatus and an institutionalized market economy (quotes from Linz and Stepan 1996:7, 10, emphasis added; see also their definitions of democratic transition and consolidation on pp. 3–7).

In their work, Linz and Stepan consider only four country cases in South America. They argue that of these only Uruguay may be considered a consolidated (if risk-prone) democracy; Brazil was the furthest from being consolidated, and Argentina could not yet be considered consolidated. Chile was the most interesting case, because in their analytical scheme it had not yet had a successful democratic transition even though it appeared to be consolidating: thus, when the antidemocratic elements of the Chilean constitution were removed, Chile could likely have simultaneously a successful transition and consolidation of democracy (1996:150, 215).[15] This view has the merit of logical consistency within their definitional scheme and of reflecting the complex ambiguous empirical reality of the constraints on Chilean political democracy, but it also means that consolidation in this case must wait for the democratic transition to conclude rather than follow as a consequence of it.

Diamond, in turn, argues that since the principal *consequence* of consolidation is the stability and persistence of (liberal) democracy, there is a need to establish a conceptual foundation (the defining element) separate from this to avoid tautology: this foundation rests on broad and deep legitimation of democracy across all significant political actors at both the elite and mass levels that can "only be fully understood as encompassing a shift in *political culture*" (1999:65). He then provides indicators of what this means for norms and behaviors at the level of elites, organizations, and masses. On the basis of these factors, with regard to the Latin American cases, by and large he also concludes that only Costa Rica and Uruguay may be considered as consolidated.[16]

In order to avoid charges of teleology or to sidestep other conceptual problems perceived with the term consolidation, a growing number of scholars are avoiding it for other concepts. Some authors, to permit positive analysis of a larger set of countries, shift their focus of analysis from consolidation to more minimalist criteria such as electoral regimes or democratic survival (Mainwaring 1999a, 1999b), or formal or partial democracy (Panizza and Barahona de Brito 1998). In doing so, they have either avoided discussion of consolidation or acknowledged that the vast majority of the countries in the region are not consolidated. One exception here is Przeworski et al. (1996:50), who argue that consolidation (understood as greater likelihood of survival the longer a democracy has persisted in time) is an "empty term" because level of development remains a better explanation for survival than age of regime. Yet, this critique does not speak directly to the arguments presented above that consolidation refers to more than simply persistence through time. Nor does their dichotomous view of democracy enable scholars to address as effectively the contemporary situation in the region, in which the "empirical gap" between democratic and civilian nondemocratic regimes in some countries in the 1990s (e.g., the Dominican Republic, Mexico, or Peru) may not have been as great as when the military ruled in open authoritarian fashion, or in which more generally the existence of electoral democracy in most Latin American countries nevertheless hides significant differences of interest to scholars.

Others have focused on particular democratic deficits—that is, more to issues of the quality of democracy—analyzing the absence of "democratic authenticity" (Conaghan 1996), or "disjunctive democracy" and the need to extend democracy to the social sphere (Holston and Caldeir, 1998), or the need for "democratic deepening" (von

Mettenheim and Malloy 1998), or "democratic citizenship" (Alvarez, Dagnino, and Escobar 1998). A growing number of these and other scholars have explicitly criticized the concept of consolidation. The issues raised include the term's ambiguity, excessive globalism, difficult empirical application, tendency to short-change considerations of democracy for those of stability, teleological nature, and incomplete view of political democracy and of democracy more broadly. Lowenthal and Domínguez argue that it is both premature and misleading to focus on "consolidating" democratic governance because it is "still incipient, inchoate, fragile, highly uneven, incomplete, and often contradicted" (1996:6–7).

Another type of criticism comes from O'Donnell, who has argued that a large number of countries in contemporary Latin America have what might be termed informally institutionalized polyarchies, some of which have lasted for many years. Analyzing them in negative terms for "what they lack" to become "formally institutionalized" or "consolidated" (i.e., more like European democracies) should be replaced by analysis that still condemns them normatively but is "nonteleological, . . . nonethnocentric, [and] positive" (1996a:46–47). Yet, the distinction he draws between informally and formally institutionalized democracies is quite similar to the one between electoral or illiberal (e.g., Zakaria 1997) and liberal or participatory democracies. And, seeking "improvement" of the former, that is, closer approximation to the latter, comes close to framing the issue in terms similar to those of scholars cited above (Huber, Rueschemeyer, and Stephens 1997; Diamond 1999).

Other authors have made similar criticisms. Agüero (1998:8) and Agüero and Stark (1998:273) argue that the concept of consolidation as employed has often applied an inadequate, incomplete notion of political democracy, overlooking more substantive aspects of expanded procedural definitions. In an effort to determine the stability and endurance of particular regimes, scholars employing the consolidation concept have sometimes skirted the question of how "incomplete, contradictory and disjointed" these regimes are (Agüero and Stark 1998:373). They argue that the most important problems facing the countries in the region today have less to do with regime stability and more to do with the "depth, quality, and consistency" of democracy (Agüero 1998:10–11). Thus, they also reject a dichotomous view of democracy, preferring to see it less as a point of arrival and more as an ongoing, nonlinear process of institutional and symbolic construction (Agüero and Stark 1998:373).

Ultimately, for Schedler (1998:101), there are so many conceptions of consolidation that it is "an omnibus concept, a garbage-can concept, a catch-all concept, lacking a core meaning." And, depending upon how the term is employed, the categorization of cases will of course be widely disparate (cf. examples drawn above from Gasiorowski and Powe [1998] and Diamond [1999]). I concur with Schedler that it is still useful to preserve the term, and I am sympathetic to the solution he proposes, employing the term to mean "securing achieved levels of democratic rule against authoritarian regression," describing a regime that is expected by relevant observers to last well into the future. However, at least in this article (Schedler 1998), this argument remains underdeveloped, especially with regard to the conception of democracy to be employed, and to what relationships across which factors are defining elements or indicators, or instead are causal factors or consequences of consolidation.

One analytical consequence that flows logically from the empirical reality that confronts us in Latin America (as well as in other areas of the world), as well as from these re-elaborated, expanded concepts of liberal democratic consolidation or of formally institutionalized democracy, is a concomitant focus on an increased number of components viewed as necessary in order to approximate these types of political democracies. These have expanded considerably beyond those that might be viewed as tightly linked to procedural elements of democracy at the regime level. Although, as before, there are some significant differences in language and in emphasis across various analyses, there is one key commonality I seek to draw out and to build on. All of them expand, though not always in carefully delimited ways, the set of components we must consider in understanding the weakness of contemporary Latin American democracies and the possible solutions.

For example, Linz and Stepan (1996:62–64) list five broad necessary conditions or minimal components for the completion of the transition to and the consolidation of a democratic regime: (1) the rule of law and freedom for civil society; (2) the autonomy of political society and the trust and legal conditions required for it; (3) the presence of constitutional rules to allocate power democratically; (4) a state bureaucracy (including a judiciary and a military) acceptable and serviceable to democratic government; and (5) sufficient autonomy for the economy and economic actors to assure the pluralism of civil society, political society, and economic society. Diamond (1999: 74–77), in turn, lists three generic and equally expansive components that must be established by all new democracies if they are to consolidate. One he terms (unfortunately, as many other authors mean something different by this) "democratic deepening"—making the formal structures of democracy more liberal, accountable, representative, and accessible. A second is "political institutionalization," especially relating to the construction of political parties and a party system that combine and balance institutional strength and stability with adaptability, strong legislatures, an effective judiciary, and civilian democratic control over the military. A third is "regime performance," understood broadly to mean issues such as material progress, security, freedom, and order (some of which, of course, may be in tension with each other).

It may be more useful for analytical purposes to circumscribe these components to key aspects associated with rule-of-law democracy, permitting one then to consider the role of other factors in helping to realize them. This may be found, for example, in the expanded research agenda for which Agüero and Stark call. They argue that their agenda would rethink the "decoupling" of procedural and substantive versions of democracy, and would be more interdisciplinary, yet would also seek to develop clearer hypotheses in the shift toward research on the more qualitative dimensions of democracy. This, they argue, would bring benefits that would "far outweigh any loss of parsimony in our research agendas" (1998:374). Their edited volume highlights in particular three key areas for future research: the representation of societal interests and citizen participation, affecting mechanisms of accountability; the rule of law and its links to transformations of the judiciary; and issues related to organized force and violence, particularly in terms of the military and civil-military relations (p. 11).

Although criticizing what he terms the illusion of consolidation, and insisting on the polyarchic (minimally democratic) nature of most current Latin American regimes, O'Donnell has also focused on a wide set of components necessary in order to attain more formally institutionalized polyarchies. He has argued for a desirable combination of democracy, liberalism, and republicanism, as "[d]emocracy without liberalism and republicanism would become majority tyranny" (1998:115). In turn, when state agents are involved directly or indirectly in human-rights violations or violations of basic rights of due process, what he terms the liberal dimension of democracy suffers. And, when public officials do not subject themselves to the law or pursue their private interests over their public duty, the republican dimension suffers (p. 118). Most insistently, he has asserted the key problem is the "severe incompleteness of the state, especially of its legal dimension." And, this has in fact increased following recent democratic transitions, under the weight of socioeconomic crises, antistatist policies, and the construction of national-level political coalitions with politicians from "privatized" areas, highlighting vast regional disparities in the extension of basic democratic rights (O'Donnell 1999:314–315). In addition, although explicitly rejecting an identification of democracy with high levels of socioeconomic equality or welfare, he argues that there appears to be a strong link from sharply unequal social structures to the weakness of political and civil rights in the region (p. 322).

This review has raised more issues than can be resolved here. However, I do believe it has underscored some important partial convergences across a number of authors adopting what might be termed an expanded academic conception of democracy and its consolidation (or alternative term), upon which future work analyzing contemporary Latin American politics can build. There is also an overlapping categorization of country cases: for example, in spite of scholars' different terminology, countries in the region such as Costa Rica and Uruguay stand apart from the others in most of these analyses. These convergences are more consequential than whether scholarly consensus regarding the term consolidation or its meaning is fully achieved, as long as scholars are both clear in their conceptualization and consistent in its usage.

In my view, research now needs to focus more carefully on why so many countries in Latin America are currently persisting or surviving as "electoral democracies or regimes," "unconsolidated democracies," or "informally institutionalized polyarchies," rather than unmistakably advancing toward "consolidation" or "formally institutionalized polyarchies." Similarly, research should focus on the extent to which and the mechanisms through which even this limited democratic progress is at risk if these countries do not begin to assume more of the characteristics of liberal or rule-of-law democracies.

In carrying out this research, the most useful conceptions of democracy are ones that accept the importance of procedural elements narrowly associated with electoral issues, but that expand on them to incorporate those associated with what we can term liberal or rule-of-law dimensions of democracy, in areas *within the state* such as "horizontal accountability"; *between* the state and society, such as equal application of the rule of law; and, regarding the state's ability to extend its legal authority to transactions *within society*.

More work is required in specifying and in providing appropriate measures and indicators of the differences between and the possibilities of a shift from electoral (or informally institutionalized) democracy to consolidated liberal (or formally institutionalized) democracy. We are only part of the way toward specifying clearly the attitudinal, behavioral, and institutional elements that comprise a qualitative change in political patterns relating to a shift toward a greater role for formal institutions and an acceptance of the democratic and legal "rules of the game" that is not instrumental, much less toward determining how countries have evolved and might evolve in that direction.

In part because "democratic consolidation" is often used "loosely" in the political and policy world, I believe there is a utility to careful academic work based on what I have termed the expanded academic conception of the term. At the same time, it is almost certainly true that at this level the concept remains quite abstract and multidimensional. Therefore, much important empirical research should be carried out in a more disaggregated fashion with more clearly specified referents to aspects of the state and the rule of law, political institutions and political parties, and civil-military relations. At the same time, the risk remains that this type of work will generate partial parallel explanations focused on a discrete set of factors, in literatures that do not fully engage with each other.

Democratic Governance in Latin America: Toward a More Comprehensive Framework

The new realities of the region and new understandings both about the emergence and evolution of political democracy itself and about the region's historical evolution and current circumstances have generated valuable analytical efforts to understand these changes in a comprehensive fashion. Yet, should one focus more on the unmistakable advance of political democracy in the region compared to its past, or on the partial retrogressions experienced by several countries recently?

Not surprisingly, different emphases have led to different causal orderings. Focusing on the survival of electoral regimes in the region, Mainwaring (1999a, 1999b) concludes that structural transformations of modernization over the past several decades,[17] ideological depolarization, the revalorization of political democracy in the region following the bitter experience of authoritarian rule, the decline in the attractiveness of the Cuban model, the end of the Cold War, and international (especially U.S.) and growing regional support for democracy are all important. Those, in turn, who focus more on the declines in democracy in the region or the lack of progress address such factors as the nature and impact of sustained socioeconomic crisis and market-oriented reforms, the ways these have encouraged unequal distributions of power within society, the region's continued high levels of inequality (among the highest in the world), the inadequacy of political representation, and how already weak liberal elements of a democratic rule of law have deteriorated further, with dramatic consequences for public order, civility, and security (among others, many of the articles in Oxhorn and Star [1999] and in Méndez, O'Donnell, and Pinheiro [1999]).

In my view, an explanation of the region's overall patterns should ideally address both the advances as well as the retrogressions. In Latin America today, one needs to explain why so many seemingly diverse countries—in terms of such features as their historical trajectories with democracy, nature of political institutions and party systems, and socioeconomic structures—appear to have converged around similar types of weak democracies, why there has been some deterioration (in some cases with subsequent partial improvement) in terms of democracy in others, and what explains the few exceptions.

All I can do here is to present a framework within which these seemingly puzzling outcomes can be studied. In understanding successful transitions to electoral democracies and the near absence of consolidated rule-of-law democracies in Latin America over the recent past, explanations must build on an analysis of the region's different historical evolution and sequence of critical events, understanding the mode of transition primarily as features inherited from the previous authoritarian regime (cf. Hartlyn 1998b). And, in understanding both the persistence of electoral democracies, and the current nature of their challenges, one must consider the variegated consequences of globalization, of which I will highlight: the impact of dramatic international (1) political changes, (2) changes in socioeconomic models and demands, and (3) understandings of democracy on state structures, societal evolution, and political attitudes.

Much more work needs to be done to understand the complex set of historical factors that evolved and combined to make liberal or rule-of-law democracy (as opposed to simply electoral democracy) possible in the industrialized democracies. These appear related to such factors as the type and extent of social inequality and the nature of their capitalist development and consolidation of their national states, processes that evolved very differently in most Latin American countries. To the extent that arguments about political democracy purely at the level of regime type—based on the successful experience of countries in Western Europe or the United States—presuppose or ignore these elements relating to the state and the democratic rule of law, then, as many of the scholars above have noted and begun to do, these assumptions need to be clarified, made explicit, and the very different patterns and sequences observed in Latin America need to be "brought back in" to the analysis.

One example can be drawn from a classical argument about historical sequences favorable to political democracy. Robert Dahl argued that the most favorable path to polyarchy was one in which political competition preceded the expansion of participation. The result was that "the rules, the practices, and the culture of competitive politics developed first among a small elite, and the critical transition from nonparty politics to party competition also occurred initially within the restricted group" (1971:33–36). Yet, this argument alone is too narrowly focused. Prior to this must be the establishment of a national state, and prior to and alongside it must be the practice of constitutional liberalism and the rule of law, respect for basic civil rights, and not just the political right to vote in free elections. Although several countries in the region approximated Dahl's favorable sequence or key aspects of it (such as Chile, Costa Rica, and Uruguay), many did not. Furthermore, there are parallels in other countries in the region (e.g., Colombia in the context of a much weaker state) to Bolívar Lamounier's admonition that in Brazil this seemingly beneficial pattern was somewhat overshadowed by a state structure that was excessively strong vis-à-vis civil society, fostering clientelist rather than citizen ties while also perhaps yielding an excess of elite conciliation (Diamond, Hartlyn, and Linz 1999; Lamounier 1999).

A related observation may be made about the weakness of mechanisms of public accountability in the region. Practically since independence for many countries in the region, there was an early choice for an institutional design derived from constitutional thinking, with features such as representative institutions and a division of powers, rule of law, and political freedoms. Indeed, no other institutional arrangement has been able to gain full legitimacy in the region. Yet, the other reality is that in many countries these liberal democratic constitutions were often distorted, perverted, and manipulated, as constitutional hypocrisy and discretional power often comfortably coexisted. Thus, the issue today is not necessarily to create new institutions, but the equally difficult challenge of overcoming historical patterns of abuse and manipulation to infuse these formal political institutions with meaning, substance, and predictability (Diamond, Hartlyn, and Linz 1999:23–25). Although there may be many historical roads to electoral democracy, it is not totally clear what implications each may have with regard to consolidating rule of law democracy.

Another set of factors crucial in explaining current patterns of political democratization in the region relates to the contemporary impacts of globalization, and their domestic correlates. Of the many effects of globalization, I want to highlight three that I believe are especially important in terms of understanding current political trends in the region and the associated scholarly attention on the challenges of and factors conducive to the consolidation of rule-of-law democracy.

One is that international forces and governments have all supported rejection of any return to outright authoritarianism, encouraging at least minimally electoral democracies. They have done so both in the absence of perceived security threats and in the absence of the legitimacy of any other model alternative to democracy in the region. The United States has played an important role in sustaining a political-ideological floor for democracy, understood in an electoral sense. Similarly, at times neighboring countries and regional organizations, such as the Organization of American States and Mercosur, have also. They have played this role in some countries in circumstances of socioeconomic or political crisis that in other time periods might well have led to successful military coups. Thus, this international pressure is widely recognized as a crucial factor in explaining the persistence of current regimes in several countries in the region. Some quick examples would include the fact that attempted coups or an *auto-golpe* were beaten back in Paraguay and in Guatemala, and that saber rattling in Peru during the Alan García administration (1985–1990) or in Colombia under President Ernesto Samper (1994–1998) were met with a clear message of opposition from Washington. U.S. pressure was important in moving the Dominican Republic toward free and fair elections in 1996, after the highly questionable results of 1994. And, U.S. and other international pressure played an important role in delegitimizing the increasingly more fraudulent electoral process in Peru in 2000 through which President Alberto Fujimori sought his reelection. Similarly, these international forces played an important role in Fujimori's ultimate resignation from office and the scheduling of new democratic elections in April 2001.

Yet, even this floor is wobbly and insecure. During 1999, the Haitian president ruled by decree as the term of congressional representatives had expired and the country had extreme difficulty in setting the date for new elections. And, when these elections were finally realized in 2000, their fairness was sharply questioned. In Ecuador, international pressure was insufficient to prevent a coup that ousted President Jamil Mahuad in January 2000, though it did force the short-lived military-civilian junta to cede power to the vice-president. Unlike the traditional image of the conservative coup, the military overthrow in Ecuador was driven by mass mobilization, especially by indigenous groups, and the military plotters were populists who identified with the rejection of the government's controversial economic austerity and reform program.

This points to the fact that, at another level, international economic currents have played a different role, with profound consequences on the state, society, and political institutions of Latin American countries, helping us to understand some of the reasons for their "low quality."[18] The international system and associated societal changes and balances of power induced within countries are imposing severe structural constraints on the kinds of economic models that Latin American states can follow, and thus on the kinds of economic goals that can be successfully pursued through political participation. Even as the quality of state institutions in many Latin American countries has suffered, so have patterns of inequality both prior to and after the initiation of stabilization and initial reform efforts; for many countries, the same can be said for poverty levels, though these have improved somewhat in several of them over the last few years. To the extent international investment and other capital flows continue to be disproportionately distributed throughout the region, a "diverging" impact upon the countries of the area may more clearly be felt over the years ahead even as international aid flows may help some countries to rebuild more than others. It is also clear that new patterns of production are generating more diversified linkages to the global economy that cut across national boundaries and constrain what national economic policymakers can hope to act upon even as economic integration schemes open up additional sets of opportunities and constraints beyond the scope of this chapter.

In perhaps exaggerated fashion, Lechner has argued that market-oriented (neoliberal) policies have put an end to the "primacy of politics," to the ability of political processes to regulate and conduct policies of modernization. The painful paradox, however, is that this does not mean that countries can do without politics: strategies to dismantle the state are successful only where they are carried along through sustained political intervention (Lechner 1997:13, 19). The dramatic separation of "politics" (*lo político*) from "policy" (*la política*) (Garretón 1999) induced by these changes has led to dramatic challenges for states and to political institutions such as political parties, as the economic effects of globalization have helped generate new patterns of social inequality in the region. Empirically, but in an uneven process throughout the continent, the state and the sphere of politics no longer have the same kind of importance as they once did as dominant forger of identity and organizer of conflicts or as an arena or locus of conflict and decisions, even as the impact of the kinds of parties, campaigns, constitutional designs, and electoral rules that a country possesses continue to be important but in different ways than before (Garretón 1993:7–12).

A central question, as I have argued previously, is whether the state in Latin America, from having been overcommitted during the earlier era, will emerge underengaged with society or reconstituted and able to provide effective responses to societal problems and demands (Hartlyn 1998a). For example, crime rates have increased dramatically in the region. Latin America had the highest median homicide rates in the world since the 1970s, yet these increased dramatically in the 1990s, such that Latin America as a region has four times the rate of other major world regions except Africa.[19] Nowhere is the decline in state coherence and capacity clearer than in Colombia, where drug trafficking provides significant revenues to both guerrilla forces who control areas of the country where coca is cultivated and to paramilitary groups associated with drug traffickers and linked to elements of the state security forces. Indeed, large parts of the country's territory are effectively outside of state control, levels of political violence and human rights abuses remain notoriously high, and over a million people may be internally displaced refugees from the violence. Given the weak institutional capacities of the judiciary and the police, this is taking place in a context of almost complete impunity for any crime, combined in 1999 with the country's worst economic recession since the 1930s (Hartlyn and Dugas 1999). There is a reasonable fear that the proposed infusion of large-scale U.S. military assistance, rather than enhancing state coherence, inducing the guerrillas to negotiate, and reducing the supply of drugs from the country, would instead provide additional resources for violence to further escalate (Human Rights Watch 2000).

Although the severity of Colombia's problems set it somewhat apart, the other Latin American countries also are experiencing acutely the inevitable tension between governability—which seeks to maximize consensus and efficient decisionmaking—and democracy—whose exercise involves the expression of multiple interests and conflict. One of the key ways democratic regimes have moderated this tension—indeed we could say a requirement for consolidated democracy—is to have strong political institutions and parties in a coherent party system. In the dilemma between governability and democracy, these are intended to serve as channelers of demands and forgers of compromise. In previous decades, one risk that occurred in several countries was that political institutions became instruments of polarization in society (perhaps the most dramatic example was Chile in the early 1970s). However, the greater risk in the region today is that political institutions, under the weight of globalization and their perceived incapacity to address domestic demands, will be circumvented by plebiscitarian leaders or avoided by alienated voters, in either case potentially becoming irrelevant at great cost to democracy.

In several countries, institutions and parties have experienced widespread repudiation as politicians have been perceived as corrupt and inept, and blamed for their inability to solve their country's major problems. Fujimori's success in carrying out his 1992 *auto-golpe* in Peru—indeed, his ability to sustain himself in power until 2000, in the process overseeing the destruction of the country's previous political parties and further weakening the country's democratic state institutions—provides one example (McClintock 1999). There is also the dramatic presidential victory of Hugo Chávez in Venezuela in December 1998, decisively trouncing the country's two established political parties. At one level, Chávez's victory reflects a greater democratization of Venezuelan society, as well as a popular response to the country's dramatic socioeconomic problems. Yet, there are good reasons to fear that the outcome will be less one in which Venezuelan democracy will be further democratized and more one in which the possibility for a more institutionalized and accountable democracy is reduced (see Levine and Crisp 1999).

In other countries, the impact on political institutions has not been as severe, pointing to the fact that the consequences of the economic forces associated with globalization on democracy are complex. In the short term, they have tended to weaken state capacity and key organized groups in civil society. Yet, as Lamounier (1999:180) has argued for Brazil, and has also been true in some other countries in the region, because the worldwide economic agenda has narrowed the country's perceived room for choice, ideological antagonisms that used to be rampant around highly controversial issues such as trade and financial opening, inflation, and privatization have lessened. This has meant that recent elections in countries such as Argentina and Chile are not polarized around fundamental questions regarding the socioeconomic model that should be pursued. And, to the extent that globalization and regional integration provide international pressure for more accountable and transparent public institutions, they may help strengthen the efforts of domestic forces seeking to enhance a democratic rule of law. However, as these pressures have tended to focus more on issues of property rights and contract enforcement than on other areas central to democratic advancement, their impact may be limited.

Finally, there is also a third consequence of globalization that helps us to understand the need for scholarly focus on liberal or rule-of-law democracy. Paradoxically, even as globalization has weakened many social actors and helped to induce new forms of social inequality, it has also helped provoke or strengthen expanded views regarding the kinds of rights to be expected and demanded under democracy—what Garretón (1999) terms the "normative expansion" of citizenship in the region—with regard to issues such as gender, ethnicity, the environment, and local power. Understandings of democracy today are deeper and more extended, though also more fragmented.

The effects are evident in the multiplicity of social movements and demands, or in the many constitutional and legal reforms extending special rights to indigenous groups, or providing for quotas for women candidates to public office in numerous countries throughout the region. Eight constitutions in Latin America now contain language recognizing "the multiethnic, pluricultural, and/or multilingual nature of their societies" (Van Cott 2000:265). By 1998, women held an average 15 percent of legislative seats in Latin America, up from 4 percent in 1970, and nearly all Latin American countries had established women's agencies in recent decades (Diamond, Hartlyn, and Linz 1999:32). Effects are also evident in the enactment of political and fiscal decentralization in such countries as Brazil, Chile, Colombia, and Venezuela, though with quite mixed results as the devolution of power to the regions has not automatically enhanced participation or responsiveness.[20] The effects of globalization enhancing perceptions of citizenship are to be celebrated and encouraged as a real opportunity to deepen democracy, even as they also represent a profound challenge for the countries' political institutions and parties.

Conclusion

Although the return of outright military regimes in the region now seems unlikely, it is not difficult to conjure up a plausible, pessimistic scenario for democracy in Latin America. Illiberal, unconsolidated democracies lacking an effective rule of law and hybrid regimes could perdure in many countries in the absence of domestic threats to the established order and with the continued presence of a broad but not very demanding international ideological hegemony in favor of democracy.[21] In most of the region, more or less genuine electoral competition and alternation would be overshadowed by the failure of all major political parties, and of state institutions in all sectors and levels, to engage and respond to vast segments of the public, who in turn would become increasingly alienated from and distrustful (even disdainful) of formal democratic institutions. Delegative, populist, and neopatrimonial presidents would override the quest for horizontal accountability and a rule of law, and thereby eviscerate the vertical dimension of accountability as well. Unable to mobilize a policy consensus or any viable, coherent vision of a more just and dynamic country, parties and politicians would flounder in governing, failing to generate sustained economic growth, much less to relieve poverty and inequality. The current situation is not this bad for the region as a whole, and of course several countries clearly do not fit this description. At the same time, it is questionable whether such a "low-level equilibrium" of democracy in Latin America would be viable indefinitely. And even if it were viable, it is hardly desirable.

A more optimistic scenario would see the forces of globalization fostering effective regional integration throughout the continent, strengthening both vibrant market economies and political democracy while helping countries to put aside old enmities. Emerging from the painful processes of economic restructuring and second-stage reforms would be states that may be smaller in size and more modest in their goals and their reach, but also more accountable and bound by legal norms. Such states would be more efficient and more capable in what they do: implementing targeted programs of poverty alleviation, improving basic public education and health, effectively regulating private economic actors to limit market abuse, and administering justice fairly both within the state and within society. Although many issues may no longer be channeled through the state or processed by political means, political parties and institutions would reemerge as important forums for mobilizing, articulating, aggregating, and compromising interests, and for responding to an invigorated civil society. Reform-minded forces in party politics and civil society would join together to rein in corruption, increase transparency, improve human-rights protections, expand access to power, and subordinate the military—all by enhancing the political institutions of democracy within a context in which all key actors endorsed and accepted the democracy and legal "rules of the game."

Whatever the precise terminology employed, the challenge confronting most of Latin America today is to consolidate rule-of-law democracies in countries where democracy remains still, in too many respects, superficial. As I trust this exercise has suggested, there is better understanding at least at an intellectual level of what is meant by and what is required for this to be achieved. If the challenge of political institution building and reform is important, the reform of stagnant, centralized, and corrupt state structures does not happen merely on initiative from above. Even with skilled and democratically enlightened leadership, democratic reform requires pressure from below and encouragement and support from outside, in the regional and international environment. However, to improve and help consolidate democracy, civil-society actors must not only remain committed to democratic ends and means, protesting and criticizing where necessary; they must also learn to engage, cooperate, and even ally with political parties, governmental institutions at all levels, and one another.

Increasingly, as they become integrated into regional and global markets, and as the prospect of a hemispheric free-trade zone draws nearer, Latin American democracies find themselves lodged in an external setting that discourages overt authoritarian regressions. However, the focus of the research above has been to underscore the significant difference between the persistence of troubled or ineffective democracies and alternative, more hopeful futures.

Notes

1. Helpful comments by Ralph Espach, Christina Ewig, and Evelyne Huber are gratefully acknowledged, as is research assistance by Hyung-min Kim and Steven Wuhs.

2. For a review of democracy in Latin America from 1930 to the late 1980s, see Hartlyn and Valenzuela (1994).

3. For a review and analysis of these elections, see Cerdas-Cruz, Rial, and Zovatto (1992).

4. Freedom House ranks countries on separate scales for political rights and civil liberties, in which 1 is the highest score and 7 is the lowest. Countries with combined scores on these two scales of 2 to 5 are rated "free," a useful if imperfect proxy for democracy. As is true of all subjective measures of political democracy, those by Freedom House are not problem-free (for one extensive critique, see Munck and Verkuilen 2000). Studies evaluating these scores during the 1970s and 1980s have concluded that during this time period they tended to rate more highly countries in some regions (including Latin America) than in others (Bollen 1993:1223) and also countries that were "Catholic and monarchies, and not Marxist-Leninist" (Bollen and Paxton 1998:475). And, to complicate matters even more, in the late 1980s and in the 1990s Freedom House scores may have become stricter than in the earlier period (see Diamond 1999 and Mainwaring 1999a:12). To the extent we are making comparisons more within the Latin American region and in the post–Cold War era, these sources of bias may be less problematic, though still apparent (for example, in terms of Freedom House scores for Nicaragua during the 1980s compared to Brazil). In any event, below I also report scores from the "Democracy" variable of the Polity IV data set. The overall correlation between the two data sets for twenty Latin American countries during the 1972–1999 time period is extremely high: .940. Yet the correlation is .965 during the 1972–1989 time period, when both indices reflected high numbers of authoritarian regimes moving in more democratic directions, but only .439 during the politically more ambiguous and difficult to categorize 1990–1999 time period. At the country level over the entire time period, there are three cases where correlations are less than .15 (El Salvador, Mexico, and Colombia) and two additional ones where they are less than .50 (Dominican Republic and Guatemala). And, it is the case that for Latin America as a whole, Polity IV sees a more authoritarian region than Freedom House in the 1980s, and a more democratic one in the 1990s (see Table 6.2).

5. Freedom House data cited from Diamond (1999:26); countries whose combined scores on the political-rights and civil-liberties scales fall between 6 and 11 are ranked "partly free" by Freedom House.

6. For purposes of this chapter, I have considered Latin America to be the Spanish- and Portuguese-speaking countries of the region plus Haiti (a total of twenty countries).

7. For a thorough review of dichotomous versus graded measures of democracy and a reasoned defense of a pragmatic choice regarding concepts based on the goals and context of research, see Collier and Adcock (1999).

8. The next several paragraphs draw from the "Preface to the Second Edition" in Diamond, Hartlyn, Linz, and Lipset (1999).

9. Diamond 1999:7–15. For some, the term "liberal democracy" may suggest an excessively narrow focus on individual political and civil rights that is not a necessary part of the conceptualization. A more accurate, but also more awkward, term that I will occasionally employ below is "rule-of-law democracy."

10. As Diamond notes, for the political quality of democracy, the most important additional mechanism of horizontal accountability is an autonomous judiciary, but crucial as well are institutionalized means (often in a separate, autonomous agency) to monitor, investigate, and punish government corruption at all levels. On the concept of lateral, or horizontal, accountability and its importance, see Sklar (1987, 1996), O'Donnell (1994, 1998), and Schedler, Diamond, and Plattner (1999). Sklar terms the lateral form "constitutional democracy" and emphasizes its mutually reinforcing relationship to vertical accountability.

11. Most prior breakdowns of democratic or semidemocratic regimes in the region took place in periods of economic crisis and were associated with them (exceptions include Venezuela in 1948 and Colombia in 1949; see Rueschemeyer, Huber Stephens, and Stephens 1992:210).

12. In a related work focused on democratic survivability in the region, Mainwaring notes he is not arguing that most of the region's democracies are consolidated (Mainwaring 1999a:1).

13. With regard to their definition (in which social democracy presumes the existence of political democracy), a more expanded analysis would need to address the fact that in several Latin American countries advancement toward greater socioeconomic equality took place more during authoritarian periods than during democratic or semidemocratic ones and the implications for all three types of democracy that follow from this different evolution.

14. One may arrive at different conclusions with regard to specific cases depending on whether one focuses on their conceptual definition or their interacting arenas, as Agüero notes (1998:8).

15. They are careful to note that consolidated democracies can break down in the future, but they argue this should be due to a different dynamic. Furthermore, there can be many types of "low-quality" to "high-quality" consolidated democracies (Linz and Stepan 1996:6–7).

16. Not surprisingly, there is a gap then between cases categorized through this much stricter set of indicators and categorization based exclusively on Freedom House scores. For example, earlier in the same book, the Chilean case is categorized as a liberal democracy based on its Freedom House scores (along with such country cases as Argentina, Panama, Venezuela, El Salvador, and Honduras, whose classification here would also be challenged by many scholars). Yet Diamond also acknowledges that in Chile there are severe constraints imposed on civilian control over the armed forces, antidemocratic features such as the designated senators enshrined in the constitution, and low legitimacy for democracy expressed in public-opinion polls, all of

which make it doubtful Chile satisfies several key components specified in his original definition. Cf. Diamond (1999:11–12; 33).

17. One of the strongest empirical relations consistently found in the comparative literature is that between per capita GDP and democracy. Employing a minimal definition of democracy and a worldwide data set, Przeworski and Limongi (1997:170–171, quote on 167) find that "once established, democracies are likely to die in poor countries and certain to survive in wealthy ones." Yet, of the ten times that countries with incomes above $3,000 (1985 PPP in U.S. dollars) experienced democratic breakdowns, seven of them were in Latin America: Argentina (five times), Chile, and Uruguay. Given this, it is not surprising that Mainwaring (1999a:21) reports low correlations between Freedom House scores and per capita income for Latin America, as low as .10 for 1979 (when countries such as Argentina, Chile, and Uruguay were authoritarian) and with correlations in the .40 to .51 range from 1989 to 1996—the latter indicating an important relationship, though with scores lower than found in studies incorporating other regions.

18. This is not to argue that some kind of economic stabilization and market-oriented reforms were not necessary, nor that initial conditions nor continuing domestic policy decision did not matter, but to underscore in broad brush terms the consequences of the policies that were implemented. For a critical discussion of the claims of both defenders and critics of neoliberalism, see Haggard and Kaufman (1995:309–334), although it may underplay somewhat the role of international constraints on domestic policy choices.

19. Inter-American Development Bank (2000:13–14). Median homicide rates are employed, rather than average rates, to avoid the bias that could be introduced by extreme cases.

20. This is not the place to analyze the partial, uneven, and sometimes even counterproductive consequences of some of these efforts; for a brief discussion, see Diamond, Hartlyn, and Linz (1999:15–33); see also Htun (1998), Van Cott (2000), and Yashar (1996).

21. These paragraphs draw on Hartlyn (1998a) and Diamond, Hartlyn, and Linz (1999).

7

Globalization, Social Inequality, and Democratic Governance in South Korea[1]

Chung-in Moon and Jae-jin Yang

South Korea has undergone a profound transformation in the last five decades. Despite lingering colonial legacies, devastation followed by the Korean War, and protracted political instability, South Korea managed to overcome the vicious cycle of poverty and underdevelopment and to emerge as one of the most powerful economic dynamos in the world. Beneath the transformation lie forces of modernization and globalization. Although the process of modernization fundamentally reshaped its domestic social and economic landscape, globalization, through expanding networks of trade, production, and financial flow, further integrated it into the international economy. South Korea's pathway from the periphery not only defied the rigid hierarchy of the world capitalist economy, but also validated the convergence thesis of early modernization theorists. Admission into the Organization for Economic Cooperation and Development (OECD) in 1996 was the hallmark of its economic ascent.

The triumph of the South Korean economy did not last long, however. South Korea underwent its worst economic crisis in 1997. Declining international competitiveness, pervasive moral hazard, economic mismanagement, mounting foreign debt, and an acute liquidity crisis drove it to the brink of economic collapse, only to be saved by rescue financing from the International Monetary Fund (IMF). The 1997 economic crisis has placed South Korea under two challenges: one is the mandate of economic recovery and growth through structural adjustment, and the other is the minimization of backlash from the crisis and structural reforms on social equality and welfare. Restoring economic normalcy has been quite a difficult task, but minimizing negative welfare consequences has been much more daunting not only because of increasing unemployment and sharp income reduction, but also because of structural constraints imposed by neoliberal reforms embodied in IMF conditions.

South Korea has shown remarkable resilience in coping with these challenges. It was able to fulfill the mandate of economic recovery in less than two years, as several macroeconomic indicators clearly show. The growth rate increased from -5.8 percent in 1997 to 10 percent in 1999, while the current account balance showed surpluses for two consecutive years, turning a $23 billion deficit in 1996 into surpluses of $40.6 billion in 1998 and $26 billion in 1999. Foreign reserves rose from $12.4 billion in 1997 to $68.4 billion as of November 1999 (Ministry of Finance and Economy 2000a). Economic vitality has been restored. What is more outstanding is the way the Kim Dae-jung government has handled the negative welfare consequences of globalization and the economic crisis by declaring the productive welfare initiative, a daring and comprehensive measure to enhance social equality and welfare. It is ironic that the economic crisis and subsequent neoliberal reforms have served as a catalyst for the speedy transformation of the developmental state into a welfare state. An interesting question arises here: Why and how could South Korea transform itself into a new welfare state amidst forces of globalization, economic crisis, and neoliberal reforms?

This chapter aims to explore the issue by looking into the dynamic interplay of globalization, economic crisis, and domestic political and institutional changes. More specifically, the first part presents a brief overview of theoretical debates on the correlates of globalization and welfare. The second part traces the impacts of globalization and the economic crisis on social inequality and welfare in South Korea. The third part analyzes social policy responses of the Kim Dae-jung government, focusing on its productive welfare initiative, and the fourth section looks into the political and institutional determinants underlying the transformation. Finally, the chapter draws some theoretical and policy implications in comparative perspectives.

Globalization and Welfare: Contending Views

As with debates on modernization, the process of globalization has been subject to various interpretations. Three contending perspectives can be identified with regard to the correlates of globalization and welfare: the cornucopian, the globaphobic, and the contextualist. The cornucopian perspective, which is widely shared by mainstream neoclassical economists, postulates that globalization is a grand, irreversible, progressive trend in human civilization. Complex transnational networks of production, trade, and capital—all closely intertwined with advancements in transportation, communication, and information technology—will eventually demolish the artificial walls of national boundaries, evolving into "sovereignty at bay" (Vernon 1971) and a "borderless world" (Ohmae 1990).

As theorists of modernization envisaged in the 1960s, proponents of the cornucopian perspective regard globalization as a linear and eugenic process of global convergence being propelled by market forces. It is thus predicated on the global diffusion of the free market, a global standard, and greater efficiency. Transitional trauma notwithstanding, globalization is assumed to produce positive effects on social equality and welfare through the trickle-down of expanded economic pies. Global diffusion of production, capital, and technology not only fosters economic growth, but also creates new job opportunities and higher income levels. Improved efficiency and ever-expanding employment opportunities that ensue from globalization make critical contributions to leveling off global, national, and local welfare. Thus, income growth, employment, and productivity gains are inseparably interconnected with integration into the world economy through the process of globalization. Economic dislocation, social inequality, and welfare losses, if any, are viewed as temporal, and would be eventually corrected through market mechanisms, social philanthropy, and family safety nets. According to the cornucopian view, globalization brings about bounty and welfare without necessarily creating profound trade-offs between the two (Burtless et al. 1998: ch.2; Williamson 1998).

The globaphobic perspective presents a quite different portrait of globalization (Cox 1997; Mittelman 1996; Gill 1995). The global organization of production and an unregulated system of global financial transactions have fostered the diffusion of market-friendly policies such as relaxation of labor market rigidity, corporate and income tax holidays, and sweeping deregulation measures. The shift to these policies has become essential not only for maintaining international competitiveness, but for attracting foreign direct investment, while minimizing the exodus of domestic industrial capital. Along with microeconomic incentives, macroeconomic stability emerges as a new policy imperative in crafting a favorable business climate, precisely because macroeconomic instability ends up punishing owners of mobile capital assets and ultimately driving them out of the country. In order to ensure macroeconomic stability, reducing public spending, minimizing public debs, and restraining countercyclic expansionary fiscal policy become unavoidable (Teeple 1995; Pontusson 1992; Evans 1997; Heye 1993; Notermans 1993).

Proponents of the globaphobic perspective contend that realignment of microeconomic incentives and adherence to macroeconomic stability, both of which constitute the core of neoliberal reforms, bear negative consequences for welfare and social equality. While the effective rate of benefits and coverage is lowered and efforts to maintain full employment are abandoned, acceleration of privatization undermines the public sector, and entitlement is pegged more closely to work (Clayton and Pontusson 1998; Schwartz 1994; Teeple 1995). The end result of these policy changes is the retrenchment of the welfare state. It is with this observation that the globaphobic perspective concludes that the welfare state is no longer viable in the globalization era. This pessimistic vision of the inexorable dominance of neoliberal reforms over the welfare state is more applicable to developing countries, since their economic performance is getting more dependent on the inflow of foreign capital (Rudra 2000). The global dominance of capital and the subordination of the welfare state to it seems irreversible in this context.

Other scholars call into question the divergent claims of both the cornucopian and globaphobic perspectives. The third perspective, the contextualist, contends that it is misleading to establish direct causal links between globalization and welfare consequences. Globalization pressures neither shrink the welfare state nor enhance prosperity and welfare in an automatic manner. Its proponents draw attention to institutional and political foundations as intervening variables that condition the impacts of globalization on welfare and social equality (Garrett 1998; Rodrik 1997c; Rieger and Leibfried 1998; Pierson 1996; Garrett and Lange 1995). They argue that while monetary and fiscal policies may face new restrictions, most governments are not nearly as shackled by economic globalization as is commonly believed, and that welfare states can retain substantial autonomy in regulating their economies, maintaining institutions, designing social policies, and securing sufficient tax bases. Moreover, welfare states have broader bases of support, promoting the restoration of equilibrium and mitigating negative welfare consequences associated with globalization. Garrett (1998) even argues that international market exposure induces growing popular demands on social policies, eventually fostering greater government spending to reduce market-generated inequalities of risk and wealth through partisan electoral politics. His study of fourteen OECD countries demonstrates that governments' greater role in social protection is not negatively related to economic performance precisely because political and social stability forged through such social policies helps attract more investment from mobile asset holders. He concludes that "macroeconomic performance under social democratic corporatism has been as good as any other constellation of political power and labor market institutions" (p. 11). His finding is congruent with other studies by Rieger and Leibfried (1998); Pfaller, Gough, and Therborn (1991); and Katzenstein (1985).

How could mandates of the welfare state be reconciled with the forces of globalization? Political and institutional logic matters. Globalization and subsequent economic insecurity bring about the emergence of new political coalitions urging protectionism and resisting domestic deregulation. Globalization cannot smoothly proceed without placating such opposing forces through compensatory social-welfare policy. In other words, in order for a country to reap net gains from economic globalization, it should be equipped with strong social safety nets. Otherwise, globalization would precipitate formidable domestic political backlash with dismal welfare performance. Such development could victimize both growth and welfare. In view of this, developing social-welfare systems should be regarded not as an obstacle to economic growth, but as a prerequisite for growth through globalization.

What to bear in mind here are the modes of political governance, coalitional dynamics, and state capacity. Although the formalized democratic mode of governance expands space for political maneuver through which civil society can redress its concerns for social equality and welfare, coalitional dynamics allow civil society to build its political power base to translate its interests into viable social policies. But provision of social welfare ultimately rests upon state capacity. Leadership commitment, technocratic competence, and resource availability determine the nature, direction, and performance of social policy. Likewise, impacts of globalization are neither uniform nor unidirectional across countries over time. Welfare consequences of globalization are very much contextual, being dictated by the dynamic interplay of domestic politics, institutional configuration, and state capacity (Rudra 2000; Brooks 1999; Kay 1999; Niles 1999).

We concur with the contextualist perspective. Since the early 1990s, South Korea underwent a rapid process of globalization, eventually resulting in an acute economic crisis in 1997. Defying the conventional wisdom, however, economic crisis and the imposition of neoliberal reforms by the IMF have not undercut the provision of social equality and welfare. On the contrary, such developments have facilitated the transformation of a developmental state into a welfare state by not only bringing social inequality and welfare to the core of social and political discourses, but also paving the way for the new policy initiative of productive welfare. As discussed below, this anomalous reversal can be attributed to the confluence of a new mode of democratic governance, the advent of a new distributional coalition, transnational pressures, and state capacity.

Globalization, Economic Crisis, and Social Inequality in South Korea

The Developmental State and Globalization[2]

Korea's modern history was littered with bloody struggles between re-formers who favored open-door policies and conservatives who fa-vored closed-door policies. Being a victim of forced opening and sub-sequent Japanese colonial domination, xenophobic perceptions have long socialized Korean minds. Such inward-looking orientation was responsible for cultivating an ideal niche for the mercantile ethos that governed its economic management. Few would refute the idea that rapid economic growth, assertive industrialization, and the phe-nomenal expansion of manufactured exports in South Korea have re-sulted from a rather unique pattern of economic management that combined Keynesian structuralism with strategic intervention via in-dustrial policy. Amsden (1992) characterizes it as the epitome of the "late-industrialization" model, as opposed to the "Anglo-Saxonian" one. Others have touted it as the prototype of the developmental state model or *dirigisme* (Haggard and Moon 1983; Haggard 1990; Johnson 1987; Wade 1990; Amsden 1989).

The Korean state was never a minimalist one envisioned by neo-classical economists whose role was confined to the provision of col-lective goods and to the facilitation of the functioning of market mechanisms with market-conforming economic policies. It even went beyond the Keynesian state of manipulating an arsenal of macroeco-nomic parameters. The Korean state was actively interventionist with its clearly defined objectives and preferences. It made strategic inter-vention in markets, and mobilized and allocated resources in order to achieve them. The state and business maintained close ties, but not on an equal footing: the state was pacesetter and guide; business fol-lowed suit. The state occasionally commanded and disciplined the private sector.

The late-industrialization model was justified in the name of de-velopmentalism, which was framed around two normative goals—eco-nomic growth and national security. Political leadership in the 1960s and 1970s was obsessed with an imperative to expedite the process of modernization through export-led economic development. Escaping from poverty and economic backwardness was vital to its legitimacy and popular support. Economic growth and industrialization were also interpreted as a solution to South Korea's security dilemma. Since the late 1960s, South Korea faced a deteriorating security envi-ronment. The old Japanese nationalist ideology of "rich nation, strong army" (*Bukuk Gangbyung/Fukoku Kyohei*) resurfaced as the dominant paradigm in South Korea, dictating the nature and direction of its economic management (Samuels 1994). It was the political leadership's obsession with the developmentalist ideology of growth and security that shaped and steered the mercantile nature of economic management since the early 1960s (Moon 1999).

Economic growth through the developmental state has brought about unintended consequences. Although forces of spontaneous globalization began to lift the mercantile overlay through extended and intensified market interactions, the very economic success through unfair trade practices evoked enormous outside pressures for market opening and economic liberalization. In fact, more than three decades of export drive rapidly integrated the South Korean economy into a web of global economic interdependence. Total trade volume in 1965 was only a meager $650 million, accounting for 21 percent of GDP; the figure increased to $12.35 billion in 1975, $61.42 billion in 1985, and $260.18 billion in 1995. The trade volume rose more than twenty times within two decades, and, since 1975, has consistently accounted for more than 50 percent of gross domestic product, reaching 63.5 percent in 1997. Trade as percent of goods GDP reached 131.3 percent in 1997 (see Table 7.1). In comparison with other countries, South Korea has been truly a trading state.

Capital and financial flows have also been remarkable. As Table 7.1 demonstrates, inbound and outbound foreign investments have been steadily rising. Total foreign direct investment inflow, $269 million in 1983, rose more than twenty-five times by 1997, reaching $6.9 billion. Compared with foreign trade, its share in GDP remained minimal, representing 0.154 percent in 1983 and 1.167 percent in 1997. Outbound foreign investment also increased from $591 million in 1985 to $4.6 billion in 1996. Since South Korea liberalized its capital account in 1994, share of foreign equity ownership of listed companies rose sharply from 2.7 percent in 1992 to 12.3 percent in 1997. It must be noted, however, that in the case of South Korea, external borrowing rather than foreign investment has played a more important role in foreign savings. Reflecting this trend, South Korea's external borrowing grew rather drastically from $46.7 billion in 1985 to $154.4 billion in 1997.

Along with growing economic interdependence in trade and capital and financial flows, a salient change in personnel flow can be noticed.[3] There were 370,656 inbound visitors and 84,245 outbound visitors in 1972. These figures have phenomenally increased to 3.07 million inbound visitors and 4.6 million outbound visitors in 1996. This is a result partly of the government's policy to liberalize overseas

Table 7.1 Indicators of Globalization

Trade	Trade % of goods GDP[d]	Gross FDI % of GDP[a,e]	FDI inflows $ million[b]	FDI balance $ million[b]	Foreign ownership % of equity of listed companies[c]	External borrowing $ billion[b]
1983	108.3	0.154	269	—	—	—
1984	116.7	0.11	422	—	—	43.1
1985	118.9	0.499	532	—	—	46.8
1986	112.4	0.848	355	—	—	44.5
1987	119.5	0.468	1,063	101	—	35.6
1988	114.3	0.583	1,284	371	—	31.2
1989	103.6	0.567	1,090	520	—	29.4
1990	101.6	0.549	803	−263	—	31.7
1991	99.3	0.71	1,396	−309	—	39.1
1992	102.3	0.459	895	−433	2.7	42.8
1993	102.2	0.432	1,044	−752	7.6	43.9
1994	105.7	0.663	1,317	−1,652	8.0	97.4
1995	115.4	0.965	1,941	−1,776	10.0	127.4
1996	118.4	1.174	3,203	−2,345	10.5	163.5
1997	131.3	1.167	6,971	−1,605	12.3	159.2
1998	—	—	8,852	616	16.4	148.7
1999	—	—	15,541	—	19.0	136.4

Sources: a. World Bank (1999b); b. Ministry of Finance and Economy (2000b); c. J. Kim (1999).

Notes: d. Trade in goods as a share of goods GDP is the sum of merchandise exports and imports divided by the current value of GDP in U.S. dollars after subtracting value added in services. Note that this indicator differs from the standard measure of trade openness (i.e., trade share of GDP), which is skewed against advanced economies that have large service sectors, which is by nature not movable.

e. Gross foreign direct investment is the sum of the absolute values of inflows and outflows of foreign direct investment recorded in the balance of payments financial account. It includes equity capital, reinvestment of earnings, other long-term and short-term capital.

tourism for Koreans, which was strictly controlled in the past. In addition, communication networks have revolutionized the pattern of Korean life-styles.

Apart from this spontaneous pattern of globalization through market mechanisms, there have been growing outside multilateral pressures for South Korea's economic liberalization. In addition to pressure from the United States and other OECD countries for market opening and correction of unfair trade practices in the name of strategic reciprocity, the Uruguay Round of negotiations and the subsequent launch of the World Trade Organization have forced South Korea to come out of the neomercantilist closet.

It is in this context that the Kim Young Sam government undertook the *segyehwa* (globalization) campaign (Sechuwi 1995, 1996, 1998a, 1998b;

S. Kim 2000).[4] The move reflected a major shift in economic management thinking from a defensive, mercantilist adaptation to external changes to a positive accommodation of outside stimuli. Globalization was more than a political slogan or an administrative guide for economic management. It has evolved into a new hegemonic ideology replacing the old developmentalism. The *segyehwa* campaign set as its principal goal South Korea's ascension to a first-rate state in the twenty-first century, and identified productivity, flexibility, fairness, and autonomy as new guiding principles for national economic management. Its target was not limited to the economic domain, but extended to entire segments of society ranging from education, law, and foreign policy to politics, culture, environment, and the quality of life.

As part of the globalization strategy, South Korea not only ratified the Uruguay Round, but also formally applied for a membership in OECD, both of which were predicated on the liberalization of trade, investment, and foreign-exchange regimes as well as of the capital, financial, and banking sectors (Korea Trade-Investment Promotion Agency 1995). Economic liberalization under Kim was quite extensive in scope and ambitious in its implementation plans. Another related move was deregulation. South Korea began to realize negative aspects of the government's strategic intervention in the economic domain, which had been considered a major source of international competitiveness. However, strategic intervention was correlated with mounting regulations, undermining its international competitiveness. Deregulating economic life and correcting government failures were singled out as a major target of globalization. State intervention was gradually replaced by market principles, and institutional reforms aimed at rationalization and accountability were undertaken in virtually all sectors of the state and society. Globalization became a new, omnipotent ideological tool of governance in the new era (see special issues on globalization, *Quarterly Sasang* 1994, 1995; Sechuwi 1998a, 1998b).

Globalization and Economic Crisis

The *segyehwa* strategy proved disastrous. The sudden collapse of the Korean economy in November 1997 alarmed the entire world. After a series of financial and foreign-exchange crises, the Kim Young Sam government filed for national economic bankruptcy by asking the IMF for $57 billion in bailout funds on 3 December 1997. The myth of the Korean economic miracle was shattered, and national shame prevailed. During his term in office, South Korea's foreign debt increased from $43.9 billion to $160.7 billion in 1996 and $153 billion in 1997, while foreign reserve assets dwindled from \$20.2 billion in 1993 to \$12.4 billion in 1997. At the peak of the currency crisis, foreign reserves held by the central bank were less than \$8 billion, spreading the fear of default. With foreign reserves being depleted, the Korean currency rapidly depreciated. In 1993, the *won*-dollar exchange rate was KW808:1, but the Korean *won* devalued by almost twice by the end of 1997, posting an exchange rate of 1,415 *won*/dollar; at one point, it reached 2,000 *won*/dollar.

Equally troublesome, the banking and financial sectors as well as the corporate sector showed the worst performance in recent history. The stock price index is generally considered the most reliable barometer of economic vitality. Although the average annual stock price index was 808:1 in 1993 and 1,027:1 in 1994, it slid down throughout 1995 and 1996, falling to 375:1 by the end of 1997, the lowest since the opening of the securities markets. Falling stock prices amidst rapid currency devaluation drastically reduced the value of Korean firms' assets. According to an analysis by the *Financial Times* (29 December 1997), total assets of all 653 Korean firms listed on the Korean Securities Exchange Market were estimated to be only 66.3 trillion Korean *won* by the end of December 1997, which was the equivalent of the assets held by a single European company—ING Group, a Dutch banking and financial firm ranked as the seventieth largest firm in the world.

The amount of nonperforming loans is another important indicator of microeconomic health, since it reflects the magnitude of corporate bankruptcies. Total nonperforming loans were KW2.4 trillion in 1993 and KW1.9 trillion in 1994; by the end of September 1997, the figure had risen to KW4.8 trillion. Given the avalanche of corporate bankruptcies, including major *chaebols* (big businesses) such as Hanbo, Kia, Jinro, Daenong, Newcore, and Halla, the size of nonperforming loans must have been much higher than 4.8 trillion *won*. In fact, the IMF estimated that they amounted to KW32 trillion in 1997, about 7 percent of GDP (IMF 1997).[5] The sharp increase in nonperforming loans, which accounted for 6.8 percent of total bank loans as of the end of September 1997, literally paralyzed the banking and financial sector, precipitating the financial crisis. In addition, most firms in South Korea, especially small and medium-sized ones, have traditionally relied on the discount of corporate bills such as promissory notes in raising corporate funds. Thus, a high ratio of dishonored corporate bills implies a severe liquidity shortage and greater corporate delinquency. In the first three quarters of 1996, the ratio of dishonored corporate bills was 0.24 percent, a dramatic increase from 0.13 percent in 1993.

What went wrong?[6] Most attributed the genesis of the Korean economic crisis to domestic mismanagement; it was seen as home-grown (*The Economist,* November 1997). Beneath the "healthy fundamentals" of its macroeconomy, microeconomic foundations had fallen into deep trouble.[7] Declining international competitiveness, dismal corporate performance and bankruptcies, mounting nonperforming loans and the paralysis of the banking and financial sectors, and extensive government failures all contributed to the downfall of the Korean economy (Mo and Moon 1999). But equally critical were international financial instabilities and the backlash from hasty globalization. Unprepared and immature economic globalization (Moon and Mo 1999), financial panic and contagion effects (Radlet and Sachs 1998:3–4; Stiglitz 1998b; Dornbush and Park 1995; Bank of Korea 1998:17–21), and imprudence and incompetence on the part of the government (Moon and Rhyu 1999) all generated an unbearable transitional trauma.

Social Inequality and Welfare Consequences

The economic crisis in 1997 not only undermined macro- and microeconomic performance, it also created serious negative consequences for social equality and welfare. The most immediate outcome was workers' deteriorating quality of life (Kim and Moon 2000). The unemployment rate rose from 2.2 percent in July 1994 to 7.6 percent in July 1998, the highest since 1966 when the rate of unemployment reached 8.4 percent. If the underemployed were included, the total number of unemployed was estimated to have reached 3 to 4 million as of July 1998. As Table 7.2 demonstrates, of four Asian countries inflicted with economic crisis, South Korea suffered most in terms of percentage changes in employment, which fell from 1.4 percent in 1997 to –5.8 percent in 1998. The manufacturing and construction sectors were especially hard hit, showing a 13.1 percent and 26.4 percent reduction in employment, respectively. Real consumption wage was also sharply cut by exceeding more than 10 percent. Along with this, the economic crisis brought about a fundamental change in employment structure. While the ratio of full-time workers decreased from 56.6 percent in 1996 to 50.9 percent in the first quarter of 1999 and 47.6 percent in the third quarter of 1999, the ratio of part-time/temporary workers increased from 43.4 percent in 1996 to 49.1 percent in 1998 and to over 50 percent in 1999 (Ministry of Finance and Economy 1999).

Table 7.3 presents a broader picture of poverty and inequality in South Korea. Although the headcount urban poverty index rose from

Table 7.2   Employment and Real Wages in East Asia During the Crisis (percentage change)

	Korea		Indonesia		Malaysia		Thailand	
	1997	1998	1997	1998	1997	1998	1997	1998
Total Employment	1.4	−5.8	1.8	2.6	4.6	−2.7	1.8	−3.0
Agriculture	−3.4	0.0	−4.7	13.3	−0.6	−5.3	1.3	−1.8
Non-agriculture	2.4	−6.5	6.8	−4.7	5.8	−2.2	2.2	−3.9
Manufacturing	−4.3	−13.1	4.1	−9.8	7.6	−2.9	−0.1	−1.9
Construction	1.7	−26.4	10.6	−15.9	8.9	−13.4	−5.6	−33.6
Real Consumption Wage								
Total	—	—	8.6	−41.0	—	—	5.7	−1.5
Agriculture	—	—	4.1	−35.0	—	—	10.0	−8.9
Non-agriculture	2.6	−10.0	9.9	−42.0	—	—	5.0	−0.5
Manufacturing	0.7	−10.6	11.1	−44.0	6.0	−2.4	7.1	−4.5
Construction	3.3	−14.7	8.5	−42.0	—	—	3.8	−2.2

Source: World Bank (2000: 57).

Table 7.3   Poverty and Inequality in South Korea Pre- and Post-Economic Crisis

	1996	1997	1998	1999.1/4	1999.2/4	1999.3/4
Headcount Poverty Index (urban)[a]	9.6	8.6	19.2	—	—	—
Wage Income Share[b]						
Highest 20%	37.9	37.2	39.8	41.3	39.5	39.0
Middle 60%	53.9	54.5	52.8	51.6	53.0	53.6
Lowest 20%	8.2	8.3	7.4	7.1	7.5	7.4
Wage Income Ratio[b]	4.63	4.49	5.41	5.85	5.24	5.29
Asset Income Ratio[c]	—	17.1	—	—	—	38.6
Gini Coefficient[b]	0.291	0.283	0.316	0.333	0.311	0.310

Sources: a. World Bank (2000:53); b. Ministry of Finance and Economy (1999); c. Hankook Ilbo (4 January 2000).
Notes: Wage Income Ratio = Highest 20%'s share ÷ Lowest 20%'s share; Asset Income Ratio = Highest 10%'s share ÷ Lowest 10%'s share.

9.6 in 1996 to 19.2 in 1998, overall inequality has worsened as a result of the economic crisis. The Gini coefficient, a relatively reliable indicator of income distribution, increased from 0.291 in 1996 to 0.316 in 1998 and 0.333 in the first quarter of 1999; the wage income ratio deteriorated from 4.63 in 1996 to 5.41 in 1998 and 5.85 in the first quarter of 1999. The highest 20 percent's wage income share grew from 37.9 percent in 1996 to 41.3 percent in the first quarter of 1999, and the share of the middle 60 percent reveals a slight decline from 53.9 percent in 1996 to 51.6 percent in the first quarter of 1999, but the greatest victim was the lowest 20 percent, whose wage income share decreased from 8.2 percent in 1996 to 7.4 percent in 1998 and

7.1 percent in the first quarter of 1999. A group of households earning a monthly average of 800,000 *won* in the first three months of 1997 saw a 12 percent reduction in their income during the same period in 1998. The economic crisis also widened the gap in wealth inequality. Asset-to-income ratio, which is measured by dividing the highest 10 percent share by the lowest 10 percent share in earning from interest, rent, and stock investment, shows a considerable increase from 17.1 percent in 1997 to 38.6 percent in the third quarter of 1999.

Judged on the data in the above, the economic crisis in 1997 and subsequent neoliberal reforms have been responsible for worsening income and wealth inequality in South Korea. The most controversial aspect is the hollowing out of the middle class (Rhyu and Kang 1999). South Korea's economic development has been highly commended for contributing to the expansion of the middle class, but the economic crisis severely undercut this group, jeopardizing the essence of the South Korean miracle. Not only has the economic crisis led to job loss and wage cuts, it has also robbed the middle class of its wealth through asset deflation. In South Korea, middle-income families' savings have been usually invested in real estate and stocks. Frozen real estate markets and the stock market crash critically eroded their wealth base. Ironically, the primary beneficiary of the crisis proved to be wealthy families, who took advantage of high interest rates and low asset prices in the aftermath of the economic crisis. In fact, several surveys show that the number of those who perceive themselves as having fallen into the low-income stratum from the middle-income one has considerably increased since the economic crisis. A survey by the Hyundai Economic Research Institute in June 1998 shows that before the 1997 economic crisis, 2.3 percent of respondents identified themselves as upper class, 53.1 percent as middle class, and 44.5 percent as lower class. After the crisis, however, only 0.2 percent of respondents identified themselves as upper class. But the number of those who identified themselves as middle class dwindled sharply from 53.1 percent to 34.8 percent, while that of lower class rose from 44.5 percent to 64.9 percent (Hyundai Economic Research Institute 1999). Surveys by other media agencies reveal similar results in shifting subjective perception of class identification, implying a widening inequality gap in Korean society (*Hangyera,i*, 22 July 1998; *Joongang Ilb,o*, 23 September 1998; *Chosun Ilbo*, 26 September 1998; see also Rhyu and Kang 1999).

The economic crisis has also led to a variety of other social problems, including a sharp rise in the number of the homeless. Unheard of during the economic heyday, the number of homeless increased exponentially, from about 1,000 in February 1998 to 2,000 in April, and 3,000 in June. According to a newspaper report, those laid off as a result of the economic crisis made up 71 percent of the homeless (*Chosun Ilb,o,* 18 May 1998). The crisis has also been responsible for increases in crime, divorce, and suicide (*Joongang Ilb,o,* 16 July 1998).

Coping with Social Inequality:
The Productive Welfare Initiative[8]

The Kim Dae-jung government, inaugurated in the vortex of economic turbulence in February 1998, faced the challenge of overcoming the economic crisis through comprehensive structural reforms, while mitigating social inequality and negative welfare ramifications. Corporate restructuring and downsizing, massive bankruptcies of small and medium-sized firms, financial reforms and phasing out of noncompetitive financial and banking institutions, adoption of flexible layoffs, and fiscal austerity, all of which constituted the mainstay of neoliberal reforms imposed by the IMF, critically imperiled the social-welfare system through job loss, reduced income, and social and psychological derailment. Economic vitality waned, while social ambiance became bleak. Suddenly, family became the last resort of social safety, and the state had little to offer. The gloomy predictions of the globaphobic perspective were about to be realized.

In coping with the race to the bottom, however, the Kim Dae-jung government has identified four major areas of emphasis in this regard. They are the minimization of unemployment, the creation of new jobs, occupational training and job placement, and the construction of an extensive social safety net. In 1998, a total of 10.7 trillion *won* (or 10 percent of the national budget) was allocated for the immediate measures for employment stabilization and construction of social safety nets. The creation of new jobs through public works and investments in small and medium-sized firms and venture companies was given top priority, receiving 5.2 trillion *won,* more than half of the entire budget. Unemployment benefits, minimum cost-of-living support for the destitute, and scholarships for children of the unemployed received the second-largest share, 2.1 trillion *won;* 1.9 trillion was allocated for minimizing unemployment through financial support of small and medium-sized firms; and 896 billion *won* was allocated for occupational training and job conversion. The construction of a social safety net through fiscal stimulus is one of the boldest Keynesian initiatives in South Korea's history; in 1999, the Kim Dae-jung government allocated 9.2 trillion *won* for the same purposes.

The quick-fix solution through fiscal stimulus could not, however, completely reverse the effects of globalization and the economic crisis.

Popular discontent was on the rise, and the Kim Dae-jung government was accused not only of neglecting its welfare mandates, but
also of lacking any systematic and comprehensive social-welfare policy. In the middle of this worsening social mood, President Kim Dae-
jung announced the *productive welfare* initiative in his National Independence Day speech on 15 August 1999:

> My fellow citizens, . . . [a]s the ruling party, the National Congress
> for New Politics will take the lead in a renewal. It will be born anew
> a party worthy of the people's trust and hope. Built around the mid-
> dle and working classes, the new political party will rise as a re-
> formist party of the people. It will uphold human rights and social
> welfare. . . . To nurture the middle class and enhance the living stan-
> dards of the masses, I will actively seek to implement constructive so-
> cial welfare policies built around the principle of human develop-
> ment. . . . *Now, all citizens, including those getting by with less than the
> minimum level of income, will be provided institutional guarantees of edu-
> cation, medical care, and other basic requirements of a decent living. . . .
> The medical insurance, unemployment insurance, national pension, and in-
> dustrial accident insurance systems will be beefed up so as to build a com-
> prehensive system of social security under which all citizens can enjoy stable,
> secure lives.* (D. Kim 1999, emphasis added)

As epitomized in the above passage, productive welfare can be defined as an ideology and a policy "that seeks to secure minimum living standards for all people, while expanding opportunities for self-
support in socioeconomic activities for the purpose of maintaining
human dignity" (Office of the President 2000:18). The new initiative
is pronounced on several accounts. First, it recognizes social welfare
as a basic human right, and emphasizes that the state is obliged to
guarantee and protect that right. The adoption of the Marshallian
concepts of citizenship, social rights, and entitlement reveals a radical
departure from previous social policies, which were framed around
maximal family responsibility and minimal state intervention (Marshall 1964; Jordan 1998). Second, the initiative is predicated on the
principle of welfare through work. It declares that "work is not only a
means of earning a living, but an essential means of attaining a sense
of satisfaction and value, i.e., attaining dignity" (Office of the President 2000:9). The concept of "welfare through work" also differenti-
ates the Kim government's policy from previous ones by overcoming
the dilemmas associated with simple redistribution or trickle-down
through market mechanisms. Finally, the productive welfare initiative
utilizes social-welfare policy as an instrument for enhancing social integration and achieving harmonious development between sustained
economic growth and participatory democracy (pp. 7–17). In sum,

productive welfare is designed to improve the quality of life for all citizens by promoting social development and a fair distribution of wealth.

The new policy initiative comprises four major components: distribution through an equitable market system; redistribution of wealth; social investment for self-support; and expansion of investment to enhance the quality of life. It is too early to make any meaningful assessments, but the Kim Dae-jung government has made some visible progress. Most remarkable is the tightening of the nation's loose social safety net by expanding the coverage and benefits of the four major state-administered social insurance schemes (health, pension, unemployment, work injury) and by overhauling public assistance programs thoroughly, all of which have shown profound changes since the economic crisis in 1997.

The unemployment insurance program was launched in 1995 to cover full-time workers in firms with more than thirty employees. Coverage was extended to those in companies with more than ten employees in January 1998, then to workplaces with more than five workers in March, and finally in October to all employees including part-time and temporary workers in the informal sector. As Figure 7.1 reveals, unemployment insurance coverage grew from 30 percent in 1995 to 70 percent in 1999. Duration of benefits also has been gradually extended up to one year from two months, while the qualifying work-history period was shortened to three months from one year (*Moonhwa Daily*, 20 August 1999).

Work injury insurance, which is one of the oldest and most mature social-insurance schemes in South Korea, followed a similar path.[9] The Industrial Accident Insurance Act that currently covers 7.5 million workers in industrial firms with five or more employees has been amended to include an additional 1.6 million workers in small businesses with four or less, starting July 2000. The amendment allows employers of small business to be eligible for work injury insurance coverage (Commission on Planning and Budget 1999). As a result, work-injury insurance coverage will increase from 70 percent in the precrisis period to 80 percent in the postcrisis period (see Figure 7.1).

The state-administered national pension program, which began to cover private-sector employees in 1988 and then expanded twice until it reached farmers and fishermen in 1995, was extended to provide financial security to old age, disability, and survivors for all residents in urban areas in a single pillar in April 1999. The whole economically active population, therefore, is now covered under four public pension schemes: National Pension, Government Employees Pension, Military Personnel Pension, and Private Teachers Pension (National Pen-

Figure 7.1   The Growth of Social Insurance Coverage

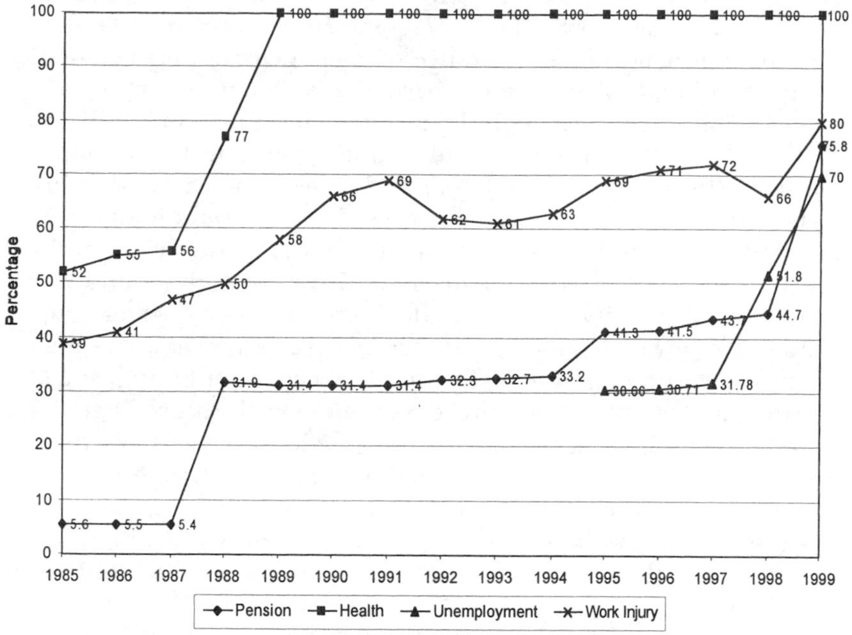

Sources: Except for health, the rates are forecasts estimated by authors based on National Statistics Office (1999) and Ministry of Planning and Budget (1999).

Notes: Coverage rate of pension = contributors/the economically active population; coverage rate of unemployment scheme = contributors/total employees; coverage rate of work injury = contributors/total employees as of 1995; work injury insurance coverage rate of 1999 is replaced by forecast for 2000 due to lack of data.

sion Corporation 1999).[10] Such development is remarkable given the rather modest coverage rate prior to the 1997 economic crisis. As Figure 7.1 shows, the coverage rate of public pension was 41 percent in 1995 and 44 percent in 1997, but jumped to 75 percent within less than two years after the crisis.

Aggressive reforms in the area of the national health insurance scheme are also expected to contribute to tightening the nation's social safety net. As Figure 7.1 illustrates, although the health insurance program began to cover the entire population in 1989, reforms have brought diverse health insurance schemes into a single integrated system.[11] Along with these integration measures, the government also enhanced the quality of benefits, including the gradual extension of the duration of benefits, from 270 to 300 days a year in 1998 and then to

330 days in 1999. The cap on benefit duration was lifted as of 1 January 2000 (National Federation of Medical Insurance 2000; The Ministry of Health and Welfare 1998: 21–22; *The Korea Herald,* 5 August 1999).

The four major social-insurance schemes generally base eligibility for pensions and other periodic payments on length of employment or self-employment. Although the redistributive function is built-in in the case of health insurance and national pension, the amount of pensions (long-term payments) and other periodic payments (short-term) in the event of unemployment, sickness, or work injury is usually tied to the level of earnings. Thus, they are insufficient and inefficient social safety nets for urban and rural marginals and those without work capacity. In order to deal with the lacunae, the Kim government renovated public-assistance programs through the enactment of the Minimum Living Standards Security Act in August 1999. Starting in October 2000, the government will ensure that basic needs, including food, clothing, housing, education, and healthcare, are met for all people below minimum living standards. And as part of the program, the government will also provide financial assistance to those who are willing to work, but are currently unemployed, on the condition that they participate in job-search activities and vocational training.

Under the old public-assistant scheme (i.e., Livelihood Protection Program), allowances were not available to households that included at least one person aged between eighteen and sixty-four deemed capable of working, even if their incomes are less than the minimum cost of living. Now the needy will receive monthly benefits from the government equivalent to the difference between their real income and the minimum cost of living under any circumstances.[12] Although the new law requires recipients to continue to seek or train for jobs, it marks a radical departure from the Elizabethan Poor-Law–style public assistance, which distinguishes the deserving from the undeserving poor and protects only the former. The anticipation that the number of people receiving government allowances for livelihood assistance will triple to 1.54 million from the present level of 0.54 million has made the South Korean government set aside an additional 900 billion *won* (or $0.8 billion) in FY 2000 (Commission on Planning and Budget 1999; *The Korea Herald,* August 19, 1999).

Likewise, substantial improvements have been made in the social-welfare system since the 1997 economic crisis. Formal social-security protection now reaches those in small business with four or fewer employees (unemployment and work injury) and the entire population (health and pension).[13] It will, however, take some time for the nation to feel the full cost of paying benefits, since those programs are not yet mature. Moreover, these schemes are basically funded by payroll contributions split between the employer and the employee, and, only in some limited cases, supplemented by general government revenues. Thus, they will not soon become a major drain on government revenues. Nonetheless, it is evident that expansion of the social safety net will call for greater government budgetary commitment. Indeed, the government's social spending has been outgrowing the total budget increase. During fiscal years 1998 and 1999, social expenditure grew by an average of 19.5 percent, while the total government outlay increased by only 5.6 percent (Commission on Planning and Budget 1999).

Along with greater social-insurance coverage and the provision of minimal cost of living, tax reforms are being undertaken in order to ensure distributive justice as well as to secure financial resources for expanded welfare needs. As part of this effort, the tax burden on middle- and lower-income families has been substantially reduced. On average, wage and salary income earners saw their tax burden reduced by 28 percent by January 2000. In order to help maintain a basic standard of living, the ceiling on tax deductions for insurance, medical, and educational expenses have also been raised. Tax reforms aimed at improving the income distribution structure will also be implemented. Inheritance and donation taxes will be more strictly imposed in order to prevent the rich from illegally inheriting or donating their wealth to their children. The government has also been employing computerized techniques to improve the accuracy of tax audits. In addition, the government plans to extend the capital gains tax by assessing the capital gains acquired from the transfer of common stock at a progressive rate of 20 to 40 percent. The gift tax on the transfer of unrealized capital gains, usually share-price gains by formerly private companies that became publicly listed companies, is designed to thwart the illegal and irregular transfer of wealth through inheritance or gift giving (Ministry of Finance and Economy 2000; Office of the President 2000:101–108).

Why Anomaly?:
Democratic Governance, State Capacity, and Social Policy

The examination of the Kim Dae-jung government's social policy responses shows a major anomaly to both the cornucopian and globaphobic perspectives. The South Korean experiences of globalization, economic crisis, and negative welfare consequences offer direct counterfactual evidence to the cornucopian claims. Although the globaphobic perspective seems persuasive, given the adverse effects of globalization on economic growth and social equality, the Kim government's countervailing strategy and a profound reversal in social-welfare policy also reveal empirical limits to its assertions. The South Korean case clearly shows that globalization, economic crisis, and neoliberal reform mandates have not unilaterally dictated the nature and direction of social-welfare policy. What matters are domestic political dynamics, institutional structure, and state capacity—all of which have served as critical intervening variables in shaping social-welfare policy.

The South Korean anomaly becomes all the more pronounced when viewed from the historical trajectory of its past social-welfare system.[14] In precrisis South Korea, social-welfare systems may best be understood in terms of "growth first, and distribution later," and "high economic growth, low unemployment" (Y. Kim 1998a). Social welfare demands involving health, housing, unemployment, old-age, and education were satisfied primarily through fast-growing real income in the market that was buttressed by stable employment, and secondarily by strong family ties and corporate welfare embedded in the Confucian cultural tradition. The South Korean state accepted limited responsibilities for health and industrial injuries, and provided only minimum protection to those neither able to participate in the labor market nor having family to rely on. Consequently, there has been a salient mismatch of domain between the miracle economy and the social-welfare system. Data in Table 7.4 aptly underscore the underdeveloped nature of South Korea's social-welfare system in comparative perspectives. Work-injury insurance and pension schemes for state and military personnel, which are most mature in South Korea, were introduced in the early 1960s, almost fifty years later than in Brazil and Chile. Introduction of health insurance, a national pension system for private sectors,[15] and unemployment insurance lags far behind not only advanced industrial countries such as the United States, Japan, Germany, and Sweden, but also developing countries such as Brazil and Chile.

Table 7.5 presents comparative data on selected governments' welfare commitment. In 1993, South Korea's per capita income reached $7,660, but budgetary share of health, housing, social security, and welfare sectors out of total government spending was 8.7 percent. The figure is far below Chile (50.8 percent) and Brazil (35.2 percent), whose per capita income was $3,170 and $2,930, respectively. The per capita income of Greece ($7,390) is comparable to that of South Korea, but the welfare share of its total government spending was 22.1 percent, far exceeding that of South Korea. Meanwhile, South Korea showed the highest ratio in economic services among the six

Table 7.4   Timing of Social Insurance Introduction

Country	Germany[a]	Sweden[a]	U.S.[a]	Japan[b]	Brazil[b]	Chile[b]	Korea[c]
Work injury	1884	1901	1930	1911	1919	1916	1963
Health	1880	1962	—	1927	1923	1924	1977
Pension	1889	1913	1935	1941	1923	1924	1960
Unemployment	1927	1934	1935	1947	1965	1937	1995

Sources: a. Flora and Heidenheimer (1981); b. U.S. Social Security Administration (1999); c. Lee (1994).

Table 7.5   Governmental Welfare Commitment: Welfare Share of Data in Central Government Welfare Budget (1993)

Country	U.S.	Germany	Singapore	Korea	Greece	Chile	Brazil
Per capita income (US $)	$24,740	$23,560	$19,850	$7,660	$7,390	$3,170	$2,930
Health (A)	17.1	16.8	6.1	1.5	7.4	11.5	5.2
Housing, soc.sec & welfare (B)	31.7	45.9	9.0	7.2	14.7	39.3	30.0
A+B	48.8	62.7	15.1	8.7	22.1	50.8	35.2
Economic services	6.2	9.7	11.5	18.8	9.4	14.6	7.5

Source: World Bank (1995).

countries under comparison by accounting for 18.8 percent of total government spending. Indeed, South Korea represents a classic example of the developmental state where the private assumption of welfare costs was routinized.

The combination of high income growth and low state commitment has forced South Koreans to prepare individual safety nets: Korea is among the highest in gross domestic savings rate (e.g., 34.25 percent of GDP in 1997; World Bank 1999b) and ranked second in the world in private insurance-premium payment rate (e.g., 15.42 percent of GDP in 1997; *Korea Economy Daily*, 11 August 1999). The paradox of maximal individual safety net and minimal state commitment, which is reminiscent of the nineteenth-century night-watch state, was a product of the developmental ideology of "growth first, distribution later" of previous authoritarian regimes. The state was willing to pull back resources from the economy to social welfare only when it was conducive to economic growth and political legitimization. The dominant social paradigm of economic growth, high employment, and individual self-reliance in welfare pacified popular discontents by serving the hegemonic ideology in the period of the developmental state. In addition, this ideology was shaped and sustained by the developmental coalition, which was composed of an authoritarian regime, technocrats, and business, especially big business (*chaebol*) (Lee 1993; Ahn 1991; Kwon 1999).

It is quite remarkable for the Kim Dae-jung government to make such a hard welfare drive by overcoming the ideological, institutional, and political legacies of the developmental state. What made such an anomalous reversal possible? Shifting coalitional dynamics mattered. The transition to the welfare state is predicated on the transfer of income and resources from one group to another: from the rich to the poor, the healthy to the weak, the young to the old, and the employed to the unemployed. Such transfers were bound to entail fierce political contestation between developmental and distributional forces. In this political debacle, the distributional coalition proved victorious for several reasons. First, the economic crisis in 1997 and subsequent structural reforms fostered the dismantling of the developmental coalition. While banking, financial, and corporate reforms severed the traditional organic ties of mutual patronage between the state and big business, the South Korean state under the Kim Dae-jung leadership undertook a hard anti-*chaebol* campaign, dissociating itself from big business. Second, the Grand National Party (GNP), which championed conservative causes as the ruling party in the past by patronizing big business, lost the presidential race in December 1997, further eroding the political foundation of the conservative ruling coalition. More important, economic crisis, the waning myth of full employment, and victimization of the poor, all of which were perceived as being its responsibility, made it difficult for the GNP to oppose welfare reform bills proposed by the government and the ruling New Party for National Congress. Ironically, reformist elements within the GNP came forward to support those bills.

Third, *chaebols* were on the defensive. Bankruptcies of selected *chaebols*, corporate reforms involving restructuring and downsizing, and widespread anti-*chaebol* public sentiment have fundamentally constrained political maneuvers by big business. Peak business-interest groups, such as the Federation of Korean Industries, the Chamber of Commerce, and the Korea Traders Association, did not engage in any significant political moves to block welfare reform bills. The retreat of big business in the wake of the economic crisis offered a decisive political impetus for the reversal.[16] Finally, the ruling regime was able to form a broad distributional coalition by including labor groups, reform-minded nongovernmental organizations, and the urban poor through various formal and informal institutional channels, such as the tripartite commission, which is composed of the government, labor, and business. For example, the tripartite commission allowed Korean labor, for the first time in its history, to participate in the policymaking process in the same status as business and the state. It has served as an important venue through which labor articulates its views on social-welfare policy. Likewise, the politics of inclusion by the new ruling regime has significantly enhanced the bargaining position of the distributional coalition.[17]

Democratic governance has played an equally critical role in several important ways. Most important, the democratic transition and consolidation paved the way for regime change without which such welfare reforms might have not been possible. South Korean voters elected center-left Kim Dae-jung as new head of the Korean government, marking the first peaceful transfer of political power in fifty years. It is through his election as president that the idea of productive welfare was put into reality. In this sense, democratic changes and the subsequent free election served as a critical necessary condition for the dramatic transition to the welfare state. Expansion of civil society and the proliferation of nongovernmental organizations, which are inevitable products of democratic opening and consolidation, have also facilitated the transformation of the developmental state into the welfare state. Unlike the past, during which they were ignored and excluded, the Kim government drew them in as core members of the inner circle, and empowered them with a new participatory role in the welfare policymaking process. For example, Kim's productive welfare initiative is by and large a reflection of proposals by the People's Solidarity for Participatory Democracy (PSPD), the most outspoken liberal civic organization in South Korea. In addition, their political activism has contributed to reshaping the social mood in favor of social equality and welfare.

Democratic governance has fundamentally realigned the overall process of policymaking in South Korea. In the past, the politics of exclusion, executive dominance, and a top-down approach had characterized its policymaking process in which most public policies including social welfare ones were formulated by government agencies in consultation only with the ruling party. Neither civil society nor the legislative branch were included in the process of policymaking. Since the inauguration of the Kim Dae-jung government, however, the process has undergone profound changes. It was the ruling party, not government agencies, that took initiatives in formulating social-welfare policies. And the ruling party's social-welfare policies have accommodated most of the demands from labor groups and civic organizations. Government agencies could no longer veto the policies. On the contrary, the Ministry of Health and Welfare has become a coalitional partner with these social forces by providing technical details for the welfare reforms. Indeed, it is democratic changes in the public policymaking process that made the anomalous reversal possible (Y. Kim 1999b).

Transnational pressures were also catalytic in ensuring the transition to the new welfare state. International lending institutions such as the IMF and the World Bank are traditionally known to impose neoliberal reforms disregarding negative social-welfare consequences. In the case of South Korea, however, both institutions have been attentive to social-welfare issues by even relaxing their conditionalities on fiscal austerity. The World Bank recommended East Asian debtor countries including South Korea to respond to the social consequences of the economic reform and to safeguard budgetary expenditures for social protection more actively. The Bank has not only assisted in designing and implementing social-protection schemes such as workfare programs, social funds, unemployment insurance, and social security systems, but also extended financial support for the protection of the poor (World Bank 1998a).[18] After admitting that "social policy has come to the forefront of the international debate," Michel Camdessus, managing director of the IMF, claimed that "Asia's experience with crisis reminds us that countries need strong social policies . . . [and] suggests making the concern for social justice truly central to the design of national policies. This calls for enhanced social welfare and protection. . . . Social safety nets are essential to protect those affected by the dislocation—such as unemployment—that remains a risk in even fast-growing economies" (Camdessus 1999:3–4). This remark nicely dovetails with Garrett's proposition that "globalization has increased the political incentives . . . to pursue economic policies that redistribute wealth and risk in favor of those adversely affected . . . by market dislocations" (1998:11).

There is a significant contextual difference between East Asia, where social safety nets are underdeveloped, and Europe, where social-welfare systems are presumably overdeveloped. Even so, one common theme connecting Camdessus and Garrett is that globalization calls for the parallel development of social welfare. Social welfare remains essential in an ever integrating world economy. Such transnational pressures favoring social-welfare reform in the process of structural adjustment have given additional support to the Kim Daejung government in formulating and implementing its productive welfare initiative.

Finally, state capacity matters. State capacity has two major dimensions: quality of executive leadership and availability of resources. South Korea under the Kim government has demonstrated a relatively high level of state capacity in terms of leadership quality and resource availability. First of all, President Kim has been profoundly committed to the promotion of social equality and welfare. Even long before his ascension to the presidency, he championed the causes of equality and welfare under the catchphrase of mass participatory democracy. In fact, he was able to win the past presidential election partly because of coalitional support from the popular sector comprised of workers, urban poor, and liberal forces, and he is obliged to deliver his election pledges to them. Thus, it was natural for him to refocus his attention on distributional dimensions as he managed to overcome the economic crisis. The leadership commitment was vital to the transition by not only stamping out bureaucratic gridlock imbued with the inertia of the developmental state, but also neutralizing the pocket of conservative offensive. Were it not for his commitment, the adoption of the productive welfare initiative could have not been possible. In this sense, President Kim has been quite successful in walking a tightrope between neoliberal reforms and populist mandates.

Beneath the ideological commitment lies a simple political logic of coalition building. From the beginning, the Kim Dae-jung government faced the complex task of meeting the demands of international lenders and foreign investors whose help it needed to recover from the economic crisis, as well as those of the lower-middle and working classes, the main support base of the current government. Despite the robust economic recovery, its effect has yet to be felt by many working and middle-class Koreans who suffered job losses and pay cuts under the structural reforms. And, as noted before, income inequality in South Korea has been reaching levels not seen since the early 1980s. The Gini coefficient rose to 0.37 in the first quarter of 1999, a seventeen-year high, contracting the ratio of the middle class to 64 percent in 1998 from 70.6 percent in 1992, which swelled the ranks of the poor (*Korea Herald,* 16 June 1999, 19 July 1999). President Kim is keenly aware of widespread popular backlash from the reform efforts among some constituencies. Such popular sentiments heightened the ruling regime's anxiety over the general election scheduled for 13 April 2000. In order to win political support from the popular sector, it was essential for President Kim to adopt a much stronger social-welfare system. Thus, his commitment was in part politically motivated.

Such political rationale explains why the South Korean welfare system is being constructed on a style closer to the traditional International Labour Organization model, which upholds the principles of postwar consensus on social welfare: social right, solidarity, and equality. Despite both the World Bank's demand for Medical Saving Accounts and preparation for the Chilean-style multipillar pension system (Kim, Lee, and Kim 1998; World Bank 1998b), and political pressures from supporters of the market-friendly social welfare schemes—such as private insurance companies, big business, medical associations, economic bureaucrats, the opposition party, and a segment of labor unions—the Kim government has taken the opposite path under the political support of and sometimes pressures from civic activist groups and democratic labor unions. It pushed forward the unification of administrative bodies and funds of numerous heath insurance associations into a single authority and incorporated the company pension fund into the unipillar national pension system, all of which are designed to enhance redistributive justice and national solidarity.[19] It is hard to say that the newly emergent welfare state in South Korea is social democratic or Scandinavian. Nonetheless, it is clear that the Korean government has taken a path quite different from its counterparts in Latin American and Eastern European regions, most of which are keen to follow the World Bank's prescriptions.

Yet history is littered with failed social welfare reforms despite the good intentions and commitment of political leaders; there must be the necessary politial capacity for the president and his government to overcome the "notorious" executive-legislative stalemate (Linz and Valenzuela 1994). Two institutional arrangements have helped President Kim consolidate his power and push for ambitious welfare reforms. One is the presidential system, and the other is a rather unique political-party system framed around personalism and factionalism. Executive leadership under the presidential system enjoys enormous political premium. In the case of South Korea, the combination of authoritarian tradition and the strong presidential system has produced almost an imperial presidency. By taking advantage of this institutional arrangement, the executive leader was often able to manufacture legislative majority (Haggard and Moon 1993). The fact that the president's party rarely loses a reliable majority in the legislature is an eloquent testimonial to the power of executive leadership. In fact, from 1948 to the present, there were only two short periods of minority government: one between 1988 and 1989 in the 13th Assembly and the other in the first half of 1998 (the current 15th Assembly) (Kang 1998:104). The Kim Dae-jung government overcame its minority position as well as executive-legislative stalemate partly by making a ruling coalition with the United Liberal Democrats and partly through *Jung-gye-gae-pyon*, or artificial reshuffling of party share in the National Assembly through co-optation of independents and opposition party members into the ruling coalition.[20]

The executive leader in South Korea also exercises enormous partisan power.[21] The president of Korea can control the ruling party and discipline its members through both formal and informal institutional channels. First, the executive leader is also president of the ruling party; thus, he has an ultimate say in the party nomination for parliamentary candidates and the allocation of political funds. Under the single-member district system, which tends to generate a stable two-party system, control over party nomination becomes the most important leverage of the president in disciplining its members.[22] Apart from this intraparty institutional arrangement, the executive leader is also the boss of the largest faction within the ruling party. Formal and informal institutions have empowered president Kim to steer his welfare reform bills through the legislative branch. The sweeping reform of the health and pension programs and the launch of a controversial public-assistance program that guarantees national minimum livelihood may be best understood in such an institutional context. Strong party discipline, stable bipartisan system, and majority in the National Assembly enabled the president and his government to implement social policies as planned. The South Korean case offers an interesting contrast to Brazil, where the combination of a fragmented party system, undisciplined parties, and federalism stalled the able President Cardoso's initiative to mend the frayed social safety net through comprehensive social-security reform.

Social welfare is by nature predicated on higher government spending. Without sufficient revenue flows, states cannot afford to develop an extensive social-welfare system. The Kim Dae-jung government was endowed with relatively good public finance at the onset of the welfare reform (see Table 7.6). Although the financial and corporate sectors rendered poor performance, amassing huge debts and triggering the economic crisis, the South Korean government prior to Kim maintained relatively balanced budgets. As Table 7.6 demonstrates, South Korea's total government debt as share of GDP was 8.6 percent as of 1996, the lowest among the upper-middle-income countries, and interest payment as share of current revenue was only 2.3 percent. Such sound public finance provided the Kim Dae-jung government with more leeway for social-welfare spending (World Bank 1999b).

In sum, South Korea's transition to the welfare state was blessed with several favorable initial conditions. Although the economic crisis was conducive to dismantling the developmental coalition, opening the way to the rise of a distributional coalition, democratic consolidation not only gave birth to the center-left government with a mandate for social-welfare reform, but also expanded space for political maneuver by civil society. Along with this, transnational pressures for the creation of social safety nets, political leadership commitment and capacity, and sound foundation of public finance have all contributed to the dramatic reversal of social-welfare policy in South Korea.

Table 7.6   Central Government Finances
             (Selected Upper-Middle-Income Countries, 1996)

Country	Total Debt (% of GDP)	Interest Payment (% of current revenue)
Argentina	—	13.0
Brazil	—	47.9
Chile	16.6	2.5
Greece	119.2	54.2
Hungary	71.9	20.3
Indonesia	49.3	31.0
Korea	8.6	2.3
Mexico	31.5	18.8
Russia	—	15.8
Turkey	37.9	18.2

Source: World Bank (1999b).

Conclusion

The South Korean experience casts several interesting theoretical, empirical, and policy implications on correlates of globalization and social inequality and welfare in comparative perspectives. First, the South Korean case falsifies both the cornucopian and globaphobic perspectives, while confirming the contextualist perspective. Forces of globalization do not automatically determine the level of social equality and welfare. They are but input variables to be translated into social-welfare policies through the dynamic interplay of the state and domestic political actors. The South Korean case clearly suggests that the rationale for social welfare has not been eroded in the globalization era and the state still retains a considerable level of policy autonomy, enough to build distinctive social-welfare systems. During economic crises and in their aftermath, government can deploy a variety of policy instruments to "shelter their economies from the competitive risks of the international economy" (Cameron 1978:1260). It is ironic to note that the worst economic crisis bred the seeds of the most comprehensive and assertive social-welfare programs in the history of South Korea. This observation directs our attention to the role of the state in mitigating the negative impacts of globalization and neoliberal reforms.

Second, the South Korean case also suggests that successful social-welfare policy requires a rather unique combination of democratic governance, coalitional dynamics, and state capacity. South Korea could have not made the transition to the welfare state unless the center-left Kim Dae-jung government came to power. And the election of Kim Dae-jung as president should have been inconceivable without democratic consolidation and free election. Democratic governance also contributed to expanding and empowering civil society and to re-aligning the structure and process of public policymaking in South Korea. Equally critical are the shifting coalitional dynamics. The waning developmental coalition in the wake of the economic crisis and structural adjustment allowed the distributional coalition to ascend to the commanding height of social-welfare policy. Along with this, political leadership commitment, formal and informal institutional arrangements to ensure the primacy of executive leadership over the legislative branch and the ruling party, and sound public finance have all played an essential role in transforming the developmental state into the welfare state. What makes South Korea distinctly different from other countries is state capacity framed around executive dominance and resource availability. In view of this, path dependence of the developmental state appears to continue to function in the era of the welfare state.

Third, the shifting emphases of international lending institutions such as the IMF and the World Bank deserve special recognition. In the past, the Washington Consensus forged and engineered by both institutions has been notorious for its welfare-busting ideology and practices. But their involvement in South Korea presents a somewhat different picture. Although they still press hard for neoliberal reforms, they have become equally sensitive to social equality and welfare. In fact, the Kim Dae-jung government could have not undertaken the productive welfare initiative without green lights from the IMF and the World Bank. It is not clear whether such a shifting attitude implies a genuine and fundamental realignment of their position on social policy, for South Korea could be an exceptional case owing to its relatively good public-finance position. Nevertheless, international lending institutions' growing concerns with equality and welfare can serve as a positive catalyst in redressing distributional issues and formulating more liberal social policy.

Finally, the declaration of the productive welfare initiative signals a welcome transition to the welfare state in South Korea, but its sustainability cannot be guaranteed. Two major challenges can undercut its viability: one is whether the Kim Dae-jung government can continue to ensure healthy public finance, and the other is whether it can sustain executive dominance and distributional coalition. As to the former, prospects are not encouraging. The share of public debt out of GDP rose from 8.6 percent in 1996 to 14.5 percent in 1997 and 22.3 percent in 1999. Given the ambitious outlay of social-welfare spending embodied in the productive welfare initiative, the burden of public debt is likely to increase. The success of the new initiative will ultimately depend on the government's ability to cope with this debt and to ensure an additional resource base for social-welfare spending. It might be equally difficult to maintain executive dominance and distributional coalition. While the return of economic normalcy has precipitated the conservative resurgence, clouding the future of distributional coalition and its political ascension, increasing intraparty democratization and growing autonomy of the legislative branch could end the era of executive dominance. Political gridlock associated with such developments could significantly weaken state capacity, which could in turn derail the productive welfare initiative. In view of this, South Korea's transition to the welfare state could be uncertain and perilous.

Notes

1. The original version of this chapter was written while Chung-in Moon was a public policy scholar at the Woodrow Wilson Center; he would like to express his thanks to the Wilson Center for its generous research support.

2. This section draws on Moon (2000:69–74).

3. South Korea has been very restrictive of inflow of foreign workers. Although acute labor shortages in the early part of the 1990s facilitated inflow of foreign guest workers, its size has been minimal. And in the wake of the recent economic crisis, there has been an exodus of foreign workers from South Korea.

4. The Roh government initially undertook a campaign for internationalization. The Kim Young Sam government, however, changed it into a globalization campaign. For the analytical and policy differences between the two, see Moon (1995:62–79).

5. The number of corporate bankruptcies rose from 9,502 in 1993 to 12,000 as of October 1997 (see *Weekly Chosun*, 1 January 1998, p. 98).

6. There is an extensive literature on the South Korean economic crisis. For a comprehensive and comparative overview, see Radelet and Sachs (1998). Roubini's website is particularly useful.

7. On the mismatch of macro- and microeconomic indicators, see *Weekly Maekyung* (24 December 1997), pp. 30–33; *Weekly Hangyerae 21* (18 December 1997), pp.74–76; *Monthly Chosun* (January 1998), pp. 30–33, all in Korean.

8. This section draws partly on Jae-jin Yang (2000).

9. It was implemented in 1963. Employers contribute 0.3 to 31.9 percent of payroll, according to risk in industry. Workers do not contribute. There is no minimum qualifying period. Temporary disability benefit is up to 70 percent of daily average earnings. As for permanent disability benefit, if it is total disability, an annual pension equal to 138–329 days of daily average earnings is paid, depending on the degree of disability. Daily average earnings are adjusted according to wage fluctuations. Free medical benefits and survivor benefits are available (U.S. Social Security Administration 1999:207).

10. The history of the public pension system goes back nearly forty years to 1960, when it started covering government employees under a special

scheme. It was followed by two other special pension plans for military personnel in 1963, and then for teachers at private schools in 1975. The government legislated the National Welfare Pension Act in 1973 to introduce a state pension program for the entire population, but implementation had to be postponed because of the oil crisis. The program was implemented in 1988 for those working at companies with ten or more employees. As of 1 April 1999, company employees pay 4.5 percent of covered monthly earnings (i.e., standard monthly remuneration) and employers must match their workers' contributions. Farmers, fishermen, and the self-employed contribute 3 percent of monthly covered earnings. The government is responsible for partial cost of administration and of programs for farmers, fishermen, and urban marginals. Average benefit level, based on forty years of contribution, is 60 percent of preretirement income (U.S. Social Security Administration 1999:206).

11. National health insurance was previously enforced by 142 insurance associations serving company employees and 227 regional insurance societies for general citizens, including the self-employed, not to mention separate administrations for public employees and private teachers. In October 1998, the 227 regional insurance societies and administrations for public employees and teachers were integrated into a new authority called the National Health Insurance Corporation (NHIC). The new National Health Insurance Act, which passed the National Assembly in January 1999, mandates the merger of the remaining associations into the NHIC starting 1 July 2000.

12. The monthly payment will be up to KW324,011 or US$270 (at KW 1,200:1) per person (Ministry of Health and Welfare 1999).

13. The expansion of statutory social-insurance schemes into the informal sector does not necessarily mean universal coverage, since workers who evade contributions are not effectively covered by social-insurance programs. It is too soon to calculate the actual evasions, but it is expected that contribution evasions would be high in the informal sector. Thus, the effective coverage rate would be lower than expected by the Kim government. Nonetheless, it is worth noting that the formal coverage expansion by the Korean government is the first necessary step toward universal coverage.

14. For good overviews of the precrisis social-welfare system in South Korea, please refer to M. Chung (1992), D. Kim (1996), Mehrotra and Jolly (1997), Krause and Park (1993), and Ramesh (1995).

15. It was enacted in 1973 and belatedly implemented in 1988. See endnote no. 11.

16. Their political activities have so far been limited to expressing concern over the unprecedentedly rapid speed at which public social-welfare systems are expanding at welfare-reform–related committee meetings in which civic groups and labor unions take initiative (interview with Jung-tae Kim, director of the social welfare research department, Korea Employers Federation, 12 August 1999). They did not give way at all, however. Ideological offensive against state-administered welfare systems is on the rise through conservative mass media and the Korea Center for Free Enterprise, an affiliate of the Federation of Korean Industries for research and public relations (see Y. Kim 1999a).

17. For details of tripartite compromise on social issues, see T. Kim (1998). Heo (1999) neatly outlines labor strategies on social-welfare issues. For a cautious prospect for the utility of the tripartite commission, see Chung (1998).

18. The $2 billion structural adjustment loan by the World Bank to South Korea, for instance, laid out conditions calling for the extension of unemployment insurance to employees in small-scale enterprises and overhaul of the nation's pension and health insurance systems (World Bank 1998b).

19. This strategy is adopted and pushed by civil activist groups led by the PSPD in alliance with the Korean Confederation of Trade Unions, a peak organization of democratic labor unions born in the wave of democratization since the July democratization movement. For more detailed strategies and tactics, see Y. Kim (1998b).

20. They are usually guaranteed party nomination and political funding for the next general election in return for their "disgraceful" defection. Under the single-member district plurality system, party nomination in the ruling party's regional bases means de facto reelection. Thus, guaranteeing nomination is a very tempting inducement to national assemblymen who seek reelection. So far, twenty-six assembly members made the switch to the ruling party (*Joongang Ilbo*, 19 October 1999). Despite rather frequent changes in party label, party discipline remains strong in terms of party vote. There is no cross-voting in Korea because it is regarded as treachery to the party and party boss. Those who cast a ballot against the party decision must risk losing party nomination in the next general election.

21. For more theoretical and empirical discussions of the partisan and constitutional power of presidents, see Mainwaring and Shugart (1997). It is also a good source for various types of presidentialism and interactions between the executive and legislative branches.

22. For a detailed theoretical discussion of the effect of electoral law and nomination rule on politicians' behavior, see Carey and Shugart (1994) and Samuels (1999).

PART 3

CONCLUSION

8

Toward a New Economic Paradigm: Crafting a Research Agenda for the Twenty-First Century

Bolivar Lamounier, Steven Friedman & Joseph S. Tulchin

As many of the preceding chapters have illustrated, economic paradigms that relied on the state to expand productive potential while distributing its fruits to all are in retreat. Reliance on the market to perform these tasks is so nearly universal that former communist parties in Eastern Europe win reelection—and then implement policies almost indistinguishable from those of their market-oriented opponents. And yet the inequality that socialism and social democracy sought to address shows no sign of disappearing.

The world today seems increasingly divided between "winning" and "losing" societies, and the divisions between haves and have-nots *within* societies seem as intractable as ever. As economies become more exposed to and dependent on the international marketplace, the constraints on the ability of individual countries to shape their own macroeconomic policies are, in the view of some analyses, increasing. Rewards for "winning" and penalties for "losing" appear to grow steadily. An entire continent, Africa, risks relegation to permanent loser status. Even within the "winning" societies of the First World, inequality in the distribution of wealth and opportunity continues to grow: some Western European countries face high unemployment and fiscal pressures that limit the resources available to address inequality. Even in the United States, some voices warn that the poverty evident on the peripheries of society may begin to spread to its core. These dangers are heightened by the unprecedented rapidity of social processes—trends that once took centuries to reach fruition now take at most a generation.

Decades ago, widening inequality between and within societies might have mattered politically far less, whatever human consequences it may have produced. Outside the small club of established representative democracies, the dominant view was that inequality was irremediable by government or collective effort. That some prospered and others did not seemed ordained by the natural order. Today, this ideological support for inequality is under unprecedented stress. The global wave of formal democratization, beginning in Portugal in the mid-1970s and spreading to southern Europe, Latin America, and then to Eastern Europe, Africa, and parts of Asia, has produced a growing desire for equality. If the state or market in these societies proves unable to provide rising living standards for all, the aspirations that the spread of formal democracy has produced may trigger enhanced social conflict, threatening a descent into anarchy or a new authoritarianism.

Effective responses to these new and potent aspirations seem as unlikely today as ever before. Enormous potential for disappointment is therefore breeding in a context in which the extension of formal democracy to all the corners of the globe is threatened by the erosion of the stable and legitimate state that is this form of democracy's precondition. Outside the industrialized North and in some cases within it, states find it increasingly difficult to fulfill their basic Hobbesian rationale: the maintenance of legitimate public order. In many societies, the relationship between citizenry and state becomes increasingly tenuous as putative citizens, faced with states that can neither offer the benefits nor impose the sanctions central to liberal democratic ideas of the state, opt out by choice or default, prompting warnings that chaos, not orderly democratic citizenship, may be the leitmotif of the twenty-first century. In some, the state dissolves entirely, giving way either to regional fiefdoms—as in parts of west Africa—or to ever-smaller, often ethnically defined, units. European statelets that seemed to have been abolished forever by World War I have rapidly reappeared over the past decade.

Population growth and urbanization in the Third World and increasing poverty may enormously expand what some call the demand for discipline, internal or externally imposed, increasing the growth potential of fundamentalist and authoritarian religious and political movements. As international migration increases, populations within most national frontiers are likely to become more heterogeneous, straining domestic and international governability and greatly expanding the potential for conflict. This challenge is daunting enough to make a mockery of the barriers that have so far insulated a few countries of the First World and made it possible for them to preserve high standards of material well-being, political order and freedom, and cultural pluralism. It also begs a rigorous analysis of the preconditions for democracy in this new world context.

It is possible that, as some have argued, the trends described in this book are merely the birth pangs of a new world order, more capable than any we have known of guaranteeing human liberty and happiness. In this view, the trends of the late twentieth century and early twenty-first century would be analogous to the industrial revolution of the early nineteenth century. The old order, economic and political, is fragmenting because it has served its purpose. The dissolution is inevitably painful, just as the previous revolution was, but the pain is the price of unprecedented human advance.

Yet the contrary view, which sees in current trends new threats to human progress, is equally plausible: it is certainly possible that the aspirations engendered by formally equal citizenship, with the inability of formally democratic states, old and new, to meet them, could prompt new and intolerable stresses on both democracy and order. And even if the optimistic view were to be conceded without debate, a postindustrial revolution in the context we have sketched would be likely to engender conflicts that may prove unmanageable.

The choice between these two views remains largely arbitrary. We simply cannot be sure at this stage whether the political and economic paradigms we have inherited are realistic, much less whether they will guide us safely to the policies we need to alleviate mass poverty, reduce social inequalities, and ensure meaningful democratic citizenship in the next century.

If, therefore, humanity is to be equipped adequately to confront the challenges of this rapidly evolving new world, it is urgently necessary to subject the familiar paradigms within which the emerging realities are now understood to critical scrutiny, conceptually and in the light of empirical reality. The aim must be to begin a debate aimed at discarding those elements that describe a past never to be recovered and at developing ones more appropriate to the world being born. But where should this debate begin? We propose a focus on three research areas—reconciling, rebuilding, and redressing.

Reconciling refers to the need to moderate and institutionalize political conflict. Research along these lines would examine the political parameters in which attempts to address poverty and inequality—and to maintain or consolidate democracy—must proceed. Under the assumption that the political viability of social policy is as important as its technical merits, this category would require an examination of the recent political history of each country, current political processes, levels and types of conflict; relevant institutional features; interest group formation and the relative influence of key interests; dominant world views among key currents of opinion in society; and the extent of access to the political system, particularly for the poor. These and other factors will help to delineate the likely coalitions under which policies will be made and implemented over the next decade.

Rebuilding addresses the need to rethink the role and probably rebuild the capabilities of the democratic state, including its interaction with nonstate actors. Here the accent falls, first, on the nature of the state machinery and its bureaucratic apparatus, with the premise that the responses to the challenges discussed above will need to be tailored to the capacity of states if they are to be workable. Possible research questions would be: How is the state machinery organized and financed, what can it do or not do well? What are the likely trends over the next decade and how do these affect the probable impact of social and economic trends and responses to them? The second part of rebuilding focuses on nonstate actors: their strengths, weaknesses, and capacities. The rationale is that policy will need the endorsement and, most likely, active participation of key interests in civil society and it is therefore necessary to evaluate its influence and capacity, particularly at the local level in terms of policy's capacity to mobilize the poor and give them a voice in the political process.

The final research category, redressing, reflects the need to respond to unsustainable inequalities that may threaten democracy and economic viability by devising affordable social-policy instruments that are within the capability of states and societies. Here the focus falls squarely on social policy—on potential to address poverty and inequality. The key theme is how poverty and inequality are perceived by actors relevant to the policy process. Which policies are seen as desirable and feasible? Which have been implemented and with what results? Which are likely to be implemented over the next decade? What are their likely impacts? How viable are current proposals and what alternatives are possible? Questions could include the costs of trying to ensure a particular minimum standard for a society's citizens and calculations of the practicability of incremental reductions in inequality.

These suggested research categories are not hermetically sealed; rather, they are interrelated. Addressing them in an interrelated way will require an interdisciplinary approach, bringing together political scientists, economists, social-policy specialists, and scholars in other branches of social science.

A formidable body of research has been conducted on specific social problems and policies. While it is important to learn as much as possible from it, the aim of future research should be to place this information—and fresh data—in a more meaningful comparative and theoretical context, one that explicitly explores the relationship between democracy on the one hand, poverty and inequality on the other. In the past, this task of subjecting paradigms to searching tests was the work of individual thinkers cloistered in a study or library. Today that approach no longer seems valid. The challenges that confront us share common features across national and even continental divides—being global, they require a globally coordinated research response. It is equally evident that, although global in nature, the impact of the problems we are considering is felt differently in different societies—in some cases, each locality—where different political, cultural, and social parameters and histories make for different experiences and recourse to differing remedies.

This task can therefore be attempted only by treating country- and locality-specific empirical realities with great respect. It is also too complex to be left to a single individual or group of individuals in a particular region. Only by comparing the insights of researchers and thinkers across regions spanning the entire globe are we likely to improve upon the explanations and remedies offered thus far. Global sameness and local difference must both be taken into account.

Several key issues will need to be addressed. One is the changing state-citizen relationship. Is the "social contract" being redefined by circumstance? In many Third World countries, is the contract still in force? If the dominant paradigm was once how to democratize the overweening state, the current one may be how to rebuild or reconstitute the state, given its declining reach. Underlying T. H. Marshall's 1964 classic essay on citizenship was a notion of the state not only as a guarantor of public order but also a deliverer of entitlements that made citizenship possible. But if the latter role is no longer viable or is being attenuated, the former may not be possible either. What sort of state is, then, emerging or can emerge and what are the implications for democracy and social policy?

A related question is whether new ways of performing the social-policy function can emerge that entail an idea of state capacity very different from that assumed until now. The emerging paradigm stresses partnership between the state and private interests or citizens. The idea of civil society—the realm of organized interest associations—as a key actor in attempts to secure greater liberty and social equality has enjoyed a revival among intellectuals and policymakers in donor agencies and multilateral financial institutions. How viable is this alternative model, and what sort of state capacity does it require? Have informal substitutes for state-made policy emerged? If so, what is their form and their implications for democracy? What is the potential for, and the constraints on, civil society's role in securing democracy and reducing poverty and inequality?

Another important issue is whether the polities of the twenty-first century will be able to achieve significant and quick changes in social structure without endangering democracy. Since the beginning of the twentieth century, revolutions or quasi-revolutions aimed to address social inequality rapidly: the result was either unstable "movement regimes" or authoritarian rule with modest or no progress to greater equality. How will the polities of the twenty-first century address this issue? Can they find ways of improving social conditions while reinforcing democracy? And can democracy survive without significant reduction in social inequality?

It is also necessary to assess states' room for maneuver in the global environment. Is there only one route to global integration or several, as the experience of some Asian societies suggested until a while ago? If the latter, what is the relationship between country-specific political contexts and feasible modes of adaptation to globalization? What are the advantages and disadvantages of different regimes and types of democracy? Are modes of interest representation such as democratic corporatism and tripartite policy negotiation still viable?

Another crucial issue is the "insider-outsider" problem. Since cross-border migration is a growing global issue, what are its implications for social policy? Traditionally, social policy was for citizens alone, as suggested by Marshall's concept of citizenship. In many cases, generous social policy regimes were achieved partly by erecting high barriers to entry. If such barriers are becoming increasingly untenable, what are the implications for social policy in the next century? Is it possible to conceive of social policy operating within the borders of a single country? Southern Africa, with its stark inequalities between countries, may illustrate the fragility of seeking to address inequalities in one country only. From another point of view, fast capital flows across borders point to the possible need to consider social policy in a cross-national or cross-regional manner. The debate on European Union social clauses may be one sign of this change in the framework of social policy. Central to Keynes's program was international financial regulation, expressed in the Bretton Woods mechanisms. Does the need to rethink social policy also entail a need to reassess these instruments? If so, what form will new ones take and what might their implications be for state sovereignty and the state-citizen relationship?

The issues we identify here are, however, not of concern to Northern countries simply because they may prompt migration from South to North or precipitate horrific acts of terrorist violence. The problems affect Northern countries' domestic polities and economies too.

The decades of postwar affluence in the North are under severe stress and current trends could also make poverty and inequality growing problems in these societies. And, while it might be assumed that Northern countries are better equipped to deal with them, this cannot be asserted without further inquiry. Northern experiences of these issues also shed light on their likely impact on established democracies, which cannot, without further examination, automatically be assumed to be less prone to challenge than the often new and fragile Southern democracies. For these reasons, studying Southern countries alone would address only part of the problem. Researching Northern countries also provides a point of comparison with which to evaluate Southern experiences and examine the contention of some analysts that there is a direct link between Northern prosperity and Southern poverty.

This book has attempted to lay a groundwork for future research on the questions raised above. The intent is not to settle debate but rather to spark debate about the relationship between democratic governance and social inequality in the twenty-first century. The preceding chapters have tried to offer some new ways of thinking about democracy and inequality in both theoretical and empirical terms. It is our hope that the ideas presented in this book will encourage further research and more informed policymaking—small steps toward a more democratic and just world.

Bibliography

Agüero, Felipe. 1998. "Conflicting Assessments of Democratization: Exploring the Fault Lines," in *Fault Lines of Democracy in Post-Transition Latin America,* edited by Felipe Agüero and Jeffrey Stark. Miami: North-South Center Press.

Agüero, Felipe, and Jeffrey Stark. 1998. "Conclusion," in *Fault Lines of Democracy in Post-Transition Latin America,* edited by Felipe Agüero and Jeffrey Stark. Miami: North-South Center Press.

Ahn, Byung-young. 1991. "A Road Toward a Welfare State" (in Korean). *Sindong-ah* (November): 122–140.

———. 1989. *Asia's Next Giant: South Korean and Late Industrialization.* New York: Oxford University Press.

Ali, Shaikh Maqsood, and Susil Sirivardana. 1996. "Towards a New Paradigm for Poverty Eradication in South Asia." *UNESCO International Social Science Journal* (June).

Alvarez, Sonia, Evelina Dagnino, and Arturo Escobar. 1998. "Introduction," in *Cultures of Politics, Politics of Cultures: Re-visioning Latin American Social Movements,* edited by Sonia E. Alvarez, Evelina Dagnino, and Arturo Escobar. Boulder, CO: Westview Press.

Amsden, Alice H. 1992. "The South Korean Economy: Is Business-Led Growth Working?" in *Korea Briefing,* edited by Donald N. Clark. Boulder, CO: Westview Press.

———. 1989. *Asia's Next Giant: South Korean and Late Industrialization.* New York: Oxford University Press.

Ardington, E., and F. Lund. 1995. "Pensions and Development: How the Social Security System Can Complement Programmes of Reconstruction and Development." Occasional Paper 61. Development Bank of Southern Africa, February.

Arrow, Kenneth J. 1963 [1951]. *Social Choice and Individual Values.* New Haven, CT: Yale University Press.

Bank of Korea. 1998. "Tongasia kumyungwigi-eui woninkwa pakeukwajung: World Bank-ui jindan" (The Causes and Impacts of Financial Crisis in East Asia). Summarized from "Global Development Finance" and "Global Economic Prospects and the Developing Countries: Short-Term Update" by the World Bank.

173

Barber, Benjamin. 1998. *A Place for Us: How to Make Society Civil and Democracy Strong.* New York: Hill and Wang.

Bell, Daniel. 1960. *The End of Ideology.* Glencoe, IL: Free Press.

Bello, Walden. 1997. "Addicted to Capital—The Ten-Year High and Present-Day Withdrawal Trauma of Southeast Asia's Economies." Bangkok: Focus on the Global South.

Benhabib, Seyla. 1999. "Citizens, Residents and Aliens in a Changing World: Political Membership in the Global Era." *Social Research* 66, no. 3 (fall).

Bhorat, H. 1999. "Income Transfers: A Viable Strategy." Job Creation Series, Policy Forum No. 3, Center for Policy Studies, Johannesburg, South Africa.

Bollen, Kenneth. 1993. "Liberal Democracy: Validity and Method Factors in Cross-National Measures." *American Journal of Political Science* 37, no. 4 (November): 1207–1230.

Bollen, Kenneth A., and Pamela Paxton. 1998. "Detection and Determinants of Bias in Subjective Measures." *American Sociological Review* 63 (June): 465–478.

Bowles, S., and H. Gintis. 1996. "Efficient Redistribution: New Rules for Markets, States and Communities." *Politics and Society* 24, no. 4 (December).

Brooks, Sarah M. 1999. "Social Protection and the Market: Pension Reform in the Era of Capital Mobility." Paper presented for the Annual Meeting of the American Political Science Association, Atlanta, Georgia, September 1–5.

Bullard, Nicola. 1998. "Taming the Tigers: The IMF and the Asian Crisis." Bangkok and London: Focus on the Global South and CAFOD, April.

Burtless, G., R. Lawrence, R. Litan, and R. Shapiro. 1998. *Globaphobia: Confronting Fears About Open Trade.* Washington, DC: Brookings Institution.

Camdessus, Michell. 1999. "Sustaining Asia's Recovery from Crisis." Remarks at the 34th South East Asian Central Banks Governors' Conference, Seoul, Korea, May 20. http://www.imf.org/external/np/speeches/1999/052099.htm1999.

Cameron, David R. 1978. "The Expansion of the Public Economy: A Comparative Analysis." *American Political Science Review* 72, no. 4: 1243–1261.

Carey, John M., and Matthew S. Shugart. 1994. "Incentives to Cultivate a Personal Vote: A Ranking Ordering of Electoral Formulas." *Electoral Studies* 14, no. 4: 417–439.

Cerdas-Cruz, Rodolfo, Juan Rial, and Daniel Zovatto, eds. 1992. *Una tarea inconclusa: Elecciones y democracia en América Latina, 1988–1991.* San José, Costa Rica: IIDH-CAPEL.

Chambers, Robert. 1983. *Rural Development: Putting the Last First.* New York: John Wiley and Sons.

Chung, Moo-kwon. 1998. "Social Policy of 'the Government of People': Evaluation and Remaining Task" (in Korean). Paper presented at the Annual Meeting of the Korean Social Science Research Council.

———. 1992. "State Autonomy, State Capacity, and Public Policy: The Development of Social Security Policy in Korea." Ph.D. dissertation, Indiana University.

Clavel, P. 1996. "The Community Option in Urban Policy." Working Papers in Planning. Ithaca, NY: Cornell University Press.

Clayton, Richard, and Jonas Pontusson. 1998. "Welfare-State Retrenchment Revisited: Entitlement Cuts, Public Sector Restructuring, and Inegalitarian Trends in Advanced Capitalist Societies." *World Politics* 51, no. 1: 67–98.

Collier, David, and Robert Adcock. 1999. "Democracy and Dichotomies: A Pragmatic Approach to Choices About Concepts." *Annual Review of Political Science* 2: 537–565.

Collier, David, and Steven Levitsky. 1997. "Democracy with Adjectives: Conceptual Innovation in Comparative Research." *World Politics* 49 (April): 430–451.

Commission on Planning and Budget. 1999. *Summary of Budget for Fiscal Year 1999* (in Korean). Seoul: CPB.

Conaghan, Catharine M. 1996. "A Deficit of Democratic Authenticity: Political Linkage and the Public in Andean Politics." *Studies in Comparative International Development* 31, no. 3 (fall): 32–55.

Cox, Robert. 1997. "Structural Issues of Global Governance: Implications for Europe," in *A New Europe in the Changing Global System,* edited by Richard Falk and Tamás Szentes. New York: United Nations University Press.

Crick, Bernard R. 1993. *In Defence of Politics.* Chicago: University of Chicago Press.

Crook, Clive. 1997. "The World Economy." *The Economist,* 20 September.

Dahl, Robert. 1999. "The Shifting Boundaries of Democratic Governments." *Social Research* 66, no. 3 (fall).

———. 1971. *Polyarchy: Participation and Opposition.* New Haven, CT: Yale University Press.

———. 1961. *Who Governs? Democracy and Power in an American City.* New Haven, CT: Yale University Press.

Davidson, James Dale, and William Rees-Mogg. 1997. *The Sovereign Individual: How to Survive and Thrive During the Collapse of the Welfare State.* New York: Simon & Schuster.

De Soto, Hernando. 1989. *The Other Path.* New York: Harper and Row.

De Souza, Amaury. 1996. "Dilemmas of Industrial Relations Reform: Learning from Brazil's Interest Representation Experience," in *Comparing Brazil and South Africa: Two Transitional States in Political and Economic Perspective,* edited by Steven Friedman and Riaan de Villiers. Johannesburg: Centre for Policy Studies, Foundation for Global Dialogue, Economic, Social, and Political Studies, Institute of São Paulo.

De Swaan, Abram. 1988. *In Care of the State.* Cambridge: Cambridge University Press.

Denzau, Arthur T., and Douglass C. North. 1994. "Shared Mental Models: Ideologies and Institutions." *Kyklos* 47, no. 1.

Diamond, Larry. 1999. *Developing Democracy: Toward Consolidation.* Baltimore: Johns Hopkins University Press.

Diamond, Larry, Jonathan Hartlyn, and Juan J. Linz. 1999. "Introduction," in *Democracy in Developing Countries: Latin America,* edited by Larry Diamond, Jonathan Hartlyn, Juan J. Linz, and Seymour Martin Lipset. Boulder, CO: Lynne Rienner Publishers.

———. 1989. *Democracy in Developing Countries: Asia.* London: Adamantine Press.

Dornbush, Rudiger, and Y.C. Park. 1995. "Financial Integration in a Second-Best World: Are We Still Sure About Our Classical Prejudices," in *Financial Opening: Policy Lessons for Korea,* edited by Rudiger Dornbush and Y. C. Park. Seoul: Korea Institute of Finance.

Douglas, William O. 1974. *Go East, Young Man.* New York: Random House.

Downs, Anthony. 1957. *An Economic Theory of Democracy.* New York: Harper and Row.

Dreze, Jean, and Amartya Sen. 1995. *India: Social and Economic Opportunity.* Oxford: Oxford University Press.

Easton, David. 1953. *The Political System.* New York: Knopf.

Eschweiler, Bernhard. 1998. "Asia Has Hit Bottom." *Asian Wall Street Journal,* 13–14 November.

Esping-Andersen, Gosta. 1990. *The Three Worlds of Welfare Capitalism.* Princeton, NJ: Princeton University Press.

———. ed. 1996. *Welfare States in Transition: National Adaptations in Global Economies.* Thousand Oaks, CA.: Sage Publications.

Evans, Peter. 1997. "The Eclipse of the 'State': Reflection in Stateness in an Era of Globalization." *World Politics* 50, no.1: 63–87.

———. 1995. *Embedded Autonomy: States and Industrial Transformation.* Princeton, NJ: Princeton University Press, 1995.

———. 1992. "The State as Problem and Solution: Predation, Embedded Autonomy and Structural Change," in *The Politics of Economic Adjustment,* edited by S. Haggard and R. R. Kaufman. Princeton, NJ: Princeton University Press.

Faux, Jeff, and Larry Mishel. 2000. "Inequality and the Global Economy," in *Global Capitalism,* edited by Will Hutton and Anthony Giddens. New York: New Press.

Feridhanusetyawan, Tubagus. 1997. "Survey of Recent Developments." *BIES* 33: 2 (August).

Fischer, Stanley. 1998. Forum Funds lecture at UCLA, Los Angeles, 20 March.

Flora, Peter, and Arnold J. Heidenheimer. 1981. *The Development of Welfare States in Europe and America.* New Brunswick, NJ: Transaction Books.

Friedman, Steven. 1999. "Who We Are: Voter Participation, Rationality and the 1999 Election." *Politikon* 26, no. 2.

———. 1993. *The Elusive "Community": The Dynamics of Negotiated Urban Development.* Johannesburg: Centre for Policy Studies.

———. 1992. "Bonaparte at the Barricades: The Colonisation of Civil Society." *Theoria* (Durban, South Africa).

Frühling, Hugo, and Joseph S. Tulchin (with Heather A. Golding), eds. Forthcoming. *Crime and Violence in Latin America: Citizen Security, Democracy, and the State.* Washington, DC: John Hopkins University Press and Woodrow Wilson Center Press.

Garretón, Manuel Antonio. 1999. "Representatividad y partidos políticos: Los problemas actuales." August. <http://www.iigov.org/wwwboard/messages>.

———. 1993. *La faz sumergida del iceberg: Estudios sobre la transformación cultural.* Santiago: CESOC-LOM.

Garrett, Geoffrey. 1998. *Partisan Politics in the Global Economy.* New York: Cambridge University Press.

Garrett, Geoffrey, and Peter Lange. 1995. "Internationalization, Institutions and Political Change." *International Organization* 49: 627–655.

Gasiorowski, Mark J., and Timothy J. Power. 1998. "The Structural Determinants of Democratic Consolidation: Evidence from the Third World." *Comparative Political Studies* (December).

George, Henry. 1948. *Progress and Poverty,* 50th anniversary edition. New York: Robert Schalkenbach Foundation.

Gilder, George. 1981. *Wealth and Poverty.* New York: Bantam Books.

Gill, S. 1995. "Globalization, Market Civilization, and Disciplinary Neoliberalism." *Millennium* 24: 399–423.

Greider, William. 1997. *One World, Ready or Not—The Manic Logic of Global Capitalism*. New York: Simon & Schuster.

Grodzins, Morton. 1960. "American Political Parties and the American System." *Western Political Quarterly* XIII.

Gunther, Richard, P. Nikiforos Diamandouros, and Hans-Jürgen Puhle. 1996. "O'Donnell's 'Illusions': A Rejoinder." *Journal of Democracy* 7, no. 4: 151–159.

Habermas, Jürgen. 1971. *Towards a Rational Society*. New York: Beacon.

Haggard, Stephan. 1990. *Pathways from the Periphery*. Ithaca, NY: Cornell University Press.

Haggard, Stephan, and Robert Kaufman. 1995. *The Political Economy of Democratic Transitions*. Princeton, NJ: Princeton University Press.

Haggard, Stephan, and Chung-in Moon. 1993. "The State, Politics and Economic Development in Post-War South Korea," in *State and Society in Contemporary Korea*, edited by Hagen Koo. Ithaca, NY: Cornell University Press.

———. 1983. "The South Korean State in the International Economy: Liberal, Dependent or Mercantile," in *Antinomies of Interdependence*, edited by John Ruggie. New York: Columbia University Press.

Hartlyn, Jonathan. 1998a. "Democracies in Contemporary South America: Convergences and Diversities," in *Argentina: The Challenges of Modernization*, edited by Joseph S. Tulchin with Allison M. Garland. Wilmington: Scholarly Resources Inc.

———. 1998b. "Political Continuities, Missed Opportunities, and Institutional Rigidities: Another Look at Democratic Transitions in Latin America," in *Politics, Society, and Democracy: Latin America*, edited by Scott Mainwaring and Arturo Valenzuela. Boulder, CO: Westview Press.

Hartlyn, Jonathan, and John Dugas. 1999. "Colombia: The Politics of Violence and Democratic Transformation," in *Democracy in Developing Countries: Latin America*, 2nd edition, edited by Larry Diamond, Jonathan Hartlyn, Juan J. Linz, and Seymour Martin Lipset. Boulder, CO: Lynne Rienner Publishers.

Hartlyn, Jonathan, and Arturo Valenzuela. 1994. "Democracy in Latin America Since 1930," in *Cambridge History of Latin America*, Vol. VI, Part 2: *Latin America Since 1930: Economy, Society and Politics*, edited by Leslie Bethell. Cambridge: Cambridge University Press.

Havel, Vaclav. 1999. "Kosovo and the End of the Nation-State." *The New York Review* (10 June): 4–6.

Heo, Young-Koo. 1999. "Social Welfare and Labor Reform" (in Korean). *Monthly Welfare Trend* (August): 13–17.

Hesion, Charles, and Hyman Saardy. 1969. *Ascent to Affluence: A History of American Economic Development*. Boston: Allyn & Bacon.

Heye, Christopher. 1993. "Labor Market Tightness and Business Confidence: An International Comparison." *Politics & Society* 21, no. 2 (June): 169–193.

Holston, James, and Teresa Caldeira. 1998. "Democracy, Law, and Violence: Disjunctions of Brazilian Citizenship," in *Fault Lines of Democracy in Post-Transition Latin America*, edited by Felipe Agüero and Jeffrey Stark. Miami: North-South Center Press.

Htun, Mala N. 1998. "Women's Political Participation, Representation, and Leadership in Latin America." Women's Leadership Conference of the

Americas, Inter-American Dialogue, and International Center for Research on Women, Washington, DC, November.

Huber, Evelyne, Dietrich Rueschemeyer, and John D. Stephens. 1997. "The Paradoxes of Contemporary Democracy: Formal, Participatory, and Social Dimensions." *Comparative Politics* (April): 323–342.

Human Rights Watch. 2000. *The Ties That Bind: Colombia and Military-Paramilitary Links.* New York: Human Rights Watch, February.

Hutchcroft, Paul. 1993. "Predatory Oligarchy, Patrimonial State: The Politics of Private, Domestic Commercial Banking in the Philippines." Ph.D. dissertation, Yale University.

Hyundai Economic Research Institute (HERI). 1999. *The Survey of Middle Class Conception.* Seoul: HERI.

Inter-American Development Bank (IDB). 2000. *Development Beyond Economics: Economic and Social Progress in Latin America.* Washington, DC: IDB and Johns Hopkins University Press.

International Monetary Fund. 1997. "Korea—Memorandum on Economic Progress." Seoul: International Monetary Fund, 3 December.

James, William E. 1995. "Survey of Recent Developments." BIES XXXI (December): 3.

Jencks, Christopher. 1992. *Rethinking Social Policy.* Cambridge, MA: Harvard University Press.

Johnson, Chalmers. 1987. "Political Institutions and Economic Performance: A Comparative Analysis of the Government-Business Relationship in Japan, South Korea, and Taiwan," in *The Political Economy of the New Asian Industrialism,* edited E. Deyo. Ithaca, NY: Cornell University Press.

Jordan, Bill. 1998. *The New Politics of Welfare.* London: Sage.

Kang, Jangseok. 1998. "A Dilemma of Presidentialism." *Korean Journal of Legislative Studies* 4, no.1: 99–119.

Katzenstein, Peter J. 1985. *Small States in World Markets: Industrial Policy in Europe.* Ithaca, NY: Cornell University Press.

Kay, Stephen J. 1999. "Unexpected Privatizations: Politics and Social Security Reform in the Southern Cone." *Comparative Politics* 31, no. 4: 403–422.

Keane, John. 1988. *Democracy and Civil Society.* London and New York: Verso.

Keller, William W., Theodore J. Lowi, and Gerry Gendlin. 2000. "Negative Capital and the Wealth of Nations." *International Studies Perspectives* 1 (January): 75–87.

Kim, Chang-yup, Tae-soo Lee, and Yeon-myung Kim. 1998."What Does IBRD Demand from US?" (in Korean). *Monthly Welfare Trend* (November): 33–41.

Kim, Dae-jung. 1999. "Presidential Address on the 54th Anniversary of National Liberation: To Open a New Millennium of Hope and Prosperity." Available at <http://www.koreaherald.co.kr/cgi-bin/sear...path=/news/1999/08/11/19990816_1134.htm>.

Kim, Dong Sung. 1996. "Social Welfare Policy in the East Asian and Latin American NICs: A Comparative Study of Social Welfare Variations." Ph.D. disseration, Government and Politics, University of Maryland at College Park.

Kim, Jin-yong, 1999."The Impact of Foreign Stock Investment Inflows on Domestic Stock Prices" (in Korean). The Bank of Korea, *Monthly Bulletin* (October): 36–56.

Kim, Samuel. 2000. "South Korea's *Segyewha* (Globalization): A Framework for Analysis," in *South Korea and* Segyewha *(Globalization),* edited by Sam Kim. New York: Cambridge University Press.

Kim, Tae-hyun. 1998. "Report! Social Security Subcommittee of the Second Tripartite Commission" (in Korean). *Monthly Welfare Trend* (November): 30–32.

Kim, Yeon-myung. 1998a. "Low-Growth—High-Unemployment Society: Let's Weave Social Safety Nets" (in Korean), in *The IMF Era and Korean Social Welfare,* edited by the Social Welfare Subcommittee of People's Solidarity for Participatory Democracy, Seoul, Korea.

———. 1998b. "Korean Labor Movement and Strategy for Social Security: Conditions for Political Alliance and Task" (in Korean). *Korean Journal of Social Welfare* 34, no. 4: 23–44.

———. 1999a. "False Press Report of Nation Pension Beyond Acceptable Level." *Monthly Welfare Trend* (June).

———. 1999b. "Great Experiment and Unclear Future" (in Korean). *Sin-dong-ah* (December).

Kim, Yong-Cheol, and Chung-in Moon. 2000. "Globalization and Workers," in *Segyehwa Strategy of South Korea,* edited by Samuel Kim. New York: Cambridge University Press.

King, D., and J. Waldron. 1988. "Citizenship, Social Citizenship and the Defence of Welfare Provision." *British Journal of Political Science* 18: 415–443.

Kissinger, Henry. 1998. "The Asian Collapse: One Fix Does Not Fit All Economies." *Washington Post,* 9 February.

Korea Trade-Investment Promotion Agency (KOTRA). 1995. *Han'guk Kyungewa OECD* (OECD and Korean Economy). Seoul: KOTRA.

Krouse, L., and F. Park, eds. 1993. *Social Issues in Korea: Korean and American Perspectives.* Seoul: Korean Development Institute.

Krugman, Paul. 1998a. *Pop Internationalism.* Cambridge, MA: MIT Press.

———. 1998b. "Asia: What Went Wrong?" *Fortune* (2 March).

Kwon, Huck-ju. 1999. *The Welfare State in Korea: The Politics of Legitimation.* New York: St. Martin's Press.

Lamounier, Bolivar. 1999. "Brazil: Inequality Against Democracy," in *Democracy in Developing Countries: Latin America,* 2nd edition, Larry Diamond, Jonathan Hartlyn, Juan J. Linz, and Seymour Martin Lipset, eds. Boulder, CO: Lynne Rienner Publishers.

———. 1997. *A democracia brasileira no limiar do século 21,* 2nd edition, São Paulo: Konrad Adenaur Stiftung.

Landman, J. P. 1999. "Is the Washington Consensus Dead?" Seminar convened by Centre for Policy Studies, Johannesburg, June.

Lechner, Norbert. 1997. "Los condicionantes de la gobernabilidad democrática en América Latina de fin de siglo," in *40 Aniversario de FLACSO: 1957–1997.* Buenos Aires: FLASCO.

Lee, He-kyung. 1994. "The Present State of the Korean Social Policy and the Direction for the Future" (in Korean). *Kyungjejungei (Economic Justice)* (fall): 87–106.

———. 1993. "Korean Social Security System: The Limitation of Compressed Growth and Task for De-Instrumentalization." *Yonsei Social Welfare Studies* 1: 63–91.

Levine, Daniel, and Brian Crisp. 1999. "Venezuela: The Character, Crisis, and Possible Future of Democracy," in *Democracy in Developing Countries: Latin America,* 2nd edition, edited by Larry Diamond, Jonathan Hartlyn, Juan J. Linz, and Seymour Martin Lipset, eds. Boulder, CO: Lynne Rienner Publishers.

Linz, Juan J., and Alfred Stepan. 1996. *Problems of Democratic Transition and Consolidation: Southern Europe, South America, and Post-Communist Europe.* Baltimore: Johns Hopkins University Press.

Linz, Juan, and Arturo Valenzuela. 1994. *The Failure of Presidential Democracy: The Case of Latin America.* Baltimore: Johns Hopkins University Press.

Lipset, Seymour Martin. 1964. "Introduction," in *Class, Citizenship and Social Development,* by T. H. Marshall. Westport, CT: Greenwood Press.

Lowenthal, Abraham F., and Jorge I. Domínguez. 1996. "Introduction," in *Constructing Democratic Governance: Latin America and the Caribbean in the 1990—Themes and Issues,* edited by Jorge I. Domínguez and Abraham F. Lowenthal. Baltimore: Johns Hopkins University Press.

Lowi, Theodore. 1998. "Think Globally, Lose Locally." *The Boston Review* (April/May).

———. 1985. "The State in Politics," in *Regulatory Policy and the Social Sciences,* edited by Roger Noll. Berkeley: University of California Press.

———. 1976. *American Government: Incomplete Conquest.* Hinsdale, IL: Dryden Press.

———. 1975. "Party, Policy and Constitution in America," in *The American Party System—Stages of Political Development,* 2nd edition, edited by William N. Chambers and Walter Dean Burnham. New York: Oxford University Press.

———. 1971. *The Politics of Disorder.* New York: Basic Books.

———. 1969. *The End of Liberalism: Ideology, Policy, and the Crisis of Public Authority.* New York: Norton.

Madison, James. 1961a. "Federalist No. 1," in *The Federalist Papers,* edited by Clinton Rossiter. New York: New American Library.

———. 1961b. "Federalist No. 51," in *The Federalist Papers,* edited by Clinton Rossiter. New York: New American Library.

Mainwaring, Scott. 1999a. "Democratic Survivability in Latin America." Working Paper #267. Kellogg Institute, Notre Dame, IN (May): 1–53.

———. 1999b. "The Surprising Resilience of Elected Governments." *Journal of Democracy* 10, no. 3: 101–114.

Mainwaring, Scott, and Matthew Soberg Shugart, eds. 1997. *Presidentialism and Democracy in Latin America.* New York: Cambridge University Press.

Mamdani, Mahmood. 1995. *Citizen and Subject: Contemporary Africa and the Politics of Late Colonialism.* Kampala, Uganda: Fountain.

Mangcu, Xolela, ed. *Community Building in the Global Age.* Unpublished manuscript.

———. 1998. Proceedings of a Rockefeller Foundation conference on community building, Bellagio, Italy.

Mannheim, Karl. 1985 [1936]. *Ideology and Utopia.* New York: Harcourt.

Marshall, T. H. 1992. *Citizenship and Social Class.* London: Pluto.

———. 1964. *Class, Citizenship, and Social Development.* Garden City, NY: Doubleday.

———. 1950. *Citizenship and Social Class.* Oxford: Oxford University Press.

———. 1950. "Citizenship and Social Class," in *Citizenship and Social Class and Other Essays,* by T. H. Marshall. Cambridge: Cambridge University Press.

McClintock, Cynthia. 1999. "Peru: Precarious Regimes, Authoritarian and Democratic," in *Democracy in Developing Countries: Latin America,* 2nd edition, edited by Larry Diamond, Jonathan Hartlyn, Juan J. Linz, and Seymour Martin Lipset. Boulder, CO: Lynne Rienner Publishers.

McGaffey, Janet. 1997. "Domination and Resistance in Zaire: Resisting the Shadow State Through the International Trade of the Second Economy."

Paper delivered at African Renewal Conference, Massachusetts Institute of Technology, March.

Mehrotra, Santosh, and Richard Jolly, eds. 1997. *Development with a Human Face: Experiences in Social Achievement and Economic Growth*. Oxford: Clarendon Press.

Méndez, Juan E., Guillermo O'Donnell, and Paulo Sérgio Pinheiro, eds. 1999. *The Rule of Law and the Underprivileged in Latin America*. Notre Dame, IN: University of Notre Dame Press.

Mettler, Suzanne. 1998. *Dividing Citizens—Gender and Federalism in New Deal Public Policy*. Ithaca, NY: Cornell University Press.

Michels, Robert. 1949. *Political Parties—A Sociological Study of the Oligarchical Tendencies of Modern Democracy*, translated from the Italian by Eden and Cedar Paul. Glencoe, IL: Free Press.

Migdal, Joel S. 1988. *Strong Societies and Weak States: State-Society Relations and State Capabilities in the Third World*. Princeton, NJ: Princeton University Press.

Ministry of Finance and Economy, Republic of Korea (MOFE). 2000a. *Korea Economic Update*. Seoul: MOFE.

———. 2000b. *Main Economic Indicators*. <http://www.mofe.go.kr/cgi-pub/listview.cgi?code=es>. (accessed 11/5/1999).

———. 1999. "Recent Trends in Income Distribution and Policy Direction" (in Korean). <http://www.mofe.go.kr/cgi-pub/listview.cgi?code=ej> (accessed 12/22/1999).

Ministry of Health and Welfare, Republic of Korea. 1999. "Health and Welfare Policy Change in the First Year of the New Millenium" (in Korean). Open document available at <http://www.mohw.go.kr> (accessed 25 January 2000).

———. 1998. *The First Long-Term Plan for Social Security Development* (in Korean). Mimeograph handout.

Ministry of Planning and Budget, Republic of Korea. 1999. *National Living 2000* (in Korean). <http://www.mpb.go.kr/list.asp>.

Mink, Gwendolyn. 1998. *Welfare's End*. Ithaca, NY: Cornell University Press.

———. 1995. *The Wages of Motherhood: Inequality and the Welfare State, 1917–1942*. Ithaca, NY: Cornell University Press.

———. 1986. *Old Labor and New Immigrant in American Political Development*. Ithaca, NY: Cornell University Press.

Mittelman, James H., ed. 1996. *Globalization: Critical Refelction*. Boulder, CO: Lynne Rienner Publishers.

Mo, Jongryn, and Chung-in Moon. 1999. "Democracy and the Origins of the 1997 Korean Economic Crisis," in *Democracy and the Korean Economy*, edited by Jongryn Mo and Chung-in Moon. Stanford, CA: Hoover Institution Press.

Montes, Manuel F. 1998. *The Currency Crisis in Southeast Asia*. Singapore: Institute of Southeast Asian Studies.

Moon, Chung-in. 2000. "Broken Cheers of Globalization: Globalization Strategy in South Korea," in *Responding to Globalization*, edited by Aseem Prakash and Jeffrey Hart. New York: Routledge.

———. 1999. "Democratization and Globalization as Ideological and Political Foundations of Economic Policy," in *Democracy and the Korean Economy*, edited by Jongryn Mo and Chung-in Moon. Stanford, CA: Hoover Institution Press.

———. 1995. "Globalization: Its Challenges and Countervailing Strategies." *Korea Focus* 3, no. 3: 62–79.

Moon, Chung-in, and Jongryn Mo, eds. 1999. *Democracy and Globalization in Korea*. Seoul: Yonsei University Press.

Moon, Chung-in, and Sang-young Rhyu. 1999. "The State, Structural Rigidity, and the End of Asian Capitalism: A Comparative Study of Japan and South Korea," in *Politics and Markets in the Wake of Asian Crisis,* edited by Richard Robison, Mark Beeson, and Kanishka Jayasuriya. New York: Routledge.

Moon, Chung-in, and Yong-cheol Kim. 2000. "Globalization and Workers," in *South Korea and Segyehwa (Globalization),* edited by Sam Kim. New York: Cambridge University Press.

Munck, Gerardo L., and Jay Verkuilen. 2000. "Measuring Democracy: Evaluating Alternative Indices." Prepared for delivery at the 2000 Annual Meeting of the American Political Science Association, Washington, DC, August 31–September 3.

Murray, Charles. 1984. *Losing Ground: American Social Policy 1950–1980.* New York: Basic Books.

National Federation of Medical Insurance (Republic of Korea). 2000. "A Chronicle of Medical Insurance" (in Korean). Open document available at <http://www.nfmi.or.kr> (accessed 25 January 2000).

National Pension Corporation (Republic of Korea). 1999. "New National Pension Law." <http://www.ncp.or.kr/eng/edata/gh-dd-01.html>.

National Statistics Office (Republic of Korea). 1999. *KOSIS.* <http://www.nso.go.kr> (accessed 8 November 1999).

Niles, Kimberly J. 1999. "Political Institutions and Redistributive Social Spending in the Developing World." Paper presented at the Annual Meeting of the American Political Science Association, Atlanta, Georgia, September 1–5.

North, Douglass C. 1995. "The Adam Smith Address: Economic Theory in a Dynamic Economic World." *Business Economics* 30, no. 1 (January).

———. 1991. "Institutions." *Journal of Economic Perspectives* 5, no. 1 (winter).

Notermans, Tom. 1993. "The Abdication from National Policy Autonomy: Why the Macroeconomic Policy Regime Has Become So Unfavorable to Labor." *Politics & Society* 21, no. 2 (June): 133–167.

Nozick, Robert. 1977. *Anarchy, State and Utopia.* New York: Basic Books.

O'Donnell, Guillermo. 1999. "Polyarchies and the (Un)Rule of Law in Latin America," in *The Rule of Law and the Underprivileged in Latin America,* edited by Juan Méndez, Guillermo O'Donnell, and Paulo Sérgio Pinheiro. Notre Dame, IN: University of Notre Dame Press.

———. 1998. "Horizontal Accountability in New Democracies." *Journal of Democracy* 9, no. 3: 112–126.

———. 1996. "Illusions About Consolidation." *Journal of Democracy* 7, no. 2 (April): 34–51.

———. 1994. "Delegative Democracy." *Journal of Democracy* 5, no. 1.

O'Donnell, Guillermo, and Philippe C. Schmitter. 1986. *Transitions from Authoritarian Rule: Tentative Conclusions About Uncertain Democracies.* Baltimore: Johns Hopkins University Press.

Office of the President (Republic of Korea). 2000. *DJ Welfarism: A New Paradigm for Productive Welfare in Korea.* Seoul: Office of the President.

Ohmae, Kenich. 1996. *The End of the Nation State: The Rise of Regional Economies.* New York: Free Press.

———. 1990. *The Borderless World.* New York: Collins.

Oliver, M., and T. Shapiro. 1997. *Black Wealth, White Wealth: A New Perspective on Racial Inequality.* New York: Routledge.

Olson, Mancur. 1971. *The Logic of Collective Action.* Cambridge, MA: Harvard University Press.

Osborne, David, and Ted Gaebler. 1993. *Reinventing Government: How the Entrepreneurial Spirit Is Transforming the Public Sector.* New York: Penguin.

Oxhorn, Philip, and Pamela K. Starr, eds. 1999. *Markets and Democracy in Latin America.* Boulder, CO: Lynne Rienner Publishers.

Panizza, Francisco, and Alexandra Barahona de Brito. 1998. "The Politics of Human Rights in Democratic Brazil: 'A Lei Não Pega.'" *Democratization* 5, no. 4 (winter): 20–51.

Perreira, Luiz Carlos Bresser, José Maria Maravall, and Adam Przeworski. 1993. *Economic Reforms in New Democracies: A Social Democratic Approach.* Cambridge: Cambridge University Press.

Peru Election 2000 web site. 2000. <http://csd.queensu.ca/peru2000/> (accessed February 2000).

Pfaller, Alfred, Ian Gough, and Göran Therborn. 1991. *Can the Welfare State Compete?: A Comparative Study of Five Advanced Capitalist Countries.* London: Macmillan.

Pierson, Paul. 1996. "The New Politics of the Welfare State." *World Politics* 48 (January): 143–179.

Piven, Frances Fox, and Richard A. Cloward. 1971. *Regulating the Poor: The Functions of Public Welfare.* New York: Pantheon Books.

Polan, A. J. 1984. *Lenin and the End of Politics.* London: Methuen.

Polanyi, Karl. 1994. *The Great Transformation.* New York and Toronto: Farrar & Rhinehart Inc.

———. 1957. *The Great Transformation.* Boston: Beacon Press.

Pollack, Sheldon D. 1996. *The Failure of U.S. Tax Policy.* University Park: Pennsylvania State University Press.

Pontusson, Jonas. 1992. *The Limits of Social Democracy: Investment Politics in Sweden.* Ithaca, NY: Cornell University Press.

Przeworski, Adam. 1987. *Capitalism and Social Democracy.* Cambridge: Cambridge University Press.

Przeworski, Adam, Michael E. Alvarez, José Antonio Cheibub, and Fernando Limongi. 1996. "What Makes Democracies Endure?" *Journal of Democracy* 7, no. 1: 39–55.

———. 2000. *Democracy and Development: Political Institutions and Well-Being in the World, 1950–1990.* New York: Cambridge University Press.

Przeworski, Adam, and Fernando Limongi. 1997. "Modernization: Theories and Facts." *World Politics* 49 (January): 155–183.

Putnam, Robert. 1995. "Bowling Alone: America's Declining Social Capital." *Journal of Democracy* 6, no. 1.

Raczynski, Dagmar, ed. 1995. *Strategies for Combatting Poverty in Latin America.* Washington DC: Inter-American Development Bank.

Radelet, Steven. 1995. "Indonesian Foreign Debt: Headed for a Crisis or Financing Sustainable Growth?" BIES XXXI (December): 3.

Radelet, Steven, and Jeffrey Sachs. 1998. "The Onset of the East Asian Financial Crisis." *Harvard Institute for International Development,* March 30.

Ramesh, M. 1995. "Social Security in South Korea and Singapore: Explaining the Difference." *Social Policy and Administration* 29, no. 3: 228–240.

Rhyu, Sangyoung, and Suk-hoon Kang. 1999. *The Change of Middle Class and the Policy Direction* (in Korean). Seoul: SERI.

Rieger, Elmar, and Stephan Leibfried. 1998. "Welfare State Limits to Globalization." *Politics & Society* 26, no. 3: 363–390.

Robinson, William I. 1996. *Promoting Polyarchy—Globalization, U.S. Intervention and Hegemony*. Cambridge: Cambridge University Press.

Rodrik, Dani. 1999. *Making Openness Work: The New Global Economy and Developing Countries*. Washington, DC: Overseas Development Council.

———. 1997a. "Sense and Nonsense in the Globalization Debate." *Foreign Policy* (summer).

———. 1997b. *Has Globalization Gone TooFar?* Washington DC: Institute for International Economics.

———. 1997c. "Trade, Social Insurance, and the Limits to Globalization." Working Paper No. 5905. Cambridge, MA: National Bureau of Economic Research.

Root, Hilton. 1998. "In Indonesia, Political Reform Has to Come First." *International Herald Tribune*, 11 August.

Rosenthal, A.M. 1997. "Lessons of the Asian Collapse." *New York Times,* 23 December, p. 19.

Rudra, Nita. 2000. "Globalization and the Decline of the Welfare State in Less Developed Countries." Ph.D. dissertation, University of Southern California.

Rueschemeyer, Dietrich, Evelyne Huber Stephens, and John Stephens. 1992. *Capitalist Development and Democracy*. Chicago: University of Chicago Press.

Rueschemeyer, Dietrich, Theda Skocpol, and Peter Evans, eds. 1985. *Bringing the State Back In*. Cambridge: Cambridge University Press.

Sabine, George. 1950. *The History of Political Theory*. New York: Henry Holt.

Sachs, Jeffrey. 1998. "IMF Prescribes Wrong Medicine." *International Herald Tribune,* 15 January.

Samuels, David. 1999. "Incentives to Cultivate a Party Vote in Candidate-Centric Electoral Systems: Evidence from Brazil." *Comparative Political Studies* 32, no. 4: 487–518.

Samuels, Richardson J. 1994. *Rich Nation, Strong Army*. Ithaca, NY: Cornell University Press.

Samson, M., O. Babson, K. MacQueane, I. Van Niekerk, and R. Van Niekerk. 2000. "The Macro-Economic Implications of Poverty-Reducing Transfers." Cape Town: Economic Policy Research Institute, 24 March.

Schattschneider, E. E. 1960. *The Semisovereign People*. New York: Holt, Reinhart and Winston.

———. 1942. *Party Government*. New York: Holt, Rinehart and Winston.

Schedler, Andreas. 1998. "What Is Democratic Consolidation?" *Journal of Democracy* 9, no. 2: 91–107.

Schedler, Andreas, Larry Diamond, and Marc F. Plattner, eds. 1999. *The Self-Restraining State: Power and Accountability in New Democracies*. Boulder, CO: Lynne Rienner Publishers.

Schmitter, Philippe C. 1999. "The Future of Democracy: Could It Be a Matter of Scale?" *Social Research* 66, no 3 (fall): 933–958.

Schwartz, Herman. 1994. "Small States in Big Trouble: State Reorganization in Australia, Denmark, New Zealand, and Sweden in the 1980s." *World Politics* 46 (July): 527–555.

Sechuwi. 1998a. *Segyehwa Baeksuh (White Paper of Segyehwa)*. Seoul: Sgyehwa Chujin Wiwonhoi.

———. 1998b. *Segyehwa Bogosuh (The Report of Segyehwa)*. Seoul: Sgyehwa Chujin Wiwonhoi.

———. 1996. *Segyehwa Baeksuh (White Paper on Globalization)*. Seoul: Sgyehwa Chujin Wiwonhoi.

———. 1995. *Segyehwaeui Bijunkwa Junryak (Vision and Strategy Segyehwa)*. Seoul: Sgyehwa Chujin Wiwonhoi.

Seidelman, Raymond, with Edward Harpham. 1985. *Disenchanted Realists—Political Science and the American Crisis, 1884–1994*. Albany: SUNY Press.

Sherraden, M. 1991. *Assets and the Poor: A New American Welfare Policy*. New York: A.M.E. Sharpe Inc.

Simone, Abdou Maliq. 1995. "Urban Societies in Africa," in *Civil Society After Apartheid*, edited by Richard Humphries and Maxine Reitzes. Johannesburg: Centre for Policy Studies/Friedrich Ebert Foundation.

———. 1994. *In Whose Image?: Political Islam and Urban Practices in Sudan*. Chicago: University of Chicago Press.

Sklar, Richard L. 1996. "Towards a Theory of Developmental Democracy," in *Democracy and Development: Theory and Practice*, edited by Adrian Leftwich. Cambridge, MA: Polity Press.

———. 1987. "Developmental Democracy." *Comparative Studies in Society and History* 29, no. 4: 686–714.

Skocpol, Theda. 1995. *Social Policy in the United States: Future Possibilities in Historical Perspective*. Princeton, NJ: Princeton University Press.

Soros, George. 1998a. "The Crisis of Global Capitalism." Testimony before the U.S. House Committee on Banking and Financial Services." 26 September.

———. 1998b. *The Crisis of Global Capitalism–Open Society Endangered*. New York: Perseus Books Group.

Stacey, Simon. 1997. *New Capacities for Old?: Public-Private Partnerships and Universal Service Delivery in South Africa, Angola and Mozambique*. Johannesburg: Centre for Policy Studies.

Stiglitz, Joseph. 1998a. "Redefining the Role of the State." Paper presented at the 10th anniversary of MITI Research Institute. Tokyo, 17 March.

———. 1998b. "International Development: Is It Possible?" *Foreign Policy* 110: 138–151.

———. 1998c. "More Instruments and Broader Goals: Moving Toward the Post-Washington Consensus." 1998 WIDER Annual Lecture, Helsinki, 7 January.

Strange, Susan. 1996. *The Retreat of the State: The Diffusion of Power in the World Economy*. Cambridge: Cambridge University Press.

Summers, Lawrence. 1998. "Opportunities out of Crises: Lessons from Asia." *Treasury News*. U.S. Treasury Department, Office of Public Affairs (19 March).

Tanner, Michael. 1996. *The End of Welfare: Fighting Poverty in the Civil Society*. Washington, DC: Cato Institute.

Tanzi, Vito, and Ludger Shuknecht. 1995. *The Growth of Government and the Reform of the State in Industrial Countries*. Washington, DC: International Monetary Fund Working Papers WP/95/130.

Teeple, Gary. 1995. *Globalization and the Decline of Social Reform*. Toronto: Garamond Press.

Tendler, J. 1999. "The Rise of Social Funds: What Are They a Model Of?" Unpublished manuscript, MIT Department of Urban Studies.

Traub, James. 2000. "What No School Can Do." *New York Times Magazine*, 16 January.

Tripp, Aili Mari. 1997. *Changing the Rules: The Politics of Liberalization and the Informal Economy in Tanzania*. Berkeley: University of California Press.

Truman, David. 1962. *The Governmental Process*. New York: Knopf.

Twala, W., and R. McCutcheon. 1999. "A Critical Evaluation of Large-Scale Development Projects and Programmes in South Africa." Paper presented at the Conference on Links Between History and Policy, University of the Witwatersrand, September.

Unger, R., and C. West. 1998. *The Future of American Progressivism: An Initiative for Political and Economic Reform.* Boston: Beacon Press.

United Nations Development Program (UNDP). 1999. *Globalization with a Human Face: Human Development Report 1999.* New York: Oxford University Press.

———. 1996. *Human Development Report 1996.* New York and Oxford: Oxford University Press.

U.S. Social Security Administration. 1999. *Social Security Programs Throughout the World.* <http://www.ssa.gov/statistics/ssptw99.html> (accessed 2 November).

Van Cott, Donna Lee. 2000. *The Friendly Liquidation of the Past: The Politics of Diversity in Latin America.* Pittsburgh, PA: University of Pittsburgh Press.

Vernon, Raymond. 1971. *Sovereignty at Bay.* New York: Basic Books.

Von Mettenheim, Kurt, and James M. Malloy. 1998. "Introduction," in *Deepening Democracy in Latin America,* edited by Kurt von Mettenheim and James M. Malloy. Pittsburgh, PA: University of Pittsburgh Press.

Wade, Robert. 1990. *Governing the Market: Economic Theory and the Role of Government in East Asian Industrialization.* Princeton, NJ: Princeton University Press.

Weber, Max. 1992. *General Economic History.* New Brunswick, NJ: Transaction Press.

Weiss, Linda. 1998. *The Myth of the Powerless State Governing the Economy in a Global Era.* Cambridge, MA: Polity Press.

White, Caroline. 1993. *Makhulu Padroni? Patron-Clientelism in Shack Areas and Some Italian Lessons for South Africa.* Johannesburg: Centre for Policy Studies.

Williamson, Jeffrey G. 1998. "Globalization and the Labor Market: Using History to Inform Policy," in *Growth, Inequality, and Globalization,* edited by P. Aghion and J. Williamson. Cambridge: Cambridge University Press.

Wilson, William Julius. 1978. *The Declining Significance of Race.* Chicago: University of Chicago Press.

Witte, Edwin. 1962. *The Development of the Social Security Act.* Madison: University of Wisconsin Press.

Wolfe, Alan. 1989. *Whose Keeper: Social Science and Moral Obligation.* Berkeley: University of California Press.

World Bank. 2000. *Global Economic Prospects and the Developing Countries—2000.* <http://www.worldbank.org/prospects/gep2000/index.html> (accessed 12/13/1999).

———. 1999a. *Annual Report 1998.* <http://www.worldbank.org/html/extpb/annrep98> (accessed 7 November 1999).

———. 1999b. *World Development Indicators* (CD-ROM version).

———. 1998a. *Annual Report 1998.* <http://www.worldbank.org/html/extpb/annrep98> (accessed 7 November 1999).

———. 1998b. "Korea Structural Adjustment Loan II Approved by the World Bank Board on Thursday, October 22." <http://www.worldbank.org/html/e...offrep/eap/krsalii/krsalii.html> (accessed 4 December 1999).

———. 1997a. *The State in a Changing World: World Development Report 1997.* New York: Oxford University Press.

———. 1997b. *Poverty Reduction and the World Bank: Progress in Fiscal 1996 and 1997.* Washington, DC: World Bank.

———. 1996. *Poverty Reduction and the World Bank: Progress and Challenges in the 1990s.* Washington, DC: World Bank.

———. 1995. *World Development Report 1995: Workers in an Integrating World.* New York: Oxford University Press.

Yang, Jae-jin. 2000. "The Rise of the Korean Welfare State amid Economic Crisis, 1997–1999." *Development Policy Review.*

Yashar, Deborah J. 1996. "Indigenous Protest and Democracy in Latin America," in *Constructing Democratic Governance: Latin America and the Caribbean in the 1990s—Themes and Issues,* edited by Jorge I. Domínguez and Abraham F. Lowenthal. Baltimore: Johns Hopkins University Press.

Zakaria, Fareed. 1997. "The Rise of Illiberal Democracy." *Foreign Affairs* 76, no. 6 (November-December): 22–43.

The Contributors

Amelia Brown is a Fulbright scholar in Ottawa, conducting research on foreign workers in Canada's high-tech sector, and a former program associate at the Latin American Program, Woodrow Wilson International Center for Scholars. Prior to her work at the Wilson Center, she was a junior fellow at the International Migration Policy Program of the Carnegie Endowment for International Peace, where she focused on U.S. immigration and border policy and immigrant communities within the United States. Ms. Brown holds a degree in international relations from Wellesley College.

Jonathan Hartlyn is professor of Political Science and department chair at the University of North Carolina at Chapel Hill, where he has also served as the director of the Institute of Latin American Studies. He is the author of *The Struggle for Democratic Politics in the Dominican Republic* and *The Politics of Coalition Rule in Colombia* (also published in Spanish); coeditor of *Democracy in Developing Countries: Latin America,* 2nd edition; *United States-Latin American Relations in the 1990s: Beyond the Cold War;* and *Latin American Political Economy,* and the author of numerous articles and book chapters on issues of democratization in Latin America.

Steven Friedman has been the director of the Centre for Policy Studies, an independent, nonprofit policy research center in South Africa, since 1992. He serves on the advisory board of the Institute for Security Studies in Midrand, South Africa, and the editorial board of the *Journal of Democracy,* and is a member of the Research Council of the International Forum for Democratic Studies. Mr. Friedman has participated in various public and private policy task forces, including the Specialist Team that drafted the Safety and Security White Paper in 1997. He is the author of regular columns in *Business Day, Mail and Guardian,* and *Reconstruct (Sunday Independent).* He has published several books and edited volumes, as well as numerous book chapters and journal articles. His most recent publications include "Agreeing to Differ: African Democracy—Its Obstacles and Prospects" (*Social Research,* 1999) and "South Africa After Mandela" (*Journal of Democracy,* October 1999).

Bolivar Lamounier holds a Ph.D. in Political Science from the University of California, Los Angeles. He has taught at the University of São Paulo and at the Catholic University of São Paulo. He was a member of the constitutional drafting commission (known as "Comissão Afonso Arinos'), appointed in 1985 by then president José Sarney. He coordinated a commission set up by the Institute for Advanced Studies of the University of São Paulo to offer suggestions on constitutional reform in the early 1990s. He was chairman of the board of directors of the Center for Public Opinion Research at the University of Campinas, São Paulo. He is presently a member of the board of the Interamerican Dialogue and in 1997 was elected to the São Paulo Academy of Letters. He has published extensively on Brazilian and comparative politics, including such recent works as "Democracy and Economic Reform in Brazil" (with Edmar Bacha, coauthor), in Joan Nelson, editor, *Precarious Balance: Democracy and Economic Reform in Latin America and East Europe* (1994); "Brazil: Inequality Against Democracy," in Larry Diamond, Jonathan Hartlyn, Seymour Martin Lipset and Juan Linz, editors, *Democracy in Developing Countries—Latin America* (1999, 2nd Edition); *A Democracia Brasileira no Limiar do Século 21* (1995); and *Rui Barbosa e a Construção Institucional da Democracia Brasileira* (1999).

Theodore J. Lowi holds a Ph.D. from Yale University. He has served on the faculty of the University of Chicago and has been the John L. Senior Professor of American Institutions at Cornell University since 1972. He has written or edited a dozen books, including *The Pursuit of Justice* (with Robert F. Kennedy, 1964) and *The End of Liberalism* (2nd Edition, 1979). His 1985 book, *The Personal President—Power Invested, Promise Unfulfilled,* won the 1986 Neustadt Prize for the best book published on the U.S. presidency. His most recent works include *American Government—Freedom and Power* (1990, 1996), *The End of the Republican Era* (1995), and *We the People* (1997). In addition to his many other distinctions, Dr. Lowi has been awarded honorary degrees from Oakland University and SUNY/Stony Brook.

Xolela Mangcu is the executive director of the Steve Biko Foundation in Johannesburg, South Africa. He holds a Ph.D. in City Planning from Cornell University and B.A. and M.S. degrees from the University of the Witwatersrand (Wits). He has held fellowships at Harvard University, the Massachusetts Institute of Technology, and the Rockefeller Foundation in New York. He is also an associate editor and columnist for the prestigious *Sunday Independent*. He was previously a senior analyst at the Centre for Policy Studies, also in Johannesburg. Dr. Mangcu has taught urban studies at the University of Maryland (College Park), worked as a specialist for the Development Bank of Southern Africa, and served as a consultant for numerous international and national development agencies, including the Rockefeller Foundation, the Kellogg Foundation, ABT Associates, and the Nelson Mandela Children's Fund. He is a regular political commentator and has been featured on the South African Broadcasting Corporation, E-TV, *NewsHour with Jim Lehrer,* National Public Radio, BBC Radio, and CNN. He is currently working on a biography of Steve Biko.

Chung-in Moon is dean of the Graduate School of International Studies and professor of political science at Yonsei University. He was a visiting fellow at the Woodrow Wilson Center in 1999. He has published sixteen books and over 150 articles in edited volumes and such scholarly journals as *World Politics, World Development,* and *Journal of Democracy.* His most recent book is *Korean Politics: An Introduction* (State University of New York Press, 2001). He is vice-president-elect of the International Studies Association.

Joel Rocamora is executive director of the Institute for Popular Democracy and president of the Akbayan (Citizens Action Party) in the Philippines. Dr. Rocamora received his Ph.D. from Cornell University in 1974. He has published extensively on the politics of the Philippines and Indonesia.

Joseph S. Tulchin holds a Ph.D. from Harvard University. He is the director of the Latin American Program at the Woodrow Wilson International Center for Scholars, in Washington, D.C. Tulchin was professor of history and director of International Programs at the University of North Carolina at Chapel Hill. In addition to teaching history at UNC, he also taught at Yale University; the Naval War College, Newport, R.I.; the University of Buenos Aires, Argentina; the Ortega y Gasset Foundation, Madrid; Georgetown University; The Johns Hopkins University School of Advanced International Studies;

several branches of the Latin American Social Science Faculty (FLACSO); and El Colegio de México, Mexico. His areas of expertise are U.S. foreign policy, inter-American relations, contemporary Latin America, strategic planning, and social-science research methodology. He was associate editor and former editor of the *Latin American Research Review*. He is often called upon to give testimony to committees of the United States Congress. He has published more than twenty books, including three monographs, on inter-American relations, Latin American affairs, Spanish foreign policy, and international relations. Dr. Tulchin's works include *Latin American Nations in World Politics* (with Heraldo Muñoz) and *Argentina and the United States: A Conflicted Relationship*. He is also the editor of *Current Studies on Latin America* for Lynne Rienner Publishers, Boulder, Colorado.

Jae-jin Yang holds a Ph.D. in political science from Rutgers University. He is a researcher at the Graduate School of Public Administration at Seoul National University in Seoul, Korea. He has written extensively on structural adjustments and social policies, with recent publications including "The Rise of the Korean Welfare State Amid Economic Crisis, 1997–99: Implications for the Globalization Debate" (*Development Policy Review*, vol. 18, no. 3, September 2000) and "Structural Adjustment and Social Welfare: The Collapse of the Developmental State Social Welfare Paradigm and the Kim Dae Jung Government's Mandate" (*Korean Political Science Review*, vol. 35, no. 1, spring 2001).

Index

About the Book

This controversial book examines the challenges that social inequities present to democratic governments.

The authors argue that issues of poverty and inequality—far from diminishing—are becoming even more important in the global environment. They consider the effects of globalization on the distribution of income and wealth within state borders, the impact of inequality on the stability and quality of democratic governance, and the future of vulnerable democracies in light of an apparent decline in the ability of governments to reduce inequality. Bridging political and economic concerns, the book is an important step toward coming to terms with the crucial socioeconomic dimensions of democracy and democratic transitions.

Joseph S. Tulchin is director of the Latin American Program at the Woodrow Wilson International Center for Scholars. **Amelia Brown** is a Fulbright scholar in Ottawa; she is a former program associate at the Latin American Program at the Woodrow Wilson International Center for Scholars.